Hollein Calling:
Architectural Dialogues

Edited by

Lorenzo De Chiffre
Benni Eder
Theresa Krenn

Architekturzentrum Wien

Index

Foreword

"There is more Hollein in contemporary architecture than you would think," say the curators of *Hollein Calling: Architectural Dialogues*. And there is still much that is new to discover in the work of Hans Hollein, who is probably the best-known Austrian architect internationally. Evidence of both these things is now available in the form of this book and the exhibition of the same name at the Architekturzentrum Wien. Previously unpublished material from the Archive Hans Hollein, Az W and MAK, Vienna provides a fresh look at the work of Austria's only Pritzker Prize winner, an architect fond of curating his own image during his lifetime. Nearly ten years after his death, fifteen contemporary architectural practices circle around the Hollein phenomenon, unsparing in both their enthusiasm and their opinions. Hollein's all-encompassing conception of architecture continues to fascinate to this day. In the twenty-first century, however, "everything is architecture" stands not only for an aspiration but also for a certain presumptuousness, which the younger participants counter with a critique of the "master" principle. On one thing, however, everyone agrees: we need to be talking more about architecture again.

The collection of the Architekturzentrum Wien provides a wealth of material for the discourse around architecture—and beyond. Founded in 1993 by the City of Vienna and the Republic of Austria, the Az W is the only museum in Austria dedicated to architecture. Its holdings, encompassing more than one hundred archives as well as unique photographic and extensive project collections, offer a diverse range of objects and documents that illuminate not only the history of art and culture but also socio-economic and technological history. Here, Hans Hollein's archive occupies a special position already on account of the sheer abundance of material: over 460 projects, hundreds of models, tens of thousands of photos and slides, as well as rolls of plans, correspondence, and, of course, sketches. With the acquisition of the archive in 2016, the Republic of Austria was able to save the internationally sought-after bequest for the nation. The agreement of a permanent loan from the MAK to the Az W marked the beginning of an interinstitutional collaboration that is unique in Austria. Since then, the Az W collection team has been working intensively to preserve and catalog the archive as well as collaborate with international researchers.

In our work at the museum, we see collecting, research, and mediation as intertwined activities. For this reason, I am particularly pleased that the *Hollein Calling* team, who began their work with the archive in the context of a research grant, went on to develop their ideas into an exhibition and publication in dialogue with the Az W. My thanks go to the curators and co-editors, Lorenzo De Chiffre, Benni Eder, and Theresa Krenn, for their simultaneously discursive and playful approach to the work of Hans Hollein and for architectural dialogues that constantly have the potential to surprise. Great thanks also to the fifteen European architectural practices that embarked on this unusual experiment, for not only sharing their inspiring work with us, but also providing new insights into the oeuvre of Hans Hollein. For the graphic design of the book and exhibition, I thank Studio Polimekanos. For the realization of the project, I thank the entire team at the Az W, especially the head of collections, Monika Platzer, for her critical guidance; Katrin Stingl, for her judicious project coordination; and Claudia Lingenhöl, for overseeing the Archive Hans Hollein, Az W and MAK, Vienna as well as Karin Lux, executive director of the Az W.

With *Hollein Calling*, the Architekturzentrum Wien once again shows how an architectural collection can be researched from the viewpoint of the present, in the process opening up the field for further explorations. The Hollein phenomenon continues to excite the imagination.

Angelika Fitz, Director Az W

Hans Hollein's workspace in his atelier in Argentinierstraße, Vienna.
Archive Hans Hollein, Az W and MAK, Vienna.

Lorenzo De Chiffre
Benni Eder
Theresa Krenn

Hollein Calling: Architectural Dialogues

During his lifetime Hans Hollein was an assiduous curator of his own work, and yet his persona, as a self-proclaimed 1960s avant-gardist and Austria's only Pritzker Prize winner, often overshadowed any objective assessment of his architecture. Now, nearly a decade after his death in 2014, it is possible to look at his work with the necessary distance and ask: How accessible is Hollein's universe today? To what extent do his ideas connect with contemporary themes in architecture?

The approach to this inquiry is purposely kaleidoscopic, yielding a multi-faceted picture that reflects both the varied nature of Hollein's oeuvre and the many voices involved in re-evaluating it here. The essential idea is to identify and make visible lines of association. Rather than being forced into an art-historical corset, Hollein's oeuvre is set into conversation with tendencies in current practice.

Hollein Calling consists of an exhibition and accompanying publication. Both are closely connected but have different focal points. In the exhibition, groundbreaking projects by Atelier Hollein are paired with buildings and projects by fifteen European practices whose work is shaping the architectural discourse today.[1] The publication, which also serves as the basis for the exhibition, grew out of the interview project, Dialogues on Hans Hollein.[2] The first part of the book contains the interviews with the contemporary architects, who relate Hollein's work to their own practice. The second part presents the selection of projects by Atelier Hollein, largely illustrated with previously unpublished archival material. The accompanying contributions by Monika Platzer and Mark Lee—on the Archive Hans Hollein, Az W and MAK, and the North American context, respectively—suggest starting points for further inquiry.

The Hollein projects—also fifteen in number—determine the structure of the exhibition, unfolding a world of ideas that visitors will find by turns resonant and discordant. All the Hollein exhibits—sketches, models, prototypes, and documents—are drawn from the extensive Archive Hans Hollein, Az W and MAK, which the Architekturzentrum Wien has been cataloging and preserving for several years. The juxtaposition of this material with selected projects by the architectural practices sets up a dialogue that focuses on working methods and processes. The curators consciously avoided a linear and project-related reading. Instead, large display tables are used to create fields of association, grouping exhibits according to shared themes, methods, and interests. Overhead video projections offer a taste of Atelier

Lorenzo De Chiffre
Benni Eder
Theresa Krenn

Hollein's vast image archive. The inclusion of many photographs and illustrations that are not in the Hollein canon of iconic (and frequently published) images opens up alternative lines of thought and provides new insight into unrealized concepts. These images are in turn in dialogue with large-format photographs conveying the approaches of the contemporary architectural practices.

Uncovering Hollein

Hollein's work is defined by his consistent pursuit of the central themes of "design" and the "architectural idea." The focus is on the "image" as a bearer of meaning, with a high value likewise ascribed to the element of iconography. Throughout, Hollein's work is concerned with architecture as a particular way of thinking with its own kind of logic. While his projects address broader social and cultural issues, their real subject is architecture—and, more specifically, how architecture can assert itself in relation to other media and forms of expression at a time of rapid social change. Finally, Hollein's works are also interesting in terms of self-presentation and the curating of a media persona. These themes and questions—equally relevant to today's discourse on architecture—form the basis for the dialogues with the contemporary practices. In the major retrospective shows that were held during Hollein's life-time and co-curated by him, the early projects were always accorded a position of prominence.[3] Posthumously, there have been two major monographic exhibition projects to date: *MAN transFORMS* at the ETH Zurich in 2016,[4] and *Hans Hollein Unpacked: The Haas Haus* at the Architekturzentrum Wien in 2019, organized following the acquisition of a large part of the archive.[5] Over the last decade, Hollein's work has also been reappraised in a number of publications. Notably, the research of art historian Eva Branscome—and in particular her monograph *Hans Hollein and Postmodernism*, 2017—has highlighted important connections between Hollein's projects and the sociopolitical context in which they were embedded.[6]

Architectural Dialogues

The selection of partners for the dialogues was guided by the assumption that it would immediately be possible to establish points of contact between the architectural practices and Hollein's work. Sometimes this common ground is quite obvious, in other cases there is only an indirect connection. What all of them share, however, is a willingness to engage with Hollein's work with an open mind, free of ideological barriers. Rather than forming a homogeneous group, the participating offices in many respects represent contradictory positions and perspectives on Hollein's work. What they nevertheless have in common is their building practice, which is closely linked to an active participation in the local and international discourses. All are fascinated by architecture as a cultural phenomenon and regard its historical dimension as a driving force for their own designs and research.

Fifteen Key Works

The interviews with the architects were based around the fifteen Hollein projects that form the framework of the exhibition as well as the book. Arranged chronologically, beginning with the Retti candle shop (1964) and ending with Vulcania (1994–2002), the selected works encompass a broad palette of typologies and different scales and uses. All of them are realized buildings or exhibitions. Key works by Atelier Hollein, they shaped not only the discourse in their own time but also the dialogues with the contemporary practices.

In the course of these conversations, it became apparent that the main focus for the interviewees was the early projects. By comparison, the later works aroused a great deal less interest. One possible explanation for this lies in Hollein's working method in his later years, which became distinctly self-referential. Christoph Monschein, Hollein's partner in practice from 2010, reports that early sketches and conceptual ideas from the 1960s and 1970s were increasingly recycled into new designs.[7]

Some Considerations on Hollein's Practice

As a starting point for discussion, the research project identified thematic categories that characterize Hollein's design practice. The subsequent interviews with the architects crystallized a specific constellation of terms and themes, which were then documented in the form of short observations. These are included in both the exhibition and the publication as interpretative notes on the following subjects: *Exhibiting, Photography, Furniture, Materiality, City, Model, References, Art, Teaching, Teamwork, Publishing*, and *Gestalt*.

These categories provide a focused approach to Hollein's complex activities and at the same time describe aspects that remain relevant to current architectural practice. Other topics of particular interest to architects today, such as ecology, energy and climate issues, or social justice, are at best implicit in Hollein's work.

Through the Eyes of a New Generation

In an essay written to accompany the Hollein retrospective at the Historical Museum of the City of Vienna in 1995, Dietmar Steiner, the former director of the Az W, positioned Hollein within a particular postwar generation of "enlightened resistance."[8] These were people, like Hollein, who went in search of a new direction, going to America to study and returning home with fresh ideas—a generation defined by a faith in the future and a spirit of technological optimism. At the same time, however, this generation was also the first to reassess early Austrian modernism, revisiting the historical positions of figures such as Adolf Loos or Rudolph M. Schindler.

From today's perspective, we could supplement Steiner's diagnosis with the observation that Hollein was also part of that first postwar cultural elite that turned their backs on the recent past and directed

Lorenzo De Chiffre
Benni Eder
Theresa Krenn

their optimistic gaze toward a future filled with promise. As his star rose, and his career was crowned with the award of the Pritzker Prize, Hollein became a powerful player in the network of actors that shaped the discourse around culture in Austria between 1970 and 2000. Hans Hollein, as Oliver Lütjens aptly puts it in one of the interviews published here effectively, hoovered everything up, gave his all, but in the process left little for others. Hollein was himself focused on design issues in architecture: a specific political stance or social commitment was not part of his professional positioning. The lacunae in Hollein's work are also more obvious to a new generation, a decade after his death. For example, he did not realize any single-family houses or residential buildings, not even in Vienna, that would have contributed to the larger discourse.

In 1973, Hollein set out his position as an architect and his reflections on the future development of the profession in a text, "Über den Beruf des Architekten."[9] Both the professional image and the field of activity of the architect" were "in flux and subject to constant change," with the independent, individual architect becoming a much rarer breed. In this uncertain context, he wrote, it would be more fruitful to conceive of the vocation of the architect in broader terms, as being "to participate in the creation of our human environment." Hollein still defined his field of operation as the "architectural studio," but did not rule out the possibility that in future he would seek out a new place to realize his work—one that potentially lay beyond architecture.

How is this stance perceived by younger contemporary architects, some of whom are well on the way to garnering the same kind of international attention that Hollein enjoyed in his early years? Even more than Hollein's generation, this new generation defies clear categorization. Architectural production is increasingly carried out by teams or collectives. The architectural discourse as a whole is becoming more diverse and inclusive: debates in architecture schools are dominated by questions of social justice, a critique of technology, and pessimism in the face of the climate crisis. A scarcity of resources, coupled with a critique of extremes, is leading to an architectural turn towards the regional, the authentic, and the specific, but also to a desire to rediscover the universal and the classical, which includes a rediscovery of the more recent past. In the interviews we find the protagonists of this "critical generation" (if they can be defined as such) raising objections to aspects of Hollein's approach but also voicing an appreciation of his work and, in particular, of his dismantling of the boundaries of architecture. Already controversial in his own time, Hollein remains an ambivalent figure even for today's architects, providing a telling barometer of the mood of a multifaceted, up-and-coming generation. Hollein was an "ideas man" who pushed the boundaries of his profession with his expanded concept of design, "everything is architecture." He was also an excellent and tireless designer, the creator of many unique buildings.

Hollein produced an incredible number of realized projects over the course of a career that spanned some fifty-five years. His most significant texts, however, were all written between the early 1960s to the early 1990s. As the interviews also reveal, people today find this early Hollein—the one who the built small shop fronts and large museums, who developed ideas, wrote texts, and conceived exhibitions—more interesting than the star architect who realized major global projects.

Our conversations with our interview partners have encouraged us to look anew at Hollein, without preconceptions, and to have the courage to reinterpret or even misinterpret his work. The focus of the exhibition and publication is therefore on what remains of Hollein: his built work, which (if not completely or partially destroyed) can still be experienced directly, including here in Vienna. Hollein, the architect of associations, stimulates thought and inspires architects and laymen in equal measure.

Hollein—Exquisite Corpse

The architects participating in this project view their own work as part of an emerging critical cultural production, and so have a particular appreciation of discursive practice. They all recognize that we need to talk more about architecture, not shying away from polemics. Their individual relations to Hollein's work, as described in the interviews, are diverse and multi-layered. Rather than being characterized solely by appreciation, they make apparent the many different facets of Hollein's work and its enduring potential to polarize. Out of this emerges a fundamental insight: the Hollein phenomenon continues to both inspire and provoke.

Aslı Çiçek, for example, locates an essential quality of Hollein's work in the fact that it is "complex and interesting to talk about, rather than particularly beautiful or praiseworthy." Conceptually, the projects are strongly rooted in the history of architecture, but at the same time they always seek to incorporate new and unexpected elements.

Hollein took up many roles on both the national and the international stage and was an influential protagonist in an anti-conformist pop architectural scene. Pier Paolo Tamburelli, for one, comments critically on the self-centered approach of the Hollein generation to this abundance of opportunity and its consequences for the discipline. Reflective architects today tend to display a fundamental skepticism towards mainstream culture. Compared to Hollein, there is more of a focus on social justice and responsibility, which does not mean they are less interested in design. In this regard, Caroline Lateur and Stefanie Everaert question the cult of the (almost invariably male) genius architect and a way of working that they do not want to pursue in their own studio.

The general tenor of the interviews is that Hollein's projects continue to provide points of reference and sources of reflection for contemporary architectural practice. His projects also find their way into the teaching of architecture, on account of their creative autonomy and "spatial mastery," as described by Wilfried Kuehn and methodically put into practice by Maria Conen and Raoul Sigl in their work with students. Rather than striving for formal reduction or programmatic

Lorenzo De Chiffre
Benni Eder
Theresa Krenn

intensification, Hollein's practice is characterized by the pursuit of enrichment, complexity, and allusion. For Pier Paolo Tamburelli, the associated work ethos and design method—protracted and labor-intensive, generating a wealth of variants—is something that many architectural practices can no longer afford given today's economic conditions and opportunities.

In this context, Claudia Cavallar reflects on Hollein's attempt to continue the Viennese tradition of striving for the superlative—for extreme achievements—and contrasts it with the "low-key" approach that is more suited to our times.

Andreas Rumpfhuber describes the general mood of the postwar period, pointing out that the rapid economic growth and cultural change of the 1960s and 1970s provided particularly fertile ground for Hollein's work, which was inspired by his years of study in America.

Job Floris also refers to the context of the times in his interview. He sees in Hollein a point of connection with an earlier tradition of Viennese modernism, particularly in works such as the small shops, which were executed with a combination of thoroughness and refinement. Hollein adopts a similar approach and architectural vocabulary, but the result, in keeping with the zeitgeist, is more modern and playful.

Overall, it can be said that many of the architects find it easier to engage with the history of Viennese modernism through the work of Hermann Czech, rather than Hans Hollein, as Reem Almannai notes. But as with Czech, it is Hollein's small-scale works that are unanimously accorded a special status. Oliver Lütjens and Thomas Padmanabhan describe how Hollein is able to create a whole world of meaning in his small projects, which are complex and subtle. Above all, these projects give a sense of Hollein's reach as an architect and a man of culture who put out feelers everywhere and brought everything into his work. For Aslı Çiçek, what is particularly exciting about Hollein's visual language is the way it incorporates many elements that are in her view not primarily architectural, but that work together nonetheless to give the projects a specific associative charge.

More easily accessible is Hollein's interpretation of the role of the architect as a "seismograph" for new developments and currents, even outside the discipline. For many of the interviewees, it is a significant and inspiring position. Linked to this interpretation, David Kohn describes Hollein's expansion of the concept of architecture as his greatest achievement. Creatively merging the different facets of the discipline, Hollein dissolved the boundaries between urban space and interior space, furniture and architecture, archaic and modern, pop and intellect, low culture and high culture. According to Kohn, this positive questioning of boundaries still provides a fruitful reference plane for an associative and inclusive understanding of the design of our environment. Dirk Somers has used Hollein projects as a direct source of design inspiration, though he adds that the more one engages with the work at the level of design, the more its complexity becomes apparent, so any attempt to produce a straight copy is bound to fail.

For Beate Hølmebakk, Hollein's works are not a direct reference, but his interest in landscape as space is something that she shares, and that is reflected in her own work.

Hølmebakk, for her part, is clearly convinced of Hollein's position as an artist-architect—a point of contention among the architects interviewed. For Martin Feiersinger, Hollein's whole conception of the world was that of a full-blooded architect, not an artist, an opinion essentially shared by Kersten Geers, who finds Hollein's work interesting only when it is the "work of an architect." Wilfried Kuehn notes that Hollein only chose between art and architecture in the early 1970s. In his view, Hollein's turn towards architecture might even have been a "mistake," given how influential he was for important artists such as Claes Oldenburg or Walter Pichler.

For all the architects, the oscillations in Hollein's position—a result of the evident inconsistencies in what he said and what he built—creates a tension that piques their interest and invites them to look more closely, with the greater objectivity granted by time. Assessing Hollein's legacy calls for a critical approach. When his work is reflected through a more associative lens, it becomes apparent that we need to rethink many of the things we thought we knew about him.

Endnotes

1 Hans Hollein in dialogue with: Reem Almannai and Florian Fischer (Almannai Fischer Architekten, Munich); Aslı Çiçek (Brussels); Pier Paolo Tamburelli (baukuh, Milan); Dirk Somers (Bovenbouw Architectuur, Antwerp); Claudia Cavallar (Vienna); Maria Conen and Raoul Sigl (Conen Sigl Architekt:innen, Zurich); Stefanie Everaert and Caroline Lateur (Doorzon, Ghent); Andreas Rumpfhuber (Expanded Design, Vienna); Martin Feiersinger (Vienna); David Kohn (David Kohn Architects, London); Wilfried Kuehn (Kuehn Malvezzi, Berlin); Oliver Lütjens and Thomas Padmanabhan (Lütjens Padmanabhan Architekt*innen, Zurich); Beate Hølmebakk (Manthey Kula, Oslo); Job Floris (Monadnock, Rotterdam); Kersten Geers (OFFICE Kersten Geers David Van Severen, Brussels).

2 Dialogues on Hollein was initiated in 2019 in the context of the research grant: Hans-Hollein-Projektstipendium (Bundeskanzleramt, Sektion II—Kunst und Kultur, Abteilung II/6—Bildende Kunst, Architektur, Design, Mode, Foto und Medienkunst).

3 *Metaphern und Metamorphosen*, Paris, Vienna, Berlin, 1986–1987; *Hans Hollein*, Historical Museum of the City of Vienna (Wien Museum), 1995; *Aufbauen und Aushöhlen*, Berlin, Vienna, 2003; *Aircraft Carrier*, Venice Biennale, 2006; *Hans Hollein*, Universalmuseum Joanneum, Graz, 2011–2012; *Hans Hollein: Everything is Architecture*, Abteiberg Museum, Mönchengladbach, 2014; *Hollein*, MAK, Vienna, 2014, curated by Wilfried Kuehn and Marlies Wirth.

4 *MAN transFORMS: The Documents*, gta exhibition space, ETH Zurich, 2016, curated by Laurent Stalder and Samuel Korn.

5 SammlungsLab, *Hans Hollein ausgepackt: Das Haas-Haus*, Az W, Vienna, 2019, curated by Mechthild Ebert.

6 Eva Branscome, *Hans Hollein and Postmodernism: Art and Architecture in Austria, 1958–1985* (London: Routledge, 2017).

7 Conversation with Christoph Monschein, January 2023. Monschein worked in the office of Hollein from the mid-1990s and in 2010 cofounded Hans Hollein & Partner ZT-GmbH.

8 Dietmar Steiner, "Die Skizze eines Namens," in *Hans Hollein—eine Ausstellung*, exh. cat. (Vienna: Eigenverlag der Museen der Stadt Wien, 1995).

9 François Burkhardt and Paulus Manker, *Hans Hollein: Writings & Manifestos* (Vienna: University of Applied Arts Vienna, 2002).

Monika Platzer

About the Collection, Collecting and Hollein

The Architekturzentrum Wien is the only museum in Austria dedicated to architecture. Its holdings on Austrian architecture of the twentieth and twenty-first centuries, already the most extensive in the country, are growing all the time. At the core of the collection are the archives and bequests of more than one hundred architects, encompassing everything from architectural drawings, plans, models, and photographs, to furniture, design objects, rare books, and written documents of various kinds. The broad spectrum of materials illustrates not only the conception and process of development of the architecture but also the context.

Whereas official bodies such as building authorities or federal or state archives are bound by legal obligations, the Az W is free to base the acquisition of an archive on an evaluation of its content. To be selected, it is important that the work makes an outstanding contribution to the building culture of Austria, has a socio-political dimension, contributes to an exchange with other disciplines concerned with the built environment, and stirs debate at an international level. All of these qualities, and many more, applied to Hans Hollein, who was himself well aware of the power of the archive as a vehicle of memory, representation, knowledge construction, and mythologizing. Dietmar Steiner, the founding director of Az W, and Hannes Pflaum, its former president, began their efforts to keep the important archive in the country immediately after Hollein's passing in 2014. The first viewing of the archive, which was spread over five locations, took place that same year.

Atelier Hollein, Vienna, 1970s. Archive Hans Hollein, Az W and MAK, Vienna.

Rare Commodity

But efforts were also made to acquire parts of Hollein's work for public collections in the early years of his career, at a time when few museums collected drawings and portfolios by contemporary architects. In 1967–1968, the Museum of Modern Art in New York hosted the legendary exhibition, *Architectural Fantasies: Drawings from the Museum Collection*, featuring the artist Walter Pichler and the architects Raimund Abraham and Hans Hollein.[1] After the show closed, all of the exhibits were purchased by MoMA's architecture department through the Philip Johnson Fund. Works described in the exhibition as "Visual Poems between poetry and prophecy"[2]—among them, Hollein's Aircraft Carrier in the Landscape from 1964—have since achieved iconic status. MoMA's curator of architecture at the time, Arthur Drexler, organized a number of these pioneering shows exploring the intersection of architecture and art. In the slipstream of Drexler's exhibitions, which promoted a dialogue between these spheres, an art market for architectural drawings began to be established.

In 1979, Heinrich Klotz was appointed founding director of the German Architecture Museum (DAM), which would open its doors five years later. The acquisition budget for building up the collection, which focuses on the work of contemporary architects, was astonishingly high by European standards, at DM 250,000 per annum. As early as 1981, Heinrich Klotz announced his intention to acquire Hans Hollein's "entire material" for DM 100,000.[3] Although the acquisition never materialized, the DAM had the largest holdings of Hollein material outside of his atelier, with a total of sixty items, ahead even of the Pompidou Center, which made some thirty-nine purchases between 1993 and 1995. In 2016, however, the balance shifted as the Pompidou Center increased its Hollein holdings to 122 items.[4] During the same period, Niall Hobhouse acquired a body of drawings from Hollein's early years for his private collection, Drawing Matter, which is open to the public.

There was great international interest in the Hans Hollein archive, then, and even though major institutions such as the Canadian Centre for Architecture and the Getty Research Institute had changed their acquisition policies in favor of donations, there was a danger that the archive would leave Austria.

Acquisition

What followed was an intensive two-year search for a solution acceptable to all parties—one that adequately compensated the heirs but also provided the conditions for an appropriate reappraisal of the work. The idea of dividing the archive between an international and a national institution was considered, but there was no agreement on the criteria for apportioning the works. It was also recognized that such a split would make things more difficult for future researchers. In 2015, under the then Federal Minister for Art and Culture, Josef Ostermayer, an Austrian solution was found. The federal government acquired the archive for 250,000 euros, with the Museum of Applied Arts (MAK) acting as legal owner of the collection, which was entrusted to the Az W on permanent loan on the basis of its many years of expertise in cataloging and conservation. This collaboration between institutions, the only one of its kind in Austria, is partly financed through federal cultural funding, though most of the work on the collection is maintained by the Az W's own resources.

In this way, a further fragmentation of the Hollein holdings was avoided, giving Austria two archival bodies for research: the private Hollein archive administered by his heirs Lilli and Max Hollein, and the Archive Hans Hollein, Az W and MAK, Vienna. The latter is characterized by its epic breadth: here, architectural thinking is manifested through the density of material. Hollein is made tangible, comprehensible, through the alternation of iconic, international, and representative works with the peripheral, the local, and the everyday.

In parallel, the state reached an agreement with the heirs to award annually a Hans Hollein Art Prize for Architecture, with prize money of 15,000 euros, and two Hans Hollein research grants of 9,000 euros each. One such grant was the starting point for this publication and the exhibition that accompanies it.

Extent

Each archive provides information about the processes of creating the projects and allows conclusions to be drawn about the office culture. On acquiring the holdings in 2017, we found a mass of material dispersed across different storage sites: stacks of tightly packed boxes in between bulging shelves, along with an impressive amount of model cases, packed furniture, and exhibition props. The entire holdings ultimately filled 263 pallets, made up of the following categories of materials:

    72 pallets: models
    62 pallets: plan material
    48 pallets: administrative documents
    43 pallets: project documentation
    18 pallets: clippings, catalogs
    12 pallets: books, journals, magazines
     8 pallets: photo archive

Holdings

This makes the archive of Hans Hollein the largest architect's bequest taken over within Austria. Preparing an archive of this scale is clearly a time-consuming process: the material has to be systematically organized and inventoried and at the same time placed in an archivally appropriate environment. Nevertheless, given the importance of the material, our primary goal was to ensure that researchers were able to access the archive while we proceeded with this work, instead of having to wait until the cataloging was complete, as is usually the case.

Az W collection depot in Möllersdorf, Hollein holdings after the acquisition in 2016. Photo: Iris Ranzinger

Az W collection depot in Möllersdorf, Hollein holdings during the process of inventory 2023. Photo: Karin Lux

In order to get to know the nature of the Hollein holdings—every acquisition is different—and to define a workflow for processing them, we selected eight case studies and systematically drilled down through all the layers of materials. As a result of this analysis, priority was given to a chronological listing of the projects and their respective portfolios of material, which were recorded in the Az W collection database. The scope and nature of the material, along with the contents of documents, can be traced in a structured database application.

The 2019 exhibition *Hans Hollein Unpacked: The Haas Haus*,[5] curated by Mechthild Ebert as part of the Az W SammlungsLab series, provided the public with their first glimpse of the wealth of archival material. The working process of the Hollein Atelier was shown in greater depth than ever before, enabling visitors to follow the genesis of the project from the urban planning considerations, through the detailed studies, to the final design. What made this exhibition unique was the sheer concentration of materials that documented the process of working through ideas and developing the project further.

The Protagonist

Hans Hollein enjoyed international recognition during his lifetime, winning the Pritzker Prize in 1985 (the only Austrian to do so to date). He took part in the contemporary architectural discourse. His experimental early work is featured in every standard work on avant-garde architecture of the 1960s, while his first major project, the Abteiberg Museum in Mönchengladbach, could be said to have initiated a postmodern turn—a "revision of the modern."[6] With that work he proclaimed himself an autonomous artist-architect, declaring: "I approached the matter of planning this museum both as an architect and as an artist: as an artist who has a close relationship to the works of art presented therein, as an artist who produces works of art (exhibited in various museums), and as an artist who interprets a built object as a work of art."[7]

This (self-)image would coalesce into a self-interpretation that merits critical reassessment by architectural historians. As early as 1968 Hollein drafted guidelines for a publication and photo archive documenting his projects.[8] In recent years, however, the idea of a body of work being single-handedly created by a heroic (predominantly male) master of architecture has increasingly been called into question. The contributions of Fritz Madl, Erich Pedevilla, Madeleine Jenewein, and Christoph Monschein,[9] to name just a few key players in the Hollein Atelier, still need to be defined. At the same time other stakeholders, such as the institutions or individual clients who commissioned the works, have become increasingly important for the research. Unlike younger utopian colleagues, such as Coop Himmelb(l)au or Haus-Rucker-Co, Hollein worked independently, rather than in a group, and trained not at the Vienna University of Technology but at the Academy of Fine Arts under Clemens Holzmeister. His 1956 diploma thesis for a "World's Fair Pavilion" clearly bears the imprint of Konrad Wachsmann, whose seminars at the Salzburg Summer Academy influenced a whole series of Holzmeister's students, among them arbeitsgruppe 4 and Ottokar Uhl. After graduating, Hollein went to Sweden, where he worked for AOS Arkitekter (Magnus Ahlgren, Torbjörn Olsson, and Sven Silow) in Stockholm until 1958. Watercolors in the archive attest to his engagement with modernist urban planning in Sweden, for example at Vällingby. After receiving a Harkness fellowship from the Commonwealth Fund of New York City, Hollein was able to study in the US, first at the Illinois Institute of Technology (IIT) from 1958 to 1959, and then at the University of California, Berkeley, where he gained a master's in architecture in 1960. Other young Austrians went to the US as Fulbright scholars: before Hollein, Eduard Sekler had studied at Harvard GSD in 1952, Wilhelm Holzbauer at the Massachusetts Institute of Technology (MIT) in 1956, and Erich Boltenstern Jr. at the University of Texas in 1958. Recent research on the "Americanization" of Austria has highlighted the importance of American exchange and educational programs in the postwar years.[10] The common purpose of this kind of cultural diplomacy was to expose Austria's elite to America's liberal, democratic value system, under the assumption that these values would be "repatriated" when they went back home. Hollein's sojourn in the United States laid the foundation for the internationalization of his architecture. However, the main transfer was at the economic level. In 1966, Hans Hollein won the annual $25,000 R.S. Reynolds Memorial Award for his Retti candle shop. The award was set up by the Reynolds Aluminum Company, which had switched to peacetime production immediately after the war, gaining a foothold first in automobile manufacturing and then in the construction industry, producing windows, doors, and entire curtainwall systems. The inaugural award in 1957 went to Spanish architects Rafael de la Joya, Manuel Barbero-Rebolledo, and Cesar Ortiz Echague for their SEAT automobile plant in Barcelona.

The dissemination of architecture—whether through image, text, or exhibition—has always played a significant role, as Hollein was well aware from very early on. In 1965, he analyzed the Austrian contribution to international surveys of postwar architecture.[11] Dissatisfied with the result, he launched a media offensive to raise awareness of the work in the journal *BAU,* where he was a member of the editorial team from 1965 to 1970. In addition to his architectural practice, Hollein held various official posts that allowed him to play a role in defining cultural policy at a national level. He was commissioner of the Austrian contribution to the Venice Art Biennale (1978–1990) and Architecture Biennale (1991–1996), as well as president of the Kunstsenat (Senate for the Arts, 1999–2012). As the long-time chairman of the Zentralvereinigung der Architekt:innen (ZV) for Vienna, Lower Austria, and Burgenland, he was an influential advocate for the profession. And through his affiliation with the University of Applied Arts, where he began teaching in 1974 and led the masterclass for architecture from 1979 to 2002, the institution became much more strongly international.

Legacy

Legacies have the potential to change the way we look at architecture. Testifying to an act of will, they lay bare the approach to the work, the solutions that were discarded, the variants, the contexts, the influences. Hollein used his archive as a kind of reservoir for future work, recycling ideas in new projects—an approach that is especially clear in his use of models. For Hollein, the model was an essential working and design tool, a means to make tangible essential aspects of the space, formal structure, proportions, and choice of materials. Whereas archiving was for him an artistic practice, archival holdings in public collections have a different role, as repositories that can provide a counterweight to an artist's biographical narrative and are open to cultural and architectural historical inquiry. With the historical distance that has come with the acquisition of the archive, a new generation is critically examining the content and the context of his work, opening up a new and differentiated view of Hollein. The relevance of Hollein to contemporary practice is the theme that runs through the dialogues with the fifteen European architects included in this publication. In the dialogues we rediscover Hollein's work as a source of stimulation but also friction, as something to appropriate or, alternatively, to keep at arm's length. The curators and their interlocutors engage with Hollein's work in a phenomenological way.

In the exhibition, the material from the Archive Hans Hollein, Az W and MAK, Vienna does not function as a historical source. Rather, in juxtaposing Hollein with contemporary architects, the curators focus on associative points of contact between the generations, on the tacit knowledge—knowledge made up of personal convictions, perspectives, and value systems—on which every architectural practice is based. The curators' strategic choices in the exhibition and the book connect history with the present day—and vice versa. The result, presented here, is a collective attempt to open up a discussion around the intrinsic qualities of architecture as the expression of an act of will.

Endnotes

1 The exhibition was held from July 27, 1967 to February 12, 1968.

2 MoMA Press Release, July 27, 1967, https://www.moma.org/documents/moma_press-release_326523.pdf.

3 According to information provided by Katja Leiskau, head of the DAM Archive, April 21, 2023.

4 https://www.centrepompidou.fr/en/recherche/oeuvres?terms=hans%20hollein&display=List.

5 SammlungsLab #4, *Hans Hollein ausgepackt: Das Haas-Haus,* was shown from June 13 to August 19, 2019, at the Architekturzentrum Wien.

6 *The Revision of the Modern* was the title of the inaugural exhibition at the German Architecture Museum. See Heinrich Klotz, *Die Revision der Moderne: Postmoderne Architektur 1960–1980,* exh. cat. (Munich: Prestel, 1984).

7 https://museum-abteiberg.de/architecture/hans-hollein-en/hans-hollein/?lang=en.

8 "Im Interesse einer besseren Büroorganisation sind nachstehende Richtlinien und Organisationshilfen ab 4.11.1968 zu beachten," typescript, Archive Hans Hollein, Az W and MAK, Vienna.

9 Christoph Monschein founded in 2010 together with Hans Hollein the firm Hans Hollein & Partner ZT-GmbH.

10 Monika Platzer, *Cold War and Architecture: The Competing Forces that Reshaped Austria after 1945,* ed. Architekturzentrum Wien (Zurich: Park Books, 2020), 151.

11 Hans Hollein, Steinbüschl [*sic.*] et al., "Architekturenzyklopädien und die Österreichische Architektur nach 1945," *BAU* 20, no. 1 (1964–1965): 31.

Interviews

Reem Almannai and Florian Fischer
Almannai Fischer Architekten

Do you have a direct point of connection with Hans Hollein? How do you see
his work and his position in relation to your own practice?

FF I've seen the shops and the Haas Haus in Vienna, but I've never
been to the museum in Mönchengladbach. Up to now, we've never
had a specific interest in Hollein, but you can't get around him—he's
a recurring presence. In a competition entry for student housing in
Weimar, we unthinkingly drew a facade with a mangled Hollein window.
It was more out of necessity than anything else, because both the facade
and the staircase were conceived in sculptural terms, and we weren't
getting anywhere with "normal" windows. What we were looking for,
then, was an art form of the window. Having rejected round windows
for "ideological" reasons, but also as a provocation, we combined
a horizontal window with two rounded off elements to create a kind of
Hollein window. Directly behind this Hollein window, there would have
been a laundry room. This was our take on a famous Hollein motif:
it wasn't theoretically grounded, but highly direct—and also mutilating.

Almannai Fischer Architekten, Hall of Residence, Weimar, Germany, 2017–2025. Rendering of east elevation.

RA In that specific case, there were other references, not just for the
sculptural facade but also for the exterior staircase, where the basis—
or better, the godmother—of our design was the staircase in the Lloyd's

building by Richard Rogers. Incorporating that was, so to speak, the wanton antithesis to our tendency to strive for restraint and objectivity in so many other aspects of the design.

FF Rather than the likes of Hollein, it's Hermann Czech who engages us in a more challenging way. If we're dealing with Czech's work in our own design, we're doing so more methodically, and not just on a one-to-one or even formalist basis involving mutated or applied motifs. Also, when Czech talks about how striving for objectivity leads to a heterogeneity of expression, he's talking about precisely the path that we would like to follow.

How would you describe your own architectural background?

Hans Hollein, Haas Haus, Vienna, Austria, 1985–1990. Main corner facing Stock-im-Eisen Platz. Archive Hans Hollein, Az W and MAK, Vienna. Photo: Franz Hubmann/ Imagno/picturedesk.com

RA We both have different architectural backgrounds and we often set our priorities differently. We got to know each other when we overlapped as teaching assistants at TU München, and not as students. During my studies I interned with Hermann Czech for a summer. I was particularly happy to have the opportunity to work for him as I really appreciated his approach to architecture. During my time in Vienna, I would pass by the Haas Haus every morning, but I didn't take the building very seriously—I had my preconceptions. In fact, going by it, I felt a distaste that would only be dispelled when I got to Singerstrasse, where Czech's office was. The question is, what do I think of the Haas Haus today, because my most intense memory of that time was walking past it.

FF Jan De Vylder once said "That it does not look good makes that it looks good." The challenge is to stand in front of the Haas Haus and visualize this.

There is a direct connection between Czech and Hollein. Czech was for many years a teaching assistant in Hans Hollein's masterclass at the University of Applied Arts in Vienna.

RA As a student, I initially looked for simple explanations of the world. How do you classify things? What's good, what's bad? But the perception of what's good or bad changes a lot over time, as you become aware of more complex connections. Looking at the architectures of Hollein and Czech, the relation between them is not immediately obvious, but in a way it's logical that in a small city like Vienna these two architectural greats of their generation would have a connection with each other.

Hollein's work with models is also interesting to us. What is your approach to working with models?

RA It's very easy to make models, even if you don't have a great deal of technical knowledge. We first discovered the model as an instrument that does not lie: it exposes many fine details that would be obscured with other methods of representation.

23

FF We've experimented with that a lot, but our approach is also changing. In the past we've used models to develop interiors, even ones that were not so complicated, then we've produced photos or perspectives from them. But over time, we began to have our doubts: were the models being overloaded to some extent?

It wasn't so long ago—with the apartment building in Goldern,[1] to be exact—that we started to think of models in less atmospheric terms. We wanted to build a more abstract model again, but on the same scale, 1:20 or 1:25. The model is also just a form of section, with the added bonus of three-dimensionality. If it is photographed in good light, the photos can also be very precise. But cutting away the model so that it's something like a "doll's house" and furnishing it down to the last piece of furniture with the correct materials is something we're now wary of— both as a method and in terms of the atmosphere it creates. It is an act of reproducing reality—not just metaphorically, but also quite directly— and in our experience it almost automatically reproduces platitudes rather than bringing new and surprising things to light. What we're looking for instead are methods that are defamiliarizing, that allow for unforeseen developments.

RA Very sectional models have never really interested us. But I do very much like those large models that let you see the overall context from all sides. For us, it's about making the structural connections visible.

FF There's another aspect, too: the practical one of the energy and resources specifically invested in architecture. Added to this, in our design process we trust the plan, i.e., the 2D drawing, even more than we did before and don't feel so compelled to check everything in three dimensions. We're increasingly moving away from the formal aspects of architecture, from a concern with defining atmosphere. What's driving our work now is the desire to pay greater attention to technology and to bring the performance form of architecture into play.

And here perhaps we could refer back to Hollein, who once said, "Architecture is not the solution, architecture is a statement." It's an assertion we would be very critical of. We would like architecture to be more of a solution than a statement. Not the solution to every problem: if someone is sick, architecture won't cure them. Without making any esoteric, exaggerated claims for architecture, we think it should provide solutions to significant contemporary problems. Models should also resolve technical issues and not just purely "architectural" ones.

Technological progress was a central theme of Hans Hollein's work. The aluminum he used in the Retti candle shop was perceived as a material of the future in the mid-1960s. Likewise, the curtain wall facade in Mönchengladbach. Technology is playing an increasingly important role in your work too, but you have a more distanced relationship to building products.

FF I'd like to be as euphoric about new materials as you could be in the 1960s or 1970s. I'd love to be the first to say, "Bring them on and we'll work with all of them." What prevents us from doing that is not a formal or aesthetic issue: the big obstacle is sustainability. It's that banal.

RA But we also face new technical problems today. In Haiming, we realized a gymnasium in timber construction.[2] It's a highly efficient structure— cheap, sustainable, effective, and easy to dismantle. A nail plate and a solid piece of wood, not glued, except for a few bottom chords, which are glulam, overall very ecological.

We don't make grand "moral" claims for our use of construction technology. We probably prefer a mineral wool brick, of the kind we used in Altötting, to thermal insulation plastered on the outside.[3] But for a private apartment building— the client was Florian's sister—we tried to up the ante. We opted for a non-insulated/filled brick, against the advice of the manufacturer. This is also the thing with technology: you're thinking, what is the state of the art, how do I fulfill all the technical conditions—but at the same time: where do I dare to make things simpler? Admittedly, we fell a bit on our face here. The sound insulation of the specific brick we chose is pretty poor.

FF That obstacle of sustainability: I would love to have that rush of always applying the latest product. There was a small window of time in the 1960s when you could have fun like that. But I have a question for you: was building technology really such a central theme for Hollein over the years?

Almannai Fischer Architekten, Townhouse near Friedrichwerder Church, Berlin, Germany, 2014–2019. Main entrance. Photo: Sebastian Schels

We think there's an ambivalence to the way Hollein dealt with material. His approach was more conceptual than craft-based. But his goal was to make architecture as progressive as possible, including from the point of view of construction.

FF When it comes to materials, we try to remain pragmatic. The client for the six-story townhouse in Berlin really wanted to have natural stone. We suggested a dolomite that is the opposite of chic. When this stone is applied to the facade, it takes on the peculiar kind of shimmer that you associate with an anonymous office building of the 1990s, which fits very well with this developer environment where the land is "contaminated" politically and socially. This stone is coupled with an aluminum facade with standard Schüco profiles that are too thick—they don't make the filigree profiles anymore. But that's how you deal with, or heal, the disruptive power of technology. You cannot escape it, so you need to embrace it. It's partly about affirmation. If there are things you can't change, then you need to find a way to make them good. For the building in Berlin, we built a 1:1 mockup of part of the facade in corrugated cardboard. That allowed us to acclimatize ourselves to the thick profiles—not just simply get used to them.

Tomb of Eurysaces the Baker, 50–20 BCE, fig. 183 from Ludwig Curtius, *Das Antike Rom* (Vienna: Anton Scholl & Co., 1944). Photo: Alfred Nawrath

Hans Hollein, Mobile Office, 1969. Photographed on the Aspern airfield, Vienna. Archive Hans Hollein, Az W and MAK, Vienna. Photo: Gino Molin-Pradel

In a lecture at the AA in London in the 1980s, Hollein talked about his life and influences.[4] He used two images to sum up his position. On the one hand there was the Tomb of Eurysaces in Rome, representing ritual, the symbolic; on the other, his Mobile Office, invoking the notion of "controlling body heat." He developed his conception of architecture between these two poles, which also formed the basis for his claim that all building ultimately evolves towards architecture. Can you understand this idiosyncratic approach, and, since we're speaking of images, what ones would you choose to represent your definition of architecture?

RA Through their juxtaposition, the pair of Hollein images sets up a powerful dialectic—the ruined tomb is incredibly powerful when seen alongside the plastic skin that encloses him. But as regards the corresponding image pair representing our understanding of architecture, we would be hard pressed to break our architecture down to just two images.

FF But we could. If we wanted to convey an expanded concept of architecture, we could show the picture of the tomatoes we harvested from our own garden, as we did in our lecture in Vienna two weeks ago, "Man and Nature—Tomatoes—Experience." This is very far removed from the formalisms of architecture.

Almannai Fischer Architekten, Man and Nature— Tomatoes—Experience, image from a lecture at TU Wien, Vienna, Austria, November 2020.

One could also say, "The architect is becoming more and more of a gardener," which suggests a completely different picture to the one of the budding starchitect Hollein, in his transparent bubble armed only with a phone…

RA …A very manly setup.

FF The garden is picturesque and very much in tune with the times. Our other experience in recent years that is the antithesis of starchitecture is the Großstadt cooperative we founded along with fourteen other people, including eleven architects. When we work together we're not acting as planning architects, but as developers of architecture and housing forms. The setup is hardly a world-first, but for us these last five years have been very interesting. The tomato is also a symbol of this: you can grow it, train the vine a certain way, but it has its own interests, and you have to take those into account. It's the same with housing: you can't pretend that your idea of life is the only valid one and that with a bit of manipulation or modeling you can make it universally palatable, so everyone will want to live that way, too. The cooperative's third project is going to be located in a gap in the middle of the *Gründerzeit* (mid-nineteenth-century) city. The question we are currently considering is: How do we approach the planning process? Do we organize a Europe-wide open competition for a house with fifteen inhabitants or do the complete opposite—an experiment in total participation? The building would then challenge the context conceptually, so to speak, and perhaps become—not un-architectural *per se*—but pure structure. There's also a bit of romance involved, in that we're saying this is perhaps the first building in Munich that has been authored but everyone involved, and not just by one or two architects.[5]

Reem, you've said you're tending to use fewer and fewer images. What do you use for teaching in Munich if you're not using pictures?

RA You effectively have this design bazaar at the beginning of each year, where you're meant to woo the students. The classic means to do this is to design a poster that combines a snazzy picture with text advertising your USP. But we're finding that we're having a hard time coming up with this image.

FF We're trying not to anticipate the outcome. For the diploma project we've been able to agree, for the moment, on a 1:1 detail of a door drop seal. That's an image, too. It's a world you can't avoid. But the point is not to indicate what the house will eventually look like: rather, it's to show a functional detail that perhaps has consequences for "collective living." Thinking about the performance of the door is a starting point for thinking about structures—as opposed to depicting a specific residential house. It's just occurred to me: that drop seal, together with a tomato, would be the picture pair to sum up our concept of architecture.

Hollein used writing as a way to explore basic assumptions about architecture, which later found their way directly into his projects. During his stay in the US, for example, he wrote about the pueblos, the settlements built by the indigenous peoples of the American Southwest. He then came back to Vienna and produced a design for a bank building that picked up certain themes of the pueblos, such as walking on the roof. What does writing about your architecture mean for you?

FF I studied philosophy before I stumbled into architecture, and I wanted to bring with me those elements of reflection and of writing. But what the two of us have never sat down together and written are texts that deal directly with our own method of design or our position towards the world as designers—as Hollein or Czech have often done.

What inspires your writing, then?

FF A couple of years ago I did a small online column for *Baumeister* magazine that helped me to assert certain themes in a pointed and also slightly aggressive way, as in, for example, "Beauty is for lazy people."[6] It's just to attract attention, but as a method it's quite revealing. In a column like that, if you phrase your opinions too delicately, they simply disappear into the silt of online content. You have to formulate things a bit more forcefully—even at the risk of feeling ashamed of yourself a few years later.

RA At the moment, preparing for lectures is the main way we reflect on our own architecture. Lectures are always linked to a specific topic, making us look at our work differently. It's like a building project, in that there's a context to consider. There can be a lot of discussion and exchange while we're preparing the lectures, as we lob ideas at each other and bring them all together at the end. We're forced to really get to the heart of things.

FF Speaking from experience, I think it's good to write retrospectively about your own projects, even if it's just for internal consumption. What forces were at play? What led to this or that decision, what were the factors, step by step, that informed the project? Though there's a danger of varnishing over or intellectualizing the end result, by writing continuously, writing becomes a tool for reflection. What were the themes of the work, what appealed to us intellectually? Putting something down in writing is different from expressing it orally.

Let's finish with another topic. It could be argued that Hollein's best works are found in the context of the established city. As soon as he works in a diffuse, peri-urban context, it becomes more difficult to find his buildings interesting. How do you deal with this issue?

RA We approach the context in a neutral way: it is as it is, and it is given. We haven't often had the chance to build in an inner-city or more established context. I don't think the townhouse in Berlin counts, as the urban planning decisions played a peripheral role and did not affect the formation of the building in a wider sense. The issues there were relatively minor, along the lines of how far can a bay window protrude? In less dense or more rural areas, more fundamental decisions are required. The question then is really: how do we want to respond to this place?

FF You could say that our attitude towards the context is the gesture of the open hand. We meet the context as it is and try to respect and develop (in the best sense) its quality. We try to understand the rules, to find a modest response. We do not want to idealize the context, to prettify it in the way that preservationists love to do, because we think that disorder, rupture, and imperfection are all part of the world we live in. We practice contextual design, meaning we don't exclude elements that fail to match the preservationists' concept of beauty. 1970s horizontal windows in a farming village, for example, would have a relevance for us as part of the context that needs to be considered and reflected on.

RA Our other problem with historic preservation is that it has a very selective understanding of context. It chooses one particular moment in history and elevates it to the status of a benchmark.

Does that mean you design from the context?

FF We wouldn't say that our projects can only be explained by the context. They have a technical or also typological impetus as well, along with a connection to a certain social context.

The Haas Haus, on the other hand, is a building designed out of context…

FF My prediction about the Haas Haus is that it will become less divisive when the technology of the glass facade is old enough to be seen through the lens of nostalgia. A veil of craftsmanship will then be drawn over the industrial product. But that time is not yet come. The building doesn't yet have the patina of an old-timer, but when it does, it will be read in much more artistic and sensitive terms than it is at present, when it is still too close to a contemporary crudeness. One could criticize Hollein for this: he should have been able to manage this earlier, this veil of nostalgia shouldn't have been necessary for the technological worth of the Haas Haus to become apparent.

Endnotes

1 Four unit apartment building, 2015–2020.

2 Sports hall, 2013–2016.

3 Residential building, 2017–2020.

4 Lecture entitled "Viennese Blood" at the Architectural Association, October 26, 1981.

5 The Metso'metso project in Munich-Haidhausen follows an experimental design method developed by Kooperative Großstadt called Open Plan Open Decision (OP-OD).

6 *Baumeister*, 2014–2016.

This Dialogue on Hans Hollein took place on October 19, 2020 online.

Almannai Fischer Architekten

Almannai Fischer Architekten was founded in 2016 by Reem Almannai, who studied architecture at the ETH Zurich, and Florian Fischer, who graduated from TU München. Based in Munich and Goldern, the office has focused in recent years on exploring alternative ways of commissioning affordable housing—an interest that led to its cofounding of the initiative Kooperative Großstadt, which acts as a non-profit housing developer. In addition to realizing various residential projects, the practice has also worked on exhibition design and public projects. Both Reem Almannai and Florian Fischer have published several texts on architecture. Florian Fischer is currently a professor at the RWTH Aachen.

Aslı Çiçek

Is there a direct relationship between your practice and Hans Hollein's "universe"?

Hans Hollein, Glassware and Ceramic Museum, Tehran, Iran, 1977–1978. Detail of display cases in Room 207. Archive Hans Hollein, Az W and MAK, Vienna. Photo: Peter Lehner

AC The Tehran Museum of Glassware and Ceramic, which I visited in 2016, is a very important project for me. The whole museum is well thought out. But what fascinated me was the autonomy of the exhibits and displays. The huge display cases appear like buildings in their own right, placed in an absurd Rococo-style interior. Strictly speaking, they have no relation to the city. As soon as you enter the museum, you forget that you're in Tehran. I don't think Hollein gave much thought to the urban context, or indeed to the objects placed in these vitrines. His approach was to create a distinctive vehicle for display that people would associate with objects of high value.

How is the exhibition structured?

AC As Hollein saw it, you don't need movable walls or elements to have a flexible exhibition design. He was interested in the figure moving through space, occasionally also in the artwork itself. The focus of the spatial approach is not a fixed gaze, but rather the perception of the viewer as they move through the galleries. The displays were designed with a great deal of precision.

How has the project inspired your own work?

AC In my work I very rarely design fixed walls, rooms, or partitions. My approach is more focused on dealing with the objects and the way they're presented. This attention to the objects themselves is my point of contact with Hollein. His work gives me some license for my own designs. Rather than simply providing supports for the objects, you can have these additional elements—self-assured presences—in the space.

In a text for *OASE 94* you wrote about the first phase of OMA, reflecting on Koolhaas's construction of a new perception of the interior of a building, a silent absence.[1] Compare this with the Haas Haus in Vienna, designed by Hollein in the early 1980s. Do you see these works by Hollein and Koolhaas as counterpositions?

AC Yes, I would say that Hollein and Koolhaas were assigned—or rather chose for themselves—two different roles in cultural production. Hollein saw himself as an artist as well as an architect, Koolhaas more

30

as an author. Koolhaas was not concerned with aesthetics, form, or interior design; rather, he dealt with strategies, trying to develop a framework in which life could unfold on its own. Hollein, on the other hand, designed decors for life, controlling the projects down to the last detail. He also put himself at the very center of the work—creating or realizing a kind of universe around his ideas. In Hollein's texts the descriptions are defined but redolent with associations. He came from Vienna, after all, and had a connection with Freud and Jung. This associative thinking, as well as the images resulting from it, took on an important role, shaping Hollein's work. Think of the palm trees in the travel agencies and their very direct associations with exoticism. He had no inhibitions about placing the palm trees in his interiors as if they were props in a stage set in the theater.

"Where there is architecture nothing else is possible," Koolhaas wrote in his text, "Imagining Nothingness,"[2] whereas Hollein was repeatedly criticized for overloading his projects with ideas.

AC Yes, but I think the intention in both cases was fundamentally the same. With Hollein, everything was architecture and everything connected to it was important. What I find so exciting about his visual language is the way it incorporates elements that are not always very architectural. The addition of these associative elements gives Hollein's projects a symbolic charge. OMA and Koolhaas were more concerned to make a statement.

In your text on OMA's first decade you talk about an absence of specific qualities in the interiors of early OMA projects. Do you see Hollein's different interpretations as counterstrategies, or more as an early form of commercialization?

Aslı Çiçek, *Constantin Brancusi: Sublimation of Form*, exhibition, BOZAR, Brussels, Belgium, 2019. Exhibition view with glass display cases. Photo: Maxime Delvaux

AC Hollein saw spaces of consumption as having a certain decadence. And this quality was staged almost as an "embellishment," giving the work a kind of theatrical character. Every chance he had to make architecture, he took, using whatever means were available. His paper projects of the early years deal with these themes conceptually. But Hollein was also interested in the reality of urban space and life itself and when the moment was right he seized the opportunity to realize his ideas. He carried this theatrical approach even into his designs for very commercial spaces, lending them a certain glamor.

Where do you find this sense of theater?

AC For me, the Abteiberg Museum is a total experience—the work where this flowing transition between urban space, interior, and exterior is most palpable. You have the sense that you're walking simultaneously through the spaces of the city and the museum, from top to bottom and vice versa. The building itself was designed down to the last millimeter.

His projects also display an integrity and a consistency. If he developed a particular approach, he would work with it again and again. In my view, this is a courageous thing to do in face of the commercial pressure to always come up with something new. Hollein was an artist, an architect, a man of culture, and at the same time he took on a lot of commercial projects. The unifying element here is probably his idea of "everything is architecture," which he pursued without compromise.

In your projects you pursue a subtle approach that allows for the possibility of introducing and incorporating specific qualities or regional elements into the interior. Did Hollein have a different approach?

AC He did indeed. Subtle is a word that can't be directly applied to Hollein's work and his approach to the perception of the context. In this sense, it could perhaps be said that Hollein's work is very introverted and introspective. Already in the early paper projects you can see how the design becomes more and more inward-looking as it evolves. He is already thinking on a large scale, but not designing purely urban projects. The Haas Haus is a prime example of a built work that provoked a lot of discussion and criticism because it was inserted into this very historical context in the center of Vienna. For Hollein, each project represented an opportunity for architectural expression, but he seems to have approached the surrounding context in quite abstract terms, rather than seeing it as something defined by a particular time or place, by local or regional elements. His position on this was quite rigid and strict. I don't think he was much concerned with the environment, even if he hoped his works would change or influence the environment in some way. Hollein's projects were on the one hand very contemporary, yet on the other hand they were not, because they were very theatrical and detached from the outside world. What you have is a certain narrative with set pieces embroidered with the decor and elements associated with that narrative. I think Hollein created his own universe within this closed set.

Before he became an architect who built, Hollein was an architect who exhibited, and he also contributed as an artist to the Biennale exhibition *Life and Death*.[3] In our opinion, the exhibitions were the testing ground for his architecture. What is your view on this?

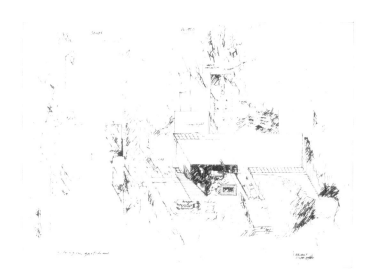

Hans Hollein, *Work and Behavior–Life and Death. Everyday Situations*, exhibition at the 36th Venice Biennale, Italy, 1972. Sketch of the Austrian Pavilion and its surroundings. Black and white photocopy. Archive Hans Hollein, Az W and MAK, Vienna.

AC I agree with you. His objects were not merely "applied art": they represented certain propositions that were important to him. Hollein cultivated his contacts with artists, who certainly influenced his work. The point, for him, was not just to talk about ideas, but to implement as many of them as possible. So, the exhibitions were undoubtedly a kind of laboratory. Exhibition designs usually have to be developed rather quickly, since opening dates cannot be postponed, but they allow certain freedoms that you don't have in other architectural projects. Often there is an interior space that is protected from the weather, so you can work more freely with materiality. In this sense, exhibition design is very rewarding, because it gives you latitude to experiment.

What was Hollein's approach to dealing with materials?

AC I think for Hollein it was more important to be seen as an artist, rather than as a "true" expert in materials. He placed a great deal of emphasis on associative, serious themes, which are also reflected in the titles of his works. He dared to attempt to translate these ideas into the spatial realm—and when he wasn't able to do so, he captured them in a pure conceptual form.

The kind of approach that Hollein pursued and applied in his projects is no longer found in architecture today. He brought something of his own personality into the work, using this freedom to develop the project further, to design and realize it as he saw fit. I think it was a very bold, creative move, using these projects as a laboratory for experimentation with as few limits as possible, because it ensured that the poetic and associative elements were not lost in the translation of the idea into architecture.

But can't these attitudes also be criticized? You could say that Hollein belonged to an egocentric generation that was also responsible for breaking quite a few things.

AC It's true that it's easy to criticize his generation. The positions they took were bold, but also very fragile, vulnerable, and open to attack. But I think this criticism is also important—there's hardly any dialogue or dispute in what passes for architectural criticism today. Very often, controversial works are quick to disappear, but Hollein's consistency, his constant, uncompromising approach, has become even clearer over time.

33

Were things easier, better in those days?

AC I don't like nostalgia, I don't think it's constructive. But of course it was a different time back then. There were these different positions developed individually as well as in design collectives in different countries such as Italy, the UK. In recent years there has been a renewed interest in that period, most of it admittedly focused on the formal language. You see individual positions being adopted as an aesthetic tool, an appealing style, even more strongly than Hollein himself asserted. But very few offices or architects are really engaging with these references. I think often it's only the visual language that is adopted, and not the content or thoughts behind it. Hollein's ideas drew on the history of architecture, yet he always tried to do something new. That's what characterizes his work: it's complex and interesting to talk about, rather than particularly beautiful or praiseworthy.

But there's also another side to Hollein's exhibitions, where he presents ideas about design, life, and ways of living, as in *MAN transFORMS* at the Cooper Hewitt, for example.[4]

AC I think it's important for institutions to be aware that exhibitions designed by architects will bear the imprint—the independent stance—of their designer. An exhibition is not just about the works on show; the installation, the spatial atmosphere or mood, can greatly enhance the experience of a visit, but it can also completely destroy it. The architect's installations themselves become part of the whole experience. I think these aspects, these meta-narratives, flowed into Hollein's exhibition designs and installations as well.

Is Hollein's design approach characterized by particular contrasts?

AC The context of turn-of-the-century Vienna certainly played a role for him. The pictorial and the associative, the search for deeper meaning, were very important elements of the culture of that time and indeed of the whole century that followed. The Freudian analyst's couch that Hollein designed is indicative of his interest. His architecture, in my opinion, went beyond establishing a simple visual connection. In the Glass Museum in Tehran I was able to experience the power of Hollein's spaces, something that cannot be fully conveyed by the photographs. This mirrored pedestal forms a self-contained universe within the museum. It's a fantastic atmospheric space, imbued with an almost nostalgic futurism. The power of this space cannot be ignored.

You've already mentioned scenography, and one of your recent projects was a set design for a dance performance. Hollein famously did the set design for Schnitzler's *Komödie der Verführung* (1980) at the Burgtheater, for example. How would you compare his work with yours?

AC I love to read and literature often provides a starting point for my work. The commission for the set design came to me before the dance performance had been choreographed. There was no text or specific narrative, so I was able to work very freely. It is this possibility of inter-pretation that develops so beautifully in a project like this, probably similar to Hollein's set design, which I know from pictures. But of course there is one essential difference between set design and exhibition

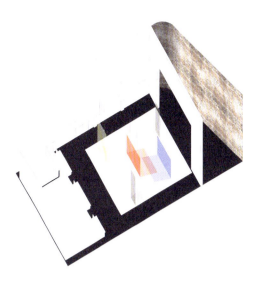

Aslı Çiçek, *Letters 2 Dance*, stage set for a dance performance, choreography by Femke Gyselinck, various theatres, Belgium, 2022. Digital drawing.

architecture, which is the position of the viewer. The audience for the performance has a fixed viewpoint and, unlike the people on the stage, they're not allowed to move. Architecture, on the other hand, involves movement. We move through spaces all the time—we don't look at them from a particular fixed viewpoint. On stage, there is a further difference between dance and theater. Dance is a little closer to architecture because words hardly figure in a performance: it's about pure movement, meaning the space is perceived differently through the figures, the dancers, who direct the viewer's gaze. In Hollein's well-known set design for the Burgtheater, this gaze is also directed by the dialogue and the canopy, as well as changes in lighting.

The 111th issue of *OASE*, which you co-edited last year, was on the theme of staging the museum.[5] Is the theatrical very zeitgeisty?

AC The theme of *OASE 111* was the museum itself, as a mechanism that stages the experience of the visitor from the entrance foyer to the storage depots. Most of the discussion around museums is centered on exhibition spaces—rarely does it address the other kinds of spaces, some of them formerly backstage, which are now accessible to visitors. We wanted to write about museum architecture, not exhibition spaces. The contributions we received on this topic dealt with the work of figures such as Stirling and Hollein, setting up a direct encounter with these architects and their production, which also entails something very theatrical. Personally, I don't see this as a problem, since the "important" architectural projects or moments of the past were always defined by a theatrical character. Often this was even expressly requested by the clients, as architecture has long been used for representational purposes, to project power.

Again, personally, I find it very fruitful to consider this element of theater and what it could contribute to the atmosphere of a place, whether it's a stage set, a museum, or an apartment. I would say it's actually a good design tool. For me, the idea of approaching spaces more theatrically is very promising. But perhaps it's being done far too little at the moment, or far too cautiously. Architecture doesn't always have to hold back, it's not just background.

That's precisely where you had this interesting split between Czech and Hollein. Czech's response to Hollein's "everything is architecture" was to say that architecture is background. There's a different kind of split in Hollein's attitude towards drawing, which was for him very much a tool, but on the other hand also an artifact, almost a work of art in itself. How do you view drawing?

AC I see drawing as a working tool. What I find particularly exciting is the way drawing lets you enter into a dialogue with yourself—to quickly sound out your thoughts and ideas as you put them down on paper. I'm interested in this process, which has a very direct bearing on the design, more than I am in drawing as a means of representation. Of course, the representational aspect is unavoidable: it already begins with the representation of my thoughts, not just to myself, but to my collaborators, the client, and the other people involved in the project. For me, however, the drawing itself is a working document, one that undergoes very few changes because it's not intended to function as a work of art. It is a document that has been prepared with care, as something to work with, from the outset.

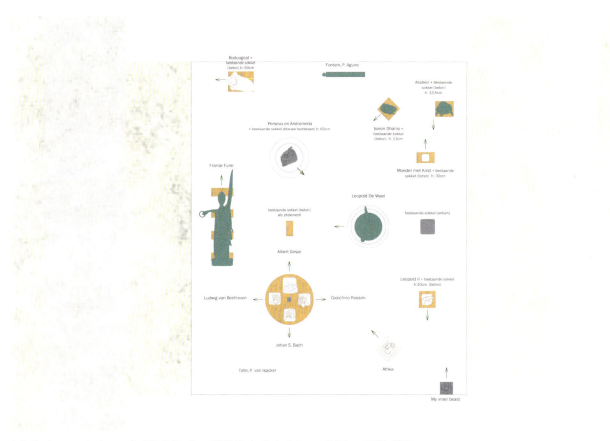

Aslı Çiçek, open air storage for KIS Collection, Middelheim Park, Antwerp, Belgium, 2020-2021.
Schematic plan showing the constellation of the discarded monuments. Digital drawing.

You have also addressed this issue in theoretical terms.

AC Yes, I wrote about Livio Vacchini's drawings for the *OASE* issue on the practices of drawing.[6] I found he had a surprising fascination with the rationality of the computer, which he attempted to translate directly into the structure. It was not a question of aesthetics per se, the computer was more a kind of mechanism that the people in his office had to work with. The flat, almost schematic aesthetics of the drawings and buildings was a consequence of this, not an apriori aim. When architectural drawings and representations have the ambition to become works of art, the original purpose shifts. Representing himself through drawings was a decision Hollein consciously pursued.

Yes, he even signed his buildings, like the Abteiberg Museum.

AC I often get the feeling that many architects start out thinking they would rather be artists and are only at peace with being an architect at a later stage of life. Over the years, they develop a certain self-assurance, and only then can they proudly say they are architects. I don't know if it was the same with Hollein, but I wouldn't be surprised if he didn't also have these thoughts.

Early on, there's this intriguing parallel development with Walter Pichler—an initial idea of almost sharing authorship.

AC These two figures worked in a very introverted and self-referential way. They were trying to make their mark, which is a very human, understandable thing to do. Because of this very subjective way of producing architecture or culture, there are moments when it's very clear that someone is doing something different. Hollein and Pichler acted in ways that were specific to them, personal. What united them was the inner urge to show themselves to the world and to formulate ideas. It's interesting that they both engaged with aspects of the same ideas—though in each case the final expression was very different.

Endnotes

1 Aslı Çiçek, "The Absence of Interior," *OMA: The First Decade, OASE,* no. 94 (April 2015): 54-59. Issue edited by Christophe Van Gerrewey and Véronique Patteeuw.

2 Rem Koolhaas "Imagining Nothingness," in *SMLXL*, ed. Rem Koolhaas, Bruce Mau, Jennifer Sigler, Hans Werlemann, and Office for Metropolitan Architecture (Rotterdam/New York: 010 Publishers/Monacelli Press, 1995), 199-202.

3 *Work and Behavior—Life and Death. Everyday Situations* (German: *Werk und Verhalten—Leben und Tod. Alltägliche Situationen.*)

4 *MAN transFORMS*, Cooper Hewitt, Smithsonian Design Museum, New York, 1976.

5 Aslı Çiçek, Jantje Engels, and Maarten Liefooghe, eds., *Staging the Museum*, *OASE*, no. 111 (May 2022).

6 Aslı Çiçek, "Calculated Aesthetics," *Practices of Drawing, OASE*, no. 105 (April 2020): 44-48.

This Dialogue on Hans Hollein took place on May 27, 2022 online.

Aslı Çiçek

Aslı Çiçek studied at the architecture and design department of the Academy of Fine Arts in Munich and founded her practice in 2015 in Brussels, where she has been based since 2005. Her work, which focuses on exhibition architecture, scenography, and furniture design, is characterized by carefully crafted displays with a high material presence. In addition to her architectural practice, she has written extensively on architecture and has been on the editorial board of *OASE* Journal for Architecture since 2017.

Pier Paolo Tamburelli
baukuh

What is your connection to Hans Hollein? Does he have any influence on
the work of baukuh, and how do you personally relate to him as a cultural figure?

PP I don't think we have any special connection with Hans Hollein.
For us, Hollein has always been part of a landscape of architects and
artists of a certain moment in time that interested us, but I would say
we were never drawn to him in the same way we were drawn to James
Stirling or Giorgio Grassi. I've visited some of his buildings. I remember
trying to see the Glass Museum in Tehran and somehow failing,
and going to Mönchengladbach because Kersten Geers insisted the
Abteiberg Museum was fundamental. I can understand why he or
Wilfried Kuehn, Simona Malvezzi, or Johannes Kuehn are interested
in the building, but it's not really our thing.

So what did you make of the Abteiberg Museum?

PP It's a very strange building. I can't even really describe it. It's like
the extension of a relatively banal spatial unit that spreads out on top
of the hill and generates this weird situation—it's really surprising
and challenging, really experimental. But again, if you were to ask me
if I think it's beautiful, I'm not really sure what I'd say…

The Architekturzentrum Wien recently showed an exhibition about the evolution
of another major project by Hollein, the Haas Haus, which included a large number
of working models.[1] What is your approach to the architectural model? Do you
see it as a presentation and communication tool or as part of the project itself?

PP We're not really model-friendly architects. The models we make are
always presentation models. They're for the client, the audience, or the
competition jury, not for ourselves. Sometimes the model is of the entire
building, other times it's just a large fragment of the project that is only
used for photographs. Anyhow, models come at the end of the project.
We don't design through models; drawings are enough.

On several occasions you've taken these models out of the office and
placed them in a public space to photograph them.

PP Yes, but we do this mainly for practical reasons. With photos of
models you always have a problem with the background, and after trying
for a while to erase everything with backdrops we decided not to waste
any more time or energy and adopt a more pragmatic approach. We just
put the model in a place that we think looks okay and don't post-produce.
We usually work with Stefano Graziani, a photographer who doesn't do
much post-production either. You bring the model some place, Stefano
takes the photo, and the photo you get is pretty much what you see.

We make very few corrections, if any. But of course, this operation also plays with the notion of context, which is undeniably a very particular Italian asset. It's easy for us to go to an extremely beautiful public space to take photographs.

baukuh, House of Memory, Milan, Italy, 2015. Scale model photographed in front of Milan Cathedral. Photo: Stefano Graziani

So, for you the model is not a tool that supports or informs the design process?

PP At baukuh we are six partners, and we have slightly different attitudes towards this. But personally, I think drawings are more than enough. I really don't believe in study models—or in testing or options, for that matter. I hate options. I believe in failure and starting over, I believe in plan B, plan C, and plan D, but I don't believe in options. I can't help but think that options are created only to justify picking the one version that was clearly the best from the beginning. And we are a relatively small office, so we don't have the luxury of generating options, or study models. No money for options, so no options, no money for models, so no models. Working without options and models is one of those things that keep the office efficient.

Hans Hollein had a very close working relationship with the photographer Franz Hubmann.[2] Could you tell us a bit about the working relationship between Stefano Graziani and your collective practice?

PP The story of how we began working together is pretty banal. We knew Stefano from university. At a certain moment, we needed photos and he took these photos for us and our collaboration just went on from there. But of course we work well with Stefano because we share certain attitudes. Stefano, as I mentioned before, does not post-produce much. And there is a certain matter-of-factness in what he does. At the same time, he has a very specific sense of humour. And even though it's not exactly our sense of humour, a relation is possible. And then there's a dark side to Stefano, a sense of death and of memory in his work. And probably this is also necessary to take pictures of our work.

And how about your experience with other photographers?

PP Stefano is very different from other photographers we've worked with, such as Armin Linke or Bas Princen. But in the end I think Stefano's work is better suited to what we're doing because it has this slightly obscure component to it. Although we are a contemporary architecture office, we are also to a certain extent archaic—not nostalgic, not conservative, but archaic, which I think is a different thing. And that quality is also present in what Stefano does.

Franz Hubmann was not just an architectural photographer. He was also a photojournalist and editor of *magnum*, the most important "magazine for modern life" in German in the 1950s and 1960s. And in addition to the photos of his buildings, installations, and interiors, Hubmann also took staged promotional portraits of Hans Hollein.

PP Hollein was born in 1934, so he's more or less part of that Rolling Stones generation—a new lifestyle, a certain idea of freedom, and so forth. Hollein's generation could play the anti-conformist intellectuals because they were living in a society where there was a place for intellectuals—at least, for more boring, "organic" intellectuals. Intellectuals aren't really relevant anymore. There are a few pop star "influencers," but they have no real influence on political and economic decisions. So, when I look back at Hollein's generation, it's the social infrastructure of that time that interests me, far more than the anarchic, pop component that somehow contributed to its destruction. That's maybe also the reason why I'm not so enamored with the pop side of Hollein. Pop is the only thing we still have left, and I can't care less about it.

What about Aldo Rossi—he's the same generation as Hollein?

PP Yes, the generation just before the baby boomers. And in fact, I so much prefer the first part of their career when, in the case of Rossi at least, they committed to a collective project. Then, at a certain moment, they took it for granted and allowed it all to be destroyed. Now that this collective project is gone, we can see how precious the situation of Western Europe in the 1950s and 1960s was. Also, in terms of artistic freedom, they had a much wider range of possibilities than we have today. Imagine someone like Hollein or Stirling trying to run an office today—they'd have to shut down immediately. Nobody would trust them—literally, nobody. Not one of these architectural experiments could have taken place without the support of at least some elements of the establishment, and of a certain political powerbase, which if we oversimplify was that of the various socialist parties of Western Europe.

One interesting thing about Hollein is that in parallel to his fascination with pop culture, he was talking about the cultic origins of architecture and about architecture as a ritual.

PP There are also those early sketches for a church which are very beautiful and probably the thing by Hollein that I like the most — a fantastic project that represents the particular tension between past and present, or between archaism and modernity (*Urmensch *und Spätkultur*, as the title of Arnold Gehlen's book of the late 1950s has it), that you find in so many other artists of his time.[3]

In one of your texts for *San Rocco* you talk about the origin of Roman architecture and how this in turn laid the basis for the ritualistic aspect of European architecture.[4] But the notion of ritual does not really figure in the thinking of our generation. Do you think Hollein's approach could be used as a kind of door to engaging with ritual today?

PP I don't know Hollein well enough to say. But on the relation between collective memory and the transformation of spaces, which I see as a possible way into this topic, you have Rossi's *Architecture of the City*[5] and Koolhaas's *Delirious New York*[6]—also some fragments by Adolf Loos. They describe a potential theory of architecture as a technology of memory, as opposed to the standard modern idea of architecture as the technology of shelter. The distinction is interesting because architecture is an art form that fundamentally addresses the public sphere. As I see it, this issue is becoming more and more problematic in the West. Contemporary art doesn't care about the public experience and is probably not even able to address it. The experiences that are addressed by contemporary art are almost exclusively private. I think architects are a bit embarrassed they aren't able to follow suit, though that doesn't prevent plenty of them from trying. You could even see it as the predominant trend nowadays—in this respect, contemporary architecture really is the architecture of neoliberalism. But it's a desperate attempt; you can devote endless attention to things like the roughness of the wall, the shininess of marble, the porosity of bricks, but in the end it is pointless, because the pure size of buildings means that architecture is incapable of addressing intimate experience. Architecture is unavoidably public.

Hans Hollein, proposal for a church on Wiedner Hauptstraße replacing the demolished Rauchfangkehrer church. Competition, Vienna, Austria, 1966. Photocopy. Archive Hans Hollein, Az W and MAK, Vienna.

And you are mainly interested in this public experience within architecture?

PP I'm interested in this because I see some potential here. This almost compulsory—or in any case unavoidable—commitment towards the public puts architecture in a special position today. It can be strangely critical, which is surprising for an art like architecture that has never been critical before. More precisely, architecture can be critical of the incredible short-termism of our civilization. We have become so anxious about the immediate future that we've stopped thinking about what is going to happen in twenty-five, fifty, or one hundred years. With buildings we address a time span that is a bit longer than the six-month timeframe in which society generally operates, which also places architecture in a particular position regarding ecological thinking.

In 1972 Hollein designed the Media Lines for the Munich Olympics. The project consists of a complex pipe system serving as a network of orientation for the Olympic village as well as a support structure for infrastructural elements like projectors, roofs, lighting, air conditioning, mobile walls, and places to sit and rest. What role do you ascribe to infrastructural elements in relation to the making of public space, and how would you describe baukuh's approach to public space in general?

baukuh, 900km Nile City, El Monshah, Egypt, 2012. Digital collage from
90 POINTS ABOUT THE 900KM NILE CITY, a research project in collaboration
with Atelier Kempe Thill.

PP It depends on the situation we're dealing with. We've had to think
about infrastructure when we've been working on large-scale planning
or research and design projects. We're currently working on large-scale
studies in Geneva and Fribourg, and earlier we did extended research
on Milan and on the Nile Valley in Egypt.

When I look at Hollein's project for the Media Lines, it reminds me
a bit of Beaubourg in Paris or those other 1970s projects defined by
a fascination for technology—an architecture supposedly of the future.
It's strange how quickly this architecture has aged. But maybe that's
also where the beauty of these projects lies. Their quality is this
sweet naivety.

Could one not draw parallels between the Media Lines and your project
for the Student City Campus in Tirana?

Hans Hollein, Media Lines, Olympic Village, Munich, Germany,
1971–1972. View along main axis. Archive Hans Hollein, Az W and
MAK, Vienna.

PP Yes, our Tirana project is about public space, but
it's also based on a rather neoclassical idea. The public
space in the Student City is defined by a super-long
porch. There are two very explicit models for this. One
is the Parque do Ibirapuera by Oscar Niemeyer, Roberto
Burle Marx, and others in São Paulo, and the other is
the University of Virginia by Thomas Jefferson. In that
sense it's a very traditional approach to designing public
space: put a portico all around and it will look just fine.

Strangely nowadays in Albania it is possible to do public
space. The country is rebuilding all its institutions,
which creates a special condition compared to the rest
of Europe. I don't think we would win any competition
in Italy, France, or Germany by proposing a 700m-long
portico. There is simply not the same sort of energy

and commitment that Albania has in this moment, even if its resources are so limited. So, the colossal portico is still an option there. There are things you can do in projects in Switzerland that you cannot do in Albania, and vice versa. Personally, I like that a lot.

baukuh, Student City Campus, Tirana, Albania, 2015. Digital collage showing portico framing the central lawn of the campus.

How do you think the contemporary discussion on public space differs from that of earlier generations?

PP We have simply lost the notion of what public space is about. It's not about organizing some play activities—"Oh, let's give the kids two buckets of paint and let them paint some chairs"—I mean, I'm sorry, but that's not what public space is about. First, you need to invest more money in public space. And public space certainly has to be free, able to be appropriated, and so forth. But it should also have a form, and have a form that can be remembered. It should somehow create spaces where it is possible to have a political rally, a strike, a funeral, or something that is not just kids playing. Public space is a serious thing, and I do not think we've gained a lot from the destruction of its formality. In this sense, Richard Sennett's *The Fall of Public Man* makes a point that I think is still relevant, because there is a collective dimension to life that needs to be staged—to be formalized and ritualized.[7] Maybe it was the cult of authenticity that destroyed this vital dimension of human co-existence. Informality is fine if there is also formality. I think it's very dangerous, and very regressive in political terms, if there is only informality in the public realm.

Are there any contemporary projects for public space that have a potential to address these issues?

PP Yes, 51N4E's design for Skanderbeg square in Tirana, for instance, which I think is one of the most interesting projects of recent years. It tries to give a contemporary interpretation of public space and monumentality. It is a very specific combination of the two.

In a lecture at the Architectural Association in London in 1981 titled "Viennese Blood," Hollein talked quite intensively about Fischer von Erlach's book, *Entwurff einer historischen Architectur*.[8] We know you are also interested in Fischer von Erlach. How would you explain your relationship to him?

PP Well, my interest in Fischer is mainly an interest in his *Entwurff*. It's a very strange amalgam of two different traditions. One is that of erudition—Villalpando's commentary on Ezekiel, and so on.[9] The other is the much more popular tradition of Roman engravings by the likes of Falda.[10] So it was also a bit like a coffee-table book, very spectacular. The end result is a very interesting mix of an intellectual and a pop dimension, which is probably also the reason why Hollein was interested in it.

Hollein was also fascinated by all the buildings that Fischer was able to recreate from the information he had gathered from historical sources.

PP The sources that Fischer uses are numerous, and he is extremely accurate in documenting them. In this sense it is a scientific book, not fantasy: all the sites in the book are in a way real. Fischer studied in Rome with a very old Gian Lorenzo Bernini. There he witnessed first-hand the disillusion of Bernini, who had been summoned to Paris to design the Louvre and had failed. By associating himself with Bernini, Fischer places himself in a lineage that is losing ground to Claude Perrault and the French tradition that would end up producing modern architecture. Again, architecture as a technology of shelter versus architecture as technology of memory. And I think Fischer's *Entwurff* is clearly an answer to this dualism. For him, architecture is a technology of memory, but one that is connected to different civilizations that in turn produce different types of architecture. And that is how we should look at architecture too—with the same open-minded attitude. Fischer is interesting for me precisely because of this perspective, where you have Chinese and Persian architecture next to Greek and Roman architecture in a book made in 1721. Fischer suggested, at least potentially, an anthropological and comparative approach to architecture.

Endnotes

1 *Hans Hollein ausgepackt: Das Haas-Haus, SammlungsLab #4*, Architekturzentrum Wien, 2019. Curator: Mechthild Ebert, Az W.

2 Franz Hubmann (1914–2007) was an Austrian photographer and photojournalist.

3 Arnold Gehlen, *Urmensch und Spätkultur: Philosophische Ergebnisse und Aussagen* (Berlin: RIAS, 1956).

4 *San Rocco* magazine 2010–2019. Editor: Matteo Ghidoni; Editorial Board: Matteo Costanzo, Francesca Pellicciari, Giovanni Piovene, Giovanna Silva, Pier Paolo Tamburelli. Founded by 2A+P/A, baukuh, Stefano Graziani, OFFICE Kersten Geers David Van Severen, pupilla grafik, Salottobuono, Giovanna Silva.

5 Aldo Rossi, *L'architettura della città* (Padua: Marsilio, 1966).

6 Rem Koolhaas, *Delirious New York: A Retroactive Manifesto for Manhattan* (New York: OUP, 1978).

7 Richard Sennett, *The Fall of Public Man* (New York: Knopf, 1977).

8 Johann Bernhard Fischer von Erlach, *Entwurff einer historischen Architectur* (Vienna, 1725).

9 Ioannes Baptista Villalpandus and Hieronymus Pradus, *In Ezechielem Explanationes*, 3 vols. (Rome, 1596–1604).

10 Giovanni Giacomo de' Rossi and Giovanni Battista Falda, *Engravings of Buildings of Rome by Rossi and Falda* (1650–1684).

This Dialogue on Hans Hollein took place on January 22, 2020 in Vienna.

baukuh / Pier Paolo Tamburelli

baukuh is a Milan-based office founded by Paolo Carpi, Silvia Lupi, Vittorio Pizzigoni, Giacomo Summa, Pier Paolo Tamburelli, and Andrea Zanderigo in 2004. The office, which is structured as a non-hierarchical collective, focuses its work on public buildings and projects at the intersection of architecture and urban design. baukuh is also active as a critical thinktank on architecture. It participates in exhibitions, and several members hold teaching positions at various universities.

Pier Paolo Tamburelli studied architecture in Genoa and Rotterdam. In 2010, he co-founded *San Rocco* magazine together with Kersten Geers (OFFICE), amongst others. Recent publications include *On Bramante* (MIT Press, 2022) and *What is Architecture?* (MACK, 2023). He is currently Chair of Design Theory at the Technical University of Vienna.

Dirk Somers
Bovenbouw Architectuur

The first question we would like to ask is what is your relationship to Hans Hollein's work?

DS I've never read anything Hollein wrote, though we have quite a few monographs on his work. I've obviously seen some of the shops in the Vienna, the Haas Haus, and the Abteiberg Museum in Mönchengladbach, which blew my socks off, it's such an amazing building. And last year, I dragged my whole office to Vulcania in France, and they still hate me for it. Vulcania was quite disappointing.

Why was it disappointing?

Hans Hollein, Vulcania, Museum of Volcanism, Saint-Ours-Les-Roches, France, 1994–2002. With Atelier 4, Clermont-Ferrand, France. Archive Hans Hollein, Az W and MAK, Vienna.

DS I learned a lot, in the sense that Hollein probably won the competition because the building got so close to the topic of the brief— you know, this volcanic setting. He built a fake volcano and also a fake crater. There's a red light flashing at the bottom of the crater and smoke coming out, as well as an erupting noise every few minutes. But the relation to the topic is so intense that it becomes like a theme park. The theme park was a difficult issue for the postmodernists. Historically, postmodernism sort of collapsed at the point when the Disney Company embraced it. I really love the idea of an intimate relation between architecture and this kind of blitheness, which Hollein embraced. But in Vulcania you feel the autonomy of the architectural object is totally consumed by its users.

With the work of your office Bovenbouw Architectuur, we found it easy to come up with obvious questions concerning Hollein—easier than with some other offices we've spoken to.

DS Well, I was trying to describe a general relation to Hollein, and I immediately launched into specific considerations. That says a lot.

One possible connection between your work and Hollein's could be the notion of the "fragment and the whole." Hollein often worked with specific architectural elements like the aedicula or the rotunda. For him, it was about bringing together these predefined elements to form a whole. There's also his use of niches and nooks, where he is defining moments of pause as integrated elements of the architecture. How do you at Bovenbouw work with these topics?

DS This is a very nice question because it touches on one of my key interests in his work. But also, on a general level, it is a significant theme in the things we do. A few months ago, I read this amazing book by Demetri Porphyrios called *The Sources of Modern Eclecticism*.[1] It's a thick book about Alvar Aalto and what I find particularly interesting is the introduction, where he defines the distinction between homotopic and heterotopic architecture. For Porphyrios, Mies van der Rohe represents the stereotype of homotopic architecture, whereas Alvar Aalto is framed as a counter-figure, working very heterotopically. Aalto's buildings are composed and collaged artefacts, bringing together different conditions in one conglomerate. Obviously, this is also true for Hollein, most of all in Mönchengladbach.

For me, the idea of producing warm and rich environments is not just a formal concern. I think it's a way of embracing the complexity of life and trying to densify the experiential richness of the world in a singular building. It's the opposite of Mies and the idea of the evenly covered field, the concept of the world as a grid.

Another topic we would like to talk about is how, and to what extent, you work with models when designing. Hans Hollein was obviously obsessed with the idea of the working model: his office built a lot of them. How important is this for your working practice? Do you also work with variants on the design?

DS I find, and also say this to my students, that all mediums are legitimate. That applies equally to computer renderings, drawings, models, or sketches, they're all viable forms of expression. I don't want to push for one medium to be superior to another. As a designer, it's important to invest in the right medium at the right moment, rather than fetishize one technique. Having said that, I also love models. One of the more unusual reasons for this is the idea of the aedicula that we touched on earlier—you know, the small building, the building within the building, and the idea of a miniature densification of architecture. And I think that the model in certain instances can be more than just the representation of a larger-scale thing. It also has its autonomy as a physical object: it's a representation of architecture, a free space of your own, that nobody can mess up. Large models especially tend to reinforce the illusion that as architects we actually have some control over the world around us.

When we researched your work, we stumbled upon your first solo exhibition at the Flanders Architecture Institute. In this exhibition, called *The House of the Explorer*, you decided not to use any photographs of your buildings, just models, drawings, and other means of representation.[2] Hans Hollein, on the other hand, was from very early on really aware of the power of the image and its capacity to sell or convey ideas and make his architecture more widely known. He developed a close working relationship with the photographer Franz Hubmann, who was a well-known photojournalist rather than a specialist in architectural photography.

Looking at your work, it's interesting that you collaborate a lot with the artist and art historian Filip Dujardin. Could you explain how you work together?

DS Yes, though my answer might disappoint you. Filip has been our photographer since 2002, so we've collaborated for a very long time. When we started working with him, he had still to make collages, he hadn't yet developed this parallel artistic practice. That started

Bovenbouw Architectuur, *The House of the Explorer*, exhibition, VAi (Vlaams Architectuurinstituut), Antwerp, Belgium, 2019. Photo: Stijn Bollaert

years later. I think he's an excellent photographer, but I'd be lying if I said there was a very intense interaction between us. Obviously, I do like how the consistency of his work also creates a consistency in the representation of our work. Maybe his graphical way of framing scenes does influence some of our design choices. But in our monograph, we also have footage by other photographers. So, we're not hyper-fixated on this exclusive relation, in the same way that Jan De Vylder is with Filip, or OFFICE is with Bas Princen.

In his work, Hollein amalgamated images from different sources. What is your attitude to reference images, especially with regard to online databases?

DS The visual overload provided by the internet reminds me a bit of the pop art fascination with magazines and advertising in the 1970s. Some architects, like Hollein, would try to process and digest all of this. Look at the way stainless steel plays a big role in Hollein's work. It's a kind of shiny new material that he likes to relate to older tropes in architecture. He likes to make columns and elevations out of stainless steel, fusing together the newest and the oldest figures—not unrelated to the way Adolf Loos designed a skyscraper as a Doric column.[3] The simultaneity of old and new feels like an embrace of multiplicity and diversity different from the restrictive attitudes of minimalism.

Hans Hollein was very involved in curating. He directed the 1996 Venice Architecture Biennale and curated many other exhibitions in Vienna as well.[4] This engagement with curating was a notable influence on his architecture: one could say it was a kind of test bed for his ideas. This year [2021] you are the curator of the Belgian Pavilion at the Biennale.[5] How would you define your role and position as curator?

DS Exhibitions provide an opportunity to think more freely about and to comment on what is happening (or not) in the current architectural

47

discourse. They allow us to frame specific questions in a particular way—to talk about the world we dream of and the ways we would like to see it improve. Similar to making drawings and models, they are a means to speed up this engagement, because trying to change the world by actually making buildings is a frustratingly slow and tedious process. Exhibitions can be a catalyst, providing a boost of oxygen that gets things moving faster. They let you tell stories in a faster and more direct way—faster, certainly, than building practice allows.

One example of this storytelling is Hollein's cool aircraft carrier (*Flugzeugträger*) image. Hollein said "Alles ist Architektur" (Everything is Architecture) and our book, *Living the Exotic Everyday*, is a bit the same.[6] Architecture is not about pre-set ideals or an idiosyncratic vision of the world. It is much more about the art of living, about appreciating and making the best out of everything that comes your way. And another thing that I sense in this image, and in his work in general, is the joy of absorbing very different impulses and influences. The aircraft carrier is an amazing structure because of its cantilevers and the way the steel curves make the top look so very flat. So putting it in a landscape makes it seem very much like a building, it allows you to appreciate it from a very formal or architectural perspective.

Speaking about the *Flugzeugträger* as a powerful architectural object in the landscape, we would contend that the best buildings by Hans Hollein are those that are set in a strong urban context—the shops, the museums, the Haas Haus, to name the most iconic examples. Conversely, when Hollein builds on the periphery the buildings are not as strong, in our opinion.

How do you approach the question of building on the urban periphery? Especially with your earlier buildings, which are often located in diffuse and weak contexts, one could say your architecture has to work hard not to drown in the bleakness of its surroundings.

DS Well, if Hollein says "Alles ist Architektur," then I would say "Alles ist Stadt" (Everything is City), which of course is not an original position. Aldo Rossi defended this idea. In this urban mindset, every building is an urban building, regardless of its location—a very small house in the mountains is an urban building because it is in dialogue with other buildings, even if it's not within sight of them.

I agree with what you're saying about Hollein. I think it's a more wide-spread Richard Meieresque, neo-modernist problem. Even Robert Venturi lamented that many buildings from the late 1980s and 1990s became about clashing volumes and perforating boxes. A preoccupation with how one shape bumps into another makes these buildings much too self-centered and a-contextual, cut off from the urban dialogue that they ought to be focused on.

Architects thought they had to mix up architectural languages to be "Venturian," which is obviously a false interpretation because it misses Venturi's social and ideological agenda, which was a very pop-inspired embrace of the everyday. Here I'm critical of the framing of Venturi by some *San Rocco* people who like to depict him as this amazing guy who made a great book but then went to Las Vegas with Denise Scott Brown

48

and it all went wrong. You can't split Venturi's legacy into before and after Las Vegas. If you study his work well, you'll see it's the same guy with the same warm, embracing attitude towards the world. So please don't suggest that Denise blurred the perspective. Having said that, weak contexts do require buildings to look beyond their surroundings, at the building culture of architecture, to construct a strong identity.

Still on this theme of urban building and context, Hollein's school in Köhlergasse—which he started working on around 1979, in parallel with Abteiberg—has its own interior world, but at the same time, in terms of how it relates to the city, we think it's possible to make a connection to Abteiberg. There's a tension between this urban situation on the one hand and the interior landscape of the school on the other.

Given your own experience of designing school buildings, what are your thoughts concerning the relation between a school and the city?

Bovenbouw Architectuur, Kindergarten in Edegem, Belgium, 2017. The street facade of the kindergarten merges with the curved morphology of the street. Photo: Stijn Bollaert

DS I don't know the Köhlergasse project well, but it has a great plan and I can obviously read some of its intentions. The building embodies what is for me one of the most fascinating aspects of postmodern architecture, namely, the idea of interiorizing the complexity of the world—of bringing the city into the building and making a very heterogeneous building with very characteristic spaces. You find it in this building as well as in Abteiberg. Also, Charles Moore did a school based around a street which feels related (Moore Lyndon Turnbull Whitaker, Haas School of Business, 1995), or there's that amazing school by Christopher Alexander in Japan, which is structured like a village (Eishin Gakuen, 1989).

These schools compress a whole world into one building complex, which I think is a beautiful metaphor because schools are parallel societies with their own rules. When you cross the threshold of the school you leave behind one universe, with its political settings and rules, and enter a new world with other leaders and other rules. To design the school as a parallel universe is a very beautiful ambition, much more interesting

Hans Hollein, Köhlergasse elementary school, Vienna, Austria, 1979–1990.
Plan showing the independent building volumes. Photocopy. Archive Hans Hollein, Az W and MAK, Vienna.

49

than the school as a box, which may be clear and simple but it doesn't trigger the imagination in the same way as complexity. That said, the metaphor can easily get a bit fake or hollow, with the design trying to be more than it actually is. That's what you can feel in Stirling and Wilford's Wissenschaftszentrum in Berlin (1979–1988), where the formal aspirations—the campanile, basilica, and so on—don't match the content, which is basically just offices. The desire for specificity clashes with the generic program Stirling was working on. I can't judge this school building by Hollein, but I love the ambition for that complexity.

Would you say there are motifs in your work that relate to Hollein's way of designing?

DS Actually, our most Hollein-inspired building is the care home we recently finished in Ostend. The care home is also a parallel universe. The people there are all around ninety years old, and they hardly ever go outside—it's sort of the last building they enter. We were working on the competition just after we came back from Mönchengladbach and we were like, "Let's not make a building. Let's build a parallel world. Like a village or a city." And we tried and tried, but it was a mess. We struggled, had sleepless nights, and it was awful—it looked so ugly. And the reason why we couldn't manage this complexity was that we're not Hollein, who was a virtuoso when it came to making all those top-notch, elegant transitions. I would say this complexity is what makes postmodernism so amazing, but at the same time it's also why it has such a bad reputation. It's so hard to do, only the best of the best of the best designers can make it work. That explains why there are so many bad postmodern buildings. We eventually submitted a planning application for Ostend, but it was still an ugly building. Fortunately, the subsidy mechanisms for care homes take forever. Over a period of a year, while the gears were in motion, we redesigned the whole

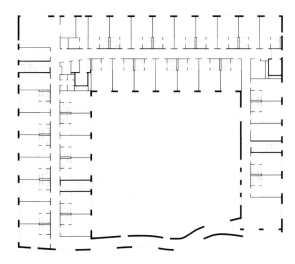

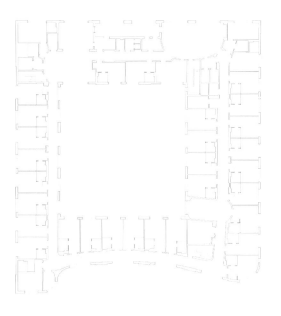

Bovenbouw Architectuur, De Drie Platanen, care home, Ostend, Belgium, 2014–2019. Competition stage, second-floor plan. Digital drawing.

Bovenbouw Architectuur, De Drie Platanen, care home, Ostend, Belgium, 2014–2019. Second-floor plan as built. Digital drawing.

building without talking to the client about it. Once the funding was granted, we said: "Well, we have the same thing for you, but now we've cleaned it up. It's still exciting, and it's going cost you less than the first version," which is something clients always like to hear. We reverted to a more careful and simpler version inspired by Gunnar Asplund's Villa Snellmann for the care home, which we could handle much better.[7] We had the level of expertise to do something Asplundish, but we couldn't pull off the Hollein.

In a previous interview you've said you wished you could be like an architect in Quattrocento Italy. What exactly did you mean by that?

DS Well, it's a bit of a romantic notion, but aren't we all fascinated with those great cities in Umbria like Urbino, Spoleto, or Perugia. There's a wonderful book by Marvin Trachtenberg, *Building-in-Time*, that describes a way of building that allowed monumental architecture and cityscapes to evolve over centuries.[8] A church might have taken 300 years to complete, but the end result was coherent, not chaotic, because everyone in society was doing their best to bring it all together. The point was to make a rich but very well sculpted, nicely composed urban setting, which each city did in its own way, trying to outshine its neighbors in the process. So yes, I'm a bit nostalgic about the civic pride people used to take in architecture and the way different places developed its own complex identity.

Endnotes

1 Demetri Porphyrios, *Sources of Modern Eclecticism: Studies on Alvar Aalto* (London: Academy Editions, 1982).

2 Bovenbouw Architectuur, *The House of The Explorer*, VAi, deSingel, Antwerp, Belgium, February 28 to June 16, 2019.

3 An entry submitted by Adolf Loos (1870–1933) for the 1922 Chicago Tribune competition, proposing an office tower in the form of a Doric column clad in black granite. In 1980 Hans Hollein incorporated the conspicuous design in his installation for the *Strada Novissima* exhibition at the Corderie dell'Arsenale at the first Venice Architecture Biennale.

4 *Sensing the Future: The Architect as Seismograph*. 6th Venice Architecture Biennale, Italy, 1996.

5 *Composite Presence*, Belgian Pavilion at the Venice Architecture Biennale, May 22 to November 21, 2021.

6 Dirk Somers, Maarten Van Den Driessche, Bart Verschaffel, Bovenbouw Architectuur, eds., *Living the Exotic Everyday* (Antwerp: VAi 2019).

7 Erik Gunnar Asplund (1885–1940) was a Swedish architect. Inspired by Italian rural houses he designed Villa Snellman in Djursholm near Stockholm in 1917. The building is an early example of Nordic classicism.

8 Marvin Trachtenberg, *Building-in-Time: From Giotto to Alberti and Modern Oblivion* (New Haven: Yale University Press, 2010).

This Dialogue on Hans Hollein took place on June 3, 2020 online.

Bovenbouw Architectuur / Dirk Somers

Bovenbouw was founded by Dirk Somers in 2011 in Antwerp. The office's work ranges from refurbishing interiors and house extensions to public buildings such as kindergartens, schools, and care homes. The work can be characterized as idiosyncratic, in as much as every project follows its own language. Bovenbouw Architectuur are collaborating with David Kohn Architects on a project in Hasselt, Belgium.

Dirk Somers studied architecture in Antwerp and Milan. In parallel to leading Bovenbouw Architectuur, he is a design professor at Ghent University. He published *Living the Exotic Everyday*, a monograph on the work of Bovenbouw, in 2019, and in 2021 curated *Composite Presence*, the Belgian contribution to the Venice Biennale.

Claudia Cavallar

What is your relation to Hollein?

CC I studied with Hollein, although studying with him wasn't always easy for me. I dropped out after a few years, stopped doing architecture altogether, and focused on other things for seven years. But when Hollein retired, I finished my studies with his successor, Greg Lynn. As a student, like many others in the class, I also worked from time to time in Hollein's studio and got to know its routines a little. But that was always paid work, and clearly separate from the university.

Was Hollein's own work an inescapable part of his teaching, or was there a clear distance between the University of Applied Arts and the work of Atelier Hollein?

CC My studies coincided exactly with the planning of those big projects in the atelier—which is also why there were so many students working there. At the university, on the other hand, it was never very clearly set out how something should be done. That was Hollein's way of teaching. You really had to be able to think for yourself. Compared to my later experience in Greg Lynn's class, the teaching was less didactic.

Why did you decide to stop studying with Hollein?

CC He had a specific idea of architecture that I could not buy into. His architecture was very insistent, he saw it as a force for bringing about change. What's more, it was always about an object and a formal solution, and I had my doubts about that. Part of the problem for me was also the way of doing architecture. I even decided to switch to studying landscape architecture with Greg Lynn because this sculptural architecture left me cold. I had nothing to say about it.

Did students have to copy Hollein?

CC Many students worked in a completely different way, very conceptually, and went on to become artists rather than architects after graduating. In that sense, you were allowed to try other things. The further you got out of your comfort zone, the more Hollein was interested. For him, questioning the nature of the task was more interesting than actually solving it. The conceptual approach was very important.

How about the ratio of women to men in the class? Was it balanced?

CC Hardly. Initially, very few of those applying to study with Hollein were women. But that was also the case with other architecture classes. Hollein treated women the same as men, there was no difference. Towards the end of my studies, there was a significant change, with a fifty/fifty gender balance, but only under Hollein.

How were the presentations?

CC Large "crits" with a host of guest jurors only became popular with Wolf Prix's professorship at the University of Applied Arts.[1] With Hollein you had individual presentations and discussed the projects with the teaching assistants. At the university, Hollein was clearly in charge, taking precedence over his collaborators when it came to framing the content of the work.

Were individual projects the norm at the university?

CC Group work was very unusual, though almost nothing was officially ruled out—I did a collaborative project with a friend at the time. In juries, Hollein was often very rational. You'd be in full flow, explaining a lot of conceptual stuff, and he'd pipe up: "Where's the entrance?" He was always concerned with the architecture itself.

Did he refer to the work of other architects?

CC Hollein didn't deal directly with references. The class was in the here and now. However, I do remember an episode when he found out that someone in the class wasn't familiar with the staircase in the Belvedere.[2] He was quite indignant: "How can you, as an architecture student, be so stupid as to not spend every free minute in museums, in lectures, in the city." I don't remember him ever mentioning classical modernism or even Loos directly, but of course you were expected to know everything anyway.

What topics did you work on at the university?

CC The two themes that you cut your teeth on in Hollein's class were the church and the bar. That says a lot…

What still connects you with Hollein today?

CC I think Hollein was a fantastic curator—a real storyteller! I often look closely at his exhibitions. The Otto Wagner show I curated for the Museum of Applied Arts in 2018[3] was very much influenced by Hollein's exhibition, *Traum und Wirklichkeit Wien* (Vienna: Dream and Reality), held at the Künstlerhaus in 1985.[4] I think *Traum und Wirklichkeit* was the reason why I wanted to study with Hollein in the first place. There was also a special publication accompanying the exhibition, which inspired me a lot.

How might this reference be read in concrete terms?

CC I designed golden walls for the Otto Wagner exhibition, for example. For me, gilding is a Wagnerian theme, but it also connects with Hollein. Wagner was criticized in his time for using gold in an unorthodox way, in secular rather than sacred spaces. Hollein did that, too.

Gold leaf was used in Hollein's school in Köhlergasse—an expression of luxury, extravagance, and ornament that is perhaps unthinkable in school construction today?

CC Hollein really loved that school. He could talk very eloquently about the importance of the spatial experiences that were created for the children there. But with its many stairs and access routes, the school is completely incompatible with contemporary barrier-free construction.

53

Hans Hollein, *Traum und Wirklichkeit: Wien 1870–1930*, exhibition at the Künstlerhaus, Vienna, Austria, 1984–1985. Scale model showing the decoration of the exterior facing Karlsplatz. Model photo. Archive Hans Hollein, Az W and MAK, Vienna.

Claudia Cavallar, *Post Otto Wagner*, exhibition, MAK, Vienna, Austria, 2018. In collaboration with Lukas Lederer. Gold-painted partition element. Photo: Robert Bodnar

Another thing that could not be built in the same way today is the famous progression that Josef Frank orchestrated through the Villa Beer.[5] A spatial impoverishment, courtesy of building regs or safety concerns, is how Hermann Czech put it on a recent tour of the house.

Do you see yourself within a tradition of Viennese architects?

CC Of course. Even if nowadays it might seem a bit kitsch or clichéd to be dealing with Loos and Wagner in Vienna, you still do it anyway. With Hollein, apart from the references I've mentioned, I would articulate more differences and distinctions between his architecture and mine: "Why does a house in Burgenland have to have something to do with the vernacular tradition of Burgenland? Are there other similar houses? How sustainable is the tradition associated with it?" These are topics that interest me, and I don't think Hollein was particularly concerned with them—they're rather low-key, whereas his Viennese tradition was above all about the superlative. What interested him, always, was the extreme: extreme achievements, extreme sizes, the mastery of something, of speed, for example.

Nevertheless, there was no getting around Hollein?

CC Even today, I'm discovering new aspects of Hollein, seeing things that we looked at in a different way back then or never even addressed in our studies. I might be looking at a photo of a project—the Schullin jewelery store or the Retti candle shop, for example—and suddenly I'll notice that he was using English fabrics, and that inspires me. You think, "Where does that narrative come from?" Although Hollein was avant-garde and the sculptural was an essential aspect of his work, you can also see this ornamental tradition that is distinctly Viennese—a continuation of the city, of the thoughts that make up Viennese architecture. This ornamental Viennese tradition is perhaps what I feel most connected to.

What I find most difficult about Hollein's work, on the other hand, is its iconic element, the first drawings, the silhouettes, the very poster-like treatment. As students, we talked a lot about wanting to find something more subtle for ourselves, not just paraphrasing wealth via a car grille, for example, but something that you could feel, that was not directly narrative.

Claudia Cavallar, Markt 67, house in Weiden am See, Austria, 2012–2014. Main space with gallery. Photo: Klaus Fritsch

How do you see the spatial qualities of Hollein's work?

CC I saw the Haas Haus while it was still a shell and it was perfect and wonderful. So much thought, so many spatial ideas, had gone into it— it was fantastic! When I saw the finished building, however, I was disappointed. It was so over-embroidered, so overwrought, that in some ways the space was submerged. Hollein could talk forever about the Haas Haus. He had this "scatter technique." Rather than have the external facade reflect the internal spatial organization, he made a conglomerate that was impossible to grasp visually as a whole. The Haas Haus was also interesting from the point of view of the changing conception of "retail." It could only have been created at that particular moment, a kind of transitional period before the idea of consumption became more globalized. We were looking again at the sketches for the facades of the Haas Haus just recently, when we were designing the Wagner exhibition. The sheer volume of existing sketches is impressive.

This brings to mind what Dietmar Steiner[6] said about Hollein never being able to let go of the space, to stop finetuning.

CC Yes, precisely. The question is, what do people need to feel comfortable in a space? How much ornamentation does it take to keep the eye engaged? He was interested in that, but in a different way from me. With Hollein, there's so much density and overload that I find myself thinking, "Just stop, it's enough already." There's something almost exotic about his architecture nowadays—we see the works at a much greater remove than we did when they were first built.

The exoticism of his work certainly resonates with many of the young architects we've spoken to about Hollein.

CC I think there was a generational shift during the time he was active, and at a certain point these younger architects began to be very critical

55

of Hollein's approach, of the overdetermination. Today we can look at it again with more distance: perhaps his architecture is really about a kind of richness of space that you move through: a consciously created density, as opposed to bareness.

The suggestion of exoticism that you see, for example, in this palm tree motif, which could also be a piece of jewelry such as a brooch—there was something about this approach that we found difficult as students. We thought you could not or should not do that, that it was an oversimplification.

At the same time as Hollein was installing these stylized gilded palm trees in the interior of a travel agency, Hundertwasser was building a house and putting trees on the roof. Both are about decoration. But is there no awareness of ecological issues in Hollein's work?

CC It has taken quite a while for the outdoor space to become more to an architect than the salad is to the steak. In my view, we still haven't fully grasped how important it is to define, incorporate, the external surroundings—nor how important this will be in the future.

We think that to some extent Hollein also thought of his interiors in terms of urban planning. Does urban planning inspire you as well?

Claudia Cavallar, *Missing Link*, exhibition, MAK, Vienna, Austria, 2022. In collaboration with Lukas Lederer. View of installation showing plastic furniture from the MAK collection and the Mobile Office by Hans Hollein (right). Photo: Robert Bodnar

CC I am inspired, for example, by a text by the Austrian architect and theorist Oskar Strnad. At one point he asks, "Where is it narrow? Where is it wide? What do you feel?"

We're not used to working with this range of sensory impressions because we're so focused on the visual. Architecture today is communicated through visual media, magazines, pictures. People believe it is pre-eminently a visual medium. So when we go on a site visit, we're often disappointed because the actual space is not as interesting as the visual representation—sometimes in fact it turns out to be a non-experience, spatially. In my own work I'm trying to move away from what I see and deal more with how the space feels. An example of this is the *Missing Link* exhibition that I recently designed for MAK Vienna.[7] The exhibition architecture should not necessarily be seen, what's important is the content. The galleries of the MAK especially lend themselves to an approach that is almost like urban planning. Whether I'm moving around in a city or in an apartment, the process is very similar.

… and materiality and Hollein?

CC Hollein was less interested in truth to materials than he was in industrial production. He found it interesting that it's possible nowadays to cut stone just 3mm thick and use it to line an elevator.

Claudia Cavallar, *Women Artists of the Wiener Werkstätte*, exhibition, MAK, Vienna, Austria, 2021. In collaboration with Lukas Lederer. Cushions by *Wiener Times*. Display case with watercolors and ceramic objects. Photo: Robert Bodnar

Where would you position yourself in this spectrum?

> CC You can't get around the question of whether craftsmanship has become anachronistic today. Knowing how to handle stone in certain way, for example, has really become a kind of a theoretical knowledge (though the Viennese have never been particularly good at working stone anyway).

How would you describe your spatial strategies in relation to Hollein? What are the things you look out for?

> CC In exhibitions where you have a lot of the same kind of elements, in terms of content or format, I make a point of ensuring that people don't register it. The spaces have to work much harder than in other exhibitions, so that this uniformity of material is not so noticeable. An example of this architectural strategy is the *Women Artists of the Wiener Werkstätte* show I did for the MAK.[8] Those tube-like spaces in the MAK are not easy to work with.

> In the exhibitions Hollein curated the objects are overstaged—something new is put into the space to make it more memorable for the viewers. There is always the possibility of resolving the task spatially. One strategy could be this insertion, but cladding the space is another possibility. Financial considerations also come into play.

Do you have a dream project that you've yet to realize?

> CC Yes, I really want to do a palm tree [laughs]. Before I always wanted to do a hotel, to arrive in an unknown city and ask: "What defines the identity of a city?" We tend to be much more critical today. The question is more, "Why would I need to see a hotel as a basic architectural task?" Hotels are also a place of luxury.

> I think the making of exhibitions has also changed so much since Hollein's time. Some of the things that were done back then appear

rather dubious today. In current exhibition design, for example, there's a great deal of focus on materials that can be re-used or disassembled. The question is, "What can a new structure do today anyway?" There is the aesthetic approach of solving a task using as little material as possible. That doesn't necessarily interest me, though I also don't think the excesses from Hollein's time are relevant today either.

What other things have changed since Hollein's time?

CC The idea of the set piece is a very Holleinian technique. But there were also all those projections of the future. Not all the things Hollein did are feasible or applicable today. With him, it was always about the best—only the best was good enough. What does "the best" mean? The idea has become relative, if it even exists today. But for Hollein, and for generations of architects over the centuries before him, "good enough" was never good enough.

Did Hollein not care about social issues, or the scarcity of materials, or the kind of client he was building for? Was he just an opportunist who wanted to make his expensive, "dissolute" architecture at any price?

CC Hollein was interested in progress. That was his political stance. He had a real faith in the future—a hedonistic confidence, you could call it—but was rather indifferent to day-to-day politics.

Crucially, his superlative work was also enabled by networks of powerful men.

CC And that was certainly followed by a backlash against the power of architecture. But you can also see the positive aspect of that time: the fact that the government felt it was worth investing in architecture— cultural statements as a state investment. Who among our current rulers even thinks along these lines? Rather than an engagement with culture, architecture is at best vehicle of prestige. I don't think architecture has become any more social or "civic" since Hollein's time.

From this point of view, Hollein stood at a historical turning point when there was a fundamental change in how we do architecture. There's a huge difference between Hollein's time and how we build today.

Endnotes

1 Wolf D. Prix (b. 1942) was head of the studio Architectural Design 3 from 1990 to 2011 at the Institute of Architecture of the University of Applied Arts, Vienna. From 2003 to 2012 he was the head of the institute and 2003 to 2011 acted as vice-dean of the university.

2 Schloss Belvedere is a baroque building complex in Vienna built by Prince Eugene of Savoy. The Upper Belvedere, designed by Johann Lukas von Hildebrandt, was completed in 1723.

3 *Post Otto Wagner: Von der Postsparkasse zur Postmoderne*, MAK – Museum für angewandte Kunst, Vienna, 2018. Curator: Sebastian Hackenschmidt, MAK with Iris Meder and Ákos Moravánszky.

4 *Traum und Wirklichkeit: Wien 1870–1930*, Künstlerhaus, Vienna, 1984–1985. Curators: Robert Waissenberger and Sylvia Wurm.

5 Josef Frank with Oskar Wlach, 1929–1930.

6 Dietmar Steiner (1951–2020), founding director AzW, 1993–2016.

7 *Missing Link: Strategien einer Archi- tekt*innengruppe aus Wien (1970–1980)*, MAK – Museum für angewandte Kunst, Vienna, 2022. Curator: Sebastian Hackenschmidt, MAK with Anna Dabernig.

8 *Die Frauen der Wiener Werkstätte*, MAK – Museum für angewandte Kunst, Vienna, 2022. Curators: Anne-Katrin Rossberg, Elisabeth Schmuttermeier.

This Dialogue on Hans Hollein took place on September 9, 2022 in Vienna.

Claudia Cavallar

Claudia Cavallar founded her own practice in 2010 in Vienna after studying architecture under Hans Hollein and Greg Lynn at the University of Applied Arts, Vienna. Her work, which focuses on exhibition design and the interior design of residential projects and cafés, often takes early modernist Viennese architecture as its starting point. Complementary to the interiors, her work is also concerned with garden design. Alongside her architectural practice, Claudia Cavallar is also on the board of ÖGfA (Austrian Society for Architecture) and recently co-curated with Elise Feiersinger a double lecture with Hermann Czech and David Kohn, to be published in *UMBAU 32*, 2023.

Maria Conen and Raoul Sigl
Conen Sigl Architekt:innen

Let's get right down to it and ask: What is your personal connection to Hollein?
What does he mean to you?

RS Our connection is more with Vienna, rather than with Hollein directly. Maria's mother is from Austria, and I've been to Budapest a lot, as that's where my mother is from. So clearly we have this Austria-Hungary point of reference, but also a relation to Vienna as a city with its protagonists. For us, Hollein is a figure in the "Viennese cabinet" that made such a mark on architectural discourse.

MC In architecture, we associate the "Viennese tradition" with Wagner, Loos, Czech, and also Hollein. Hermann Czech gave a lecture when we came to Vienna with our students from Munich in 2016.[1] He talked about the city from the urban plan to the keyhole. What interests us in this discourse is the relation of the interior space to the public space of the city—a kind of "threshold detail" that connects the inner and the outer worlds. Hollein can also be situated in this discourse. The shops, the furniture, and especially the joyful quality of his design appeal to us very much. Building in the existing fabric is another direct point of contact, though in this regard we find Czech and Loos easier to categorize than Hollein. Their work has another degree of balance and therefore tends to stir up less discussion. With Hollein, you ultimately reach a point where you don't always know what he means to you. We once gave our students a Hollein reference as a starting point: the entrance hall of the Siemens building in Munich, with its striking stainless-steel column.

RS And we had a heated debate during the final crits in Munich about whether or not it was "allowed" to look at Hollein at all. We found it interesting that he provokes such strong emotions.

MC He also has a strong presence in the design of the interiors. We're fascinated by this enveloping, cloaking quality, which again is something we associate with Vienna. It's a strongly artistic approach, with these mysterious, stage-setting elements.

What is it about Hollein, do you think, that causes such polarization?

RS I think a lot of it comes down to the fact that he does not conform to convention and defies classification.

MC He doesn't stick to the rules, everything is possible, to the point of testing the limits of "good taste." In the case of the column in the Siemens entrance hall, however, it seems to us that he manages to pull everything together in a balanced way. The work reflects a creative will that is quite fascinating.

RS What lends the work authority is its combination of elements: on its own, the door would perhaps appear historicizing, but together with the column and the floor it creates a fresh new language—one that still looks fresh today, in my view. The craftsmanship and the choice of means of construction also contribute to this.

Not far from the Loos House (1912) on Michaelerplatz in Vienna is Hollein's first built project, the Retti candle shop. How do you see this project from the perspective of today?

Conen Sigl Architekt:innen, Zum Hinteren Hecht bar, Winterthur, Switzerland, 2018–2019. Built-in furniture with water dispenser. Photo: Roman Keller

MC Hollein designs "associatively." But Retti also has a tripartite organization and an axiality, which are implemented very freely. When you enter Retti, a new world opens up. This approach is particularly effective in the remodeling projects, where the challenge is to define the possibility of creating something new in a place where you have to work with a lot of pre-existing elements. Hollein creates a very strong presence in the city with his interventions—an atmosphere reminiscent of a stage set.

RS The Retti candle shop was made for a specific place, but at the same time it has a general validity. The choice of aluminum is special: the material fits in, but it also makes a very strong impression. It's designed very sensitively. The technology comes from the aerospace industry, and Hollein deals with it as meticulously as Loos did with his slabs of marble.

MC What's very nice with Hollein is his attention to every detail of the image he's creating. When we're working with an existing building, we also try to incorporate as much as we can into the design, from the furniture and light fixtures, to the floor and building services or ventilation.

RS With Hollein everything is *gestalt*,[2] everything is architecture. Ventilation is not a problem, but an opportunity. The question is: What do we do with those elements of architecture that we don't want to see? Do we conceal them, or try instead to work with them, to integrate them?

MC These themes are evident in our bar in Winterthur, where you can also see the Vienna connection that we've been talking about. The bar is in an existing building in the old town. We didn't touch the exterior, but only designed the interior. There were a lot of visible pipes in the middle of the space, coming down from the apartments on the upper floors. We integrated this pipework into the furnishings, to make a new composition.

Conen Sigl Architekt:innen, Fliederstrasse apartment building extension, Zurich, Switzerland, 2014–2016. Photo: Roman Keller

RS The client was keen that people should be able to sit without immediately feeling pressure to consume something. Anyone can get water for free—the bar is also thought of as a fountain.

With any project, whether it's a conversion or an extension, we always ask ourselves what stories we want to tell. For example, with the glazed extension in Mühlezelgstrasse, it was important to open up to the green surroundings, and for the glassed-in bays to become like a garden element. The column that stands on the threshold between the old and the new parts then acts as the linchpin of these very different spaces. In the case of Fliederstrasse, on the other hand, the existing building was strongly articulated. And here, because we did not want to recreate historicizing cornices and friezes, we worked with different window proportions on each floor in the new part of the building. The exposed concrete elements tie the new construction to the existing one. The question is always: how can we continue to build meaningfully, using the possibilities and methods of current building technologies?

Then there's also the spatial, scenographic qualities of the work. How is it approached, how do you read it, what is the atmosphere? How do the new spaces relate to the existing ones? You have to find a language that gives them equal value. We think it's important to work with a degree of freedom to bring a historic, listed building to life, rather than attempt to conserve everything.

For Hollein the framework of the exhibition provided another testing ground—a place for developing something new. You've already realized some exhibition architecture, what is your approach here?

Conen Sigl Architekt:innen, Swiss Art Awards 2017, exhibition design, Basel, Switzerland, 2017. Digital drawing.

RS Our designs respond to concrete tasks. We don't see them as a testing ground, but as our own reality. That said, there are certain fundamental issues that we engage with in our projects, whether they're exhibitions, conversions, or new constructions.

MC *Best Of* at EPF Lausanne,[3] Manifesta in Zurich,[4] and the Swiss Art Awards,[5] which we did regularly—those are our exhibition architectures. The first thing we look at when we design a show is the place. What is being exhibited? How accessible is it? What's the scale? Ultimately, it's a similar mindset to the rest of our work. With the Swiss Art Awards, which are shown in a large trade fair hall, accessibility was at the center of our thinking. We thought of a city, of squares, houses, a place that you walk through. The question was how to create scale and density so that you don't feel like you're in a big hall, but are instead moving around an exhibition, going from work to work along a sequence of spaces.

RS The focus in the Swiss Art Awards was on the common project, because there are so many different artists and architects exhibiting there.

MC The first exhibition was based around the idea of four houses and a village square. But the works still seemed a bit adrift—the space of the hall was too big to create a feeling of delicate density. For the second exhibition, instead of houses, we developed the idea of a block arranged in various ways to give visitors the sense of a denser spatial situation. People should consciously come closer together. So we modified our concept between the first and the second exhibitions.

Hans Hollein engaged with a complex framework of references, just as you do. How does this engagement translate into concrete terms in your teaching and practice?

MC When we work with students, we're very precise when we look at a reference project, because we're interested in passing something on. As an architect, you build up over time an internal library of buildings, places, images, texts, books, and art projects that inspire and engage you. What's interesting then is the way this whole subjective cosmos is perceived as a "reference," though the transfer is not as clear as it is in teaching. In our case, it's not only the actual building that interests us, but also its context. How does it stand in its place, city or village, and why was it built that way? Rather than just looking at the figure of a column, say, our students discuss its wider cultural, social, and economic contexts and then try to incorporate this analysis into their designs, but not necessarily figuratively. It is the concept, the idea, that is adopted, rather than the image.

Hans Hollein, Carl Friedrich von Siemens Foundation, Nymphenburg, Munich, Germany, 1969–1972. Stainless-steel twin column in the entrance hall. Archive Hans Hollein, Az W and MAK, Vienna. Photo: Franz Hubmann/Imagno/picturedesk.com

RS The moment you come to build a column yourself, you inevitably find yourself asking how others have approached this task. How did Palladio or Bramante do it? What proportions did they use? A column is a formal element that has its own rules and poses its own questions, but always stands in relation to a space. When you see it that way, it takes on a life of its own.

MC When our students were working with Hollein's column in the Siemens building in Munich, they found it difficult to take something new from it. The themes had already been heavily "processed" by Hollein himself. How do you deal with architecture like this without falling into the trap of copying? Not that copying is not allowed; the point is more that the object should not remain an artifact, but become part of a new space. It's difficult to work with Hollein as a reference because he is so specific. It would perhaps be more interesting to take a Hollein building and extend it.

RS It's also more fruitful to explore the working methods and design process, rather than trying to copy the end result.

We have here a pair of images that Hollein put together. On the left is the Tomb of Eurysaces the Baker in Rome and on the right is Hollein's Mobile Office [see page 26]. When Hollein showed these two images in a lecture, "Viennese Blood," at the Architectural Association in 1981, he said that for him they represented the fundamental aspects of architecture. What would your image pair look like, and which of the two images do you feel closer to?

RS I find the pair of images very apposite and illustrative of the special qualities of Hollein's work—the pleasure, the lightness, the joy of

Conen Sigl Architekt:innen, *Wand, Boden, Decke, Säule = Raum*, installation, Swiss Art Awards 2015, Basel, Switzerland, 2015. Bundesamt für Kultur. Photo: Guadalupe Ruiz

architecture, where you don't feel bound by a set of rules but freely appropriate the things that fascinate you, from your travels, photos, everyday life. And where do we see ourselves in this pair of images? Either precisely in between them—or in neither one. The image on the left is too heavy, the one on the right too light.

MC The two images embody the rigor of the discipline, which Hollein certainly absorbed, but on the other hand they allow for something playful and light—a combination that for us is the essence of Viennese charm. We see the same thing with Czech, in his admirably light reworking of the Thonet chairs, despite the weight of history attached to them.

When we were studying at the ETH, there was this whole doctrine of right and wrong that really bugged us: "Structure and statics have to come together, you have to be able to see what is loadbearing and what is not." Loos stood for a different world and was an important figure for us even during our studies.

At the same time, we were taught to avoid cladding and only to build monolithically, if possible. Layered construction was a no-go area. We wanted to free ourselves from this way of looking at things, and Hollein, Czech, Loos—this Viennese world—helped us to do so.

RS If we're talking about studying at the ETH, we should also mention Hans Kollhoff or Peter Märkli. With Kollhoff, too, there was a world that was self-contained, but a different one. Kollhoff also worked for Hollein—there were points of contact.

Hermann Czech told us that Hollein's approach to teaching was very modern for his time. It was not necessarily about what was right or wrong, and it was not directly aimed at creating a Hollein school. Rather, it focused on strengthening the personalities of the students through dialogue—albeit without questioning the principle of the masterclass. Maria, you're also very involved in teaching, how free can you be here?

MC The idea that teaching is a dialogue really chimes with me. It's something we push with our students in the studio. While we often work with references, we don't want to take away their freedom to make their own discoveries. There are always different discussions in the group, depending on its composition, and the projects that emerge from this discourse are very varied.

With references, what interests us is the search for something. And that can be different every time. This kind of level dialogue is very productive and constantly amazing. We can't—won't—come up with fourteen projects for the students. I'm interested in the discussion and in new and surprising way of looking at things. Of course, we provide input and steer in certain directions, but the students have their autonomy. We see this collaboration as something enriching, which also inspires us.

Independent thinking is what we want to promote. We're interested in diversifying the language and want to give students the opportunity to discover their own means of expression. Which is perhaps the opposite of how we were taught.

Hollein's authorship of the work was clearly formulated, even though he worked with partners in his office. How do you work as a team, as a pair?

MC We're both involved in the initial phase of a project. We talk about the core ideas that interest us, and because we've been working together like this for a long time, we soon understand each other. Our collaborators and the experts from other disciplines are very important in this phase. In joint discussions, they challenge the ideas critically and we continue to develop the project in this way.

And while we talk, we also sketch. We use language, images, and sketches in parallel. We then attach the corresponding reference images to the drawings.

RS There are also models that inform the project. Then all of a sudden, these images will recede into the background and new ones will emerge. It's a process.

With Hollein, we were struck by how self-referential his work was, particularly towards the end, when he quoted himself again and again. This prompted us to think about how you can stay fresh. What strategies have you developed for this?

MC I have the feeling we're still searching, so this question doesn't really arise for us. But the longer you're in this profession, the more you have to consider the return on your efforts. Early on, the energy we put in was unlimited. We didn't have a big office infrastructure and during that time we discovered a lot of the themes that interest us. Then we entered a new phase—the one we're still in now—where we employed more people in the office. The projects also got bigger. The infrastructure became more important. Now there's less freedom, because many aspects of the design have to be firmed up earlier. That's why it's so important not to lose sight of the core ideas during the long process of developing the project.

64

RS We often struggle in our work to focus on just one essential element—we have too many ideas and need to learn to rein them in. We haven't yet got to the point where we feel we're repeating ourselves.

We asked Hermann Czech about Hollein's legacy: which of Hollein's projects was the "good" one, in his view? He said that what would remain of Hollein was the dissolution of the concept of design, and he went on to give two concrete examples, the *MAN transFORMS* and *Austriennale* exhibitions. What is your take on this?

RS Hollein knew how to provoke, how to create atmospheres. The aircraft carrier series has an independent, purely formal or sculptural quality. It immediately makes an impression, but it also sparks further ideas and makes you think more deeply. It is also very political. For us that's a good thing.

But what interests us the most are the earlier, small-scale works, the furniture, as well as the grand piano or the dressing table. There's also the Retti shop and the exhibition architecture—I find Hollein more interesting here than in his very large projects.

What we also admire about Hollein today is the intellectual dimension of his persona, his method, and his work. These are aspects that are not so much in evidence in the current Viennese discourse.

MC On our study trip to Vienna, we also asked ourselves where the next Czech or Hollein was. I think it's really good that you're wanting to look at these themes from today's perspective. After all, this Viennese-Hollein cosmos has had a decisive influence on generations of architects beyond the city. The strong will to shape and create a place is impressive. The same goes for the often political statements that can be found in the work.

Endnotes

1   Maria Conen and Raoul Sigl were visiting professors during the 2016–2017 winter term at the Chair of Urban Architecture, TUM School of Engineering and Design, TU München.

2   An organized whole that is perceived as more than the sum of its parts. Origin, 1920s: from German *Gestalt*, meaning "form, shape."

3   *BestOf Architecture* of the École Polytechnique Fédérale de Lausanne (EPFL). Exhibition design by Victoria Easton and Raoul Sigl, 2009.

4   *Manifesta 11*, Löwenbräu and Helmhaus, Zurich, 2016.

5   Conen Sigl Architekt:innen were commissioned to design the *Swiss Art Awards* exhibitions in Basel 2017 and 2018.

This Dialogue on Hans Hollein took place on April 7, 2021 online.

Conen Sigl Architekt:innen

Conen Sigl Architekt:innen was founded by Maria Conen and Raoul Sigl in 2011 in Zurich. Both completed their studies at the ETH Zurich. The main focus of the office is on residential projects, but they have also worked on exhibitions and the preservation of cultural buildings. In addition to their built work, both partners have taught at various architecture schools in Europe. Maria Conen is currently a full professor at the ETH Zurich. They have also published several essays on contemporary architecture.

David Kohn
David Kohn Architects

What is your relationship to Hans Hollein's work?

> DK Hollein designed through a process of assimilation and translation and his built projects have a very direct, enriching experience of association—an approach that feels connected with the work of my practice. Hollein's projects have strong forms and characters, but at the same time the layers of cultural complexity are immediately discernible. His work feels irreverent and subversive towards what is fixed in our culture. This elicits excitement and pleasure—I find Hollein emboldening.

Have you ever looked at his work as a reference for your own work?

> DK Yes, one of the first projects I designed as a student at Cambridge University was a florist's shop. I remember looking at Hollein's Retti and Schullin shops in Vienna as references. In a way his work was a delicious antidote to some of the constraints of a typical 1990s modernist education, when you were expected to be doing substantial institutional projects. Designing a shop was not condoned by all—probably best avoid commerce, smallness, and impermanence altogether. The need to

David Kohn Architects, A4 Building, Design District, London, United Kingdom, 2022.
Frontal view of A4 building at dusk. Photo: Max Creasy

engage your audience directly, an unavoidable aspect of commercial environments, was not much discussed either. I remember my project was considered kitsch, and not in a good, Josef Frank-kind of way, but I was proud of it nonetheless. Even then, twenty-five years ago, I found Hollein's work very nourishing and I have kept up that interest.

That process of association and transformation can also be related to the work of Hermann Czech. Is he possibly a Viennese architect who is even closer to the work of your practice?

DK It's true that Hermann Czech is probably the architect I have discussed most often in public. Czech's work was very important to me when I started my practice around fourteen years ago. I was interested in his use of collage and the juxtaposition of unalike things, the potential of projects to disrupt expectations. Projects like Czech's Kleines Café (1970, 1973–1974) or Palais Schwarzenberg (1984) make you return to architectural history with a kind of magpie interest in subverting codes. And this is something I also see in Hollein's work, though he seems less preoccupied with the status of all the facets of architecture, and consequently has a greater freedom to juxtapose high and low architectural registers.

And how do you connect this approach, which is inherently linked to an interest in mannerist architecture, to today's practice?

DK I understand mannerism as a kind of playfulness towards architectural history, but potentially incorporating other disciplines too. One interesting phenomenon of contemporary architectural practice is its capacity to look outside of itself, to engage with other design disciplines, like fashion or digital technology, and explore what they might mean in relation to architecture culture. Today, we have to position ourselves closer to cultural practitioners in a broader sense, asking: What is architecture? Do "we" collectively allow this or that to be within "our" discipline? There still seem to be strong disciplinary boundaries. What Hollein did, very effectively, was to question those boundaries in a positive way. And it seems there is even more at stake today, in terms of what constitutes valid practice.

One point about Hollein's working method is that he was obsessed with building models and his office produced endless working models during the design process. Just now, we walked through your office and looked at several types of models. How do you work with this medium?

DK Working with models plays an important role in our practice. Every design decision embodies a vast amount of labor because we believe slight aesthetic adjustments can have a major impact on the overall design. I think this kind of precision is a potent thing in contemporary architecture, as in many instances, and certainly in the UK, the possibility of precision is being slowly obliterated by standard procurement procedures. For us, it's not just about a need to be precise: it's about creating the spatial context in which the precise judgment can be observed and appreciated—that's where the potential for radicality lies. And models are a way of establishing that context.

Does this also have something to do with creating a narrative basis for a project?

DK Using models does connect to telling stories through the notion of *gestalt*. Models give you an opportunity to check and affirm the character of an object. By character, I mean the way an object adds up to more than the sum of its parts, much like a face is read as more than two eyes, a nose, and a mouth. This character is something that will remain when scaled up to the size of a building, even though you might not be able to perceive the whole of the building at once. And when objects are identified as having a character or wholeness, they are able to leap the boundaries of architecture to occupy other cultural spheres. A building can be an individual figure or part of an ensemble, a chorus. It forms part of the theatrical cast that animates the city.

David Kohn Architects, V&A Photography Centre, London, United Kingdom, 2018. Model study of the "Dark Tent" film theater. Photo: David Kohn Architects

David Kohn Architects, *Play for Today: The Performance of Architecture*, 2019–2020. Student performance in Birmingham, Diploma Unit 19, AA School of Architecture, London, United Kingdom, in collaboration with Bushra Mohamed. Photo: Luca Bosco

What you were saying about the model embodying the character of the project brings to mind the role that photographs played for Hollein. Once he had arrived at his *gestalt*, the photographing of the project was also the point of closure. After the pictures were taken, it did not really matter to him if the building was demolished or not, because he had the idealized images of the work.

DK I think it's quite interesting that the images of Hollein's shops, for example the 1965 Retti candle shop, feel very frontal. There's clearly a controlling aspect to these photographs. They definitely feel part of the work. But this also poses the question of whether in fact demolishing the building is a requirement of realizing Hollein's vision. Given that any experience of the real building will depart from the singular perspective of the Hollein-commissioned photograph, reality can be seen as an impediment to achieving the closure you mention.

68

Do you give your photographers total freedom or is it very important for you to be part of the process of image production?

DK I've always liked the idea of being able to control the production of images and directing a photographer to realize this vision. But though the idea appeals to me, it's not how I work. I prefer to give photographers license to look for themselves—I'm happy to be surprised. In part this approach is driven by my hope that the project is able to absorb this new perspective as well, that its story is not fixed but can be retold and re-elaborated by others. Whereas Hollein sought a singular image, I want the image-making process to confound my own expectations and demonstrate that the work is polysemic. Architecture may be inarticulate in practice, but a building can nonetheless communicate in a very present and forceful way, with different people taking different things from it.

Hollein's Media Lines could be described as a performative project. In fact, it was a guidance system for the Olympic village in Munich realized as a public art project in 1972. Colored pipes carry infrastructural elements like lighting, sunshading, heating, cooling facilities, but also interactive elements like projections. In some of your urban projects we see a related interest. Could one say they follow a similar idea, three generations apart?

DK Yes, true. We've done a number of public realm projects in the London boroughs of Harrow[1] and Hounslow[2], and now in Birmingham,[3] in which lighting and signage as well as pavilions and pocket parks are conceived as characters playing a distinct role in an urban performance. Right now I'm thinking about the notion of the "performative" in relation to the theme of my diploma unit at the Architectural Association, "Play for Today: The Performance of Architecture." Many of the students are doing projects with a focus on public space. They're asking: What is allowed and what is not allowed? Who's in and who's out? What do we think is celebration, and what isn't? Given the privatization of so much space in our cities, there's an inevitable need to reassert or recover types of publicness. And what is clear is that this project cannot be done once and set in stone—it has to be repeated by every generation. There's something reassuring about this constant struggle to create a performative city, yet at the same time you feel a kind of mournfulness in the face of its impermanence.

Hans Hollein, Media Lines, Olympic Village, Munich, Germany, 1971–1972.
Amphitheater. Archive Hans Hollein, Az W and MAK, Vienna.

There's also something mournful about the current state of Media Lines, with its faded colors …

DK I wonder whether the apparent provisionality of the Media Lines project creates this impression. Temporary projects are more often than not regarded as being inferior to permanent projects. Similarly, there's an underlying assumption in architecture that interiors are less important than their more permanent structures. I believe in another version where temporality in architecture is important because certain projects need to be constantly redone. Both Hollein's Media Lines and the work of my students illustrate this. They show that ritual and public space in the city need to be reclaimed again and again because there isn't a natural state of publicness.

You've already mentioned the teaching program where you focus on the performance as a spatial act. Could you tell us more about how you've framed this topic?

DK We did an exercise with the students in Birmingham about six weeks ago, where we organized workshops with a dancer and a theater academic and each student had to script a performance. The validation of the exercise is the actual and immediate experience of doing these performances together, which reminds you that architecture is something that is enacted, and not only described. And that being an architect might involve a lot more of this attitude and approach. Then a week later, there was an interesting conversation at the AA, where we speculated about how this is connected to architecture practice. I think many architects are not quite sure what they're going to be doing in the future.

Are you saying that as architects we have to radically reinvent what we do and how we teach new generations of architects?

DK I think that in order to address the climate crisis for example, we must learn to occupy existing structures in completely new ways. There is so much doubt and speculation, we have to be very proactive in doing primary research, actually experiencing change for ourselves, because we're not going to be able to just wait for things to resolve themselves. That's not going to happen. We have to be incredibly adventurous, meeting people and encouraging collaboration across disciplines. Where do we find the answers to what we ought to be doing in the future? They're not going to come through being in school and rehashing the same old questions with people in the same discipline. So even though it's not primarily intended as such, this approach can perhaps be seen as a starting point for a different kind of practice.

Would you say this has to do with an interest in unpredictability in your teaching?

DK So much of our life and work right now is online, and thus mediated. It's not often that people come together and do things that are entirely unscripted, where the outcome is not known in advance. In recent years I have been going to the theater a lot more than before, partly because my partner is a theater academic. I have a growing appreciation of what theater offers: it's a space for testing publicness, for finding out what is or is not allowed—or what is onstage or offstage. In a way we're asking the students to go out and perform a kind of publicness.

One could also see it as a project of re-humanizing digital society?

DK Yes, I think it has to do with human experience. When I was a student there was a different discourse about what was happening in the world. Nonetheless, there was still a question about what would be going on in a floor plan, whether the drawing was talking sufficiently about the human activity happening within the space. But as soon as you acquire the title of an Architect the instrumental aspect of this expertise overrides the quality of being an expert in human experience. The professional trappings, the weight of procedural issues, can often blind you to the need to actually train yourself to understand experience. I think the humanizing of these processes should somehow be a constant aspect of the architect's role.

Hollein had a keen interest in technical innovation. How do you reflect on this topic from today's perspective?

DK Well, I would think it's not that clear-cut at the moment. I'm currently reading *The Age of Surveillance Capitalism* by Shoshana Zubott, which is a reminder that absolutely every digital fragment of our experience is endered to capitalism and used to sell us things.[4] But at the same time, I'm having conversations with clients who are pushing beyond Building Information Modelling (BIM) to the next level, where buildings have a digital twin. In this case, every element within the real building communicates with its twin within a digital model. If a tile falls off the real building, it falls off the digital model too. A maintenance operative, potentially located halfway around the world, could fix the twin in digital space and the tile would be reattached correctly in the real building. So, while I'm learning about the dangers of surveillance capitalism, I'm also having to engage with other dimensions of the same technology. It is difficult to imagine how one would like it to be. I wonder, if Hollein were around today, if he would just find a way of pulling these questions into the immediate experience of the architecture. Can there be a pleasure to experiencing a digital twin in the real world? Will people craft tiles and digital models simultaneously? Could refining the making and using of the real and the digital lead to a point where the twin acquires a strange hybrid beauty and we find something lacking about a tile that does not have one?

Does this have concrete implications for your current work?

DK Recently we collaborated with the artist Simon Fujiwara on an installation at the Whitechapel Gallery that looked at the "lost" work of Leonardo da Vinci, the *Salvator Mundi*, and the idea of making a museum built around this one painting. The installation was like a themed experience around a single painting.

Simon is interested in the copy, the fake, and asking what constitutes authentic experience. He's working in quite a difficult territory, dealing with forces in contemporary culture that perhaps one would rather avoid. I think he's trying to understand how relevant authenticity is to everyday life, and whether as an artist one can even aspire to produce something authentic.

71

David Kohn Architects, The Salvator Mundi Experience, 2019. Project exploring possible museums of the near future for the *Is This Tomorrow?* exhibition, Whitechapel Gallery, London, United Kingdom, in collaboration with artist Simon Fujiwara. Interior space of the installation. Model photo: David Kohn Architects

One wonders what Hans Hollein would make of this question…

> DK Well, I don't think it's credible as a cultural practitioner today to say "I'm not interested" in technology or in challenging notions of originality. And I believe Hollein was someone who on a subversive level wanted to provoke awareness of all these complex issues.

Do you think the agency of art can be an ally for the future of our profession, in similar terms to how you talked about performance and performers?

> DK Yes, definitely. We are constantly learning, expanding what we think of as our professional territory, through our collaborations with different practitioners. At the same time, whilst we are being informed and challenged by these practices to expand the discipline of architecture, I don't feel any need to be an artist, or to call myself an actor or a designer.

That's one difference between us and Hans Hollein. He thought of himself
as an artist as well as an architect.

DK I feel there's a lot of responsibility attached to calling yourself an artist, and I don't want to treat that lightly. I am not an artist, but I have a lot of respect for them. The artists that I know take a lot of personal risks and possibly Hollein did so as well. I think another big difference between us is a result of the increasing division of labor and specialization within architecture over the past decades.

More and more the architect is becoming someone who has to be able to think
in multiple directions and have agency. The ability to moderate, mediate,
and collaborate is also gaining in importance, which opens up a new potential,
because at the moment, at least in Austria, the profession is going through
intellectually hard times.

DK Perhaps in future an architect will be more like an artist who will choose from the options made available by artificial intelligence. Working with Simon Fujiwara has certainly made me think that is possible! However, we have been through technological paradigm shifts before, and though the tools have got better they still haven't removed the need for architects to reimagine the design process to provide more and better design outcomes. But I also feel there are lots of things where fifteen years ago you would have thought, "That's going to require a human," and yet it doesn't anymore. And maybe it will evolve very quickly in the near future.

Endnotes

1 High Street Harrow, a reconfigured public space for a North London town center, 2012.

2 Hounslow High Street, 2012.

3 Birmingham Smithfield Market, new market halls for Birmingham with performance spaces, workshops and offices, in collaboration with Eastside Projects, ongoing.

4 Shoshana Zuboff, *The Age of Surveillance Capitalism: The Fight for a Human Future at the New Frontier of Power* (London: Profile Books, 2019).

This Dialogue on Hans Hollein took place on February 27, 2020 in London.

David Kohn

David Kohn studied architecture at the University of Cambridge and Columbia University. He established his office, David Kohn Architects, in 2007. His work, rich in subtle historical references, ranges from exhibition design, interiors, and small conversions to houses and large institutional buildings. In addition to his architectural work, he has published several essays and articles on architecture. Finally, he has taught at various universities in the UK and Europe and is currently a lecturer at the Architectural Association in London.

David Kohn Architects are collaborating with Bovenbouw Architectuur on a project in Hasselt, Belgium.

Stefanie Everaert and Caroline Lateur
Doorzon

What is your relationship to Hans Hollein's work?

CL Well, we've used Hans Hollein's work as a direct reference and source of inspiration for several projects.

SE There are a lot of Hollein images floating around our office.

CL We were commissioned to do the interior design for the swimming pool in Châteauroux, France (2019). It was an intimidating space, a large project where most of the building had already been designed by the time we got involved.

SE The reference to Hans Hollein had to do with scale. We were drawing lanterns that did not match the human scale any longer because of their size. So the lamps became artificial palm trees, and the palm trees, of course, referred to Hollein.

Is Hollein "famous" in Belgium at all?

SE Not remotely. But there's a particular group of architects from our generation, probably only a small number of us, who know Hollein's work and like to study it or refer to it. We were children when postmodernism was big and we grew up with those images and playful objects.

Hans Hollein, Austrian Travel Agency, Opernringhof branch, Vienna, Austria, 1976–1978. Entrance space. Archive Hans Hollein, Az W and MAK, Vienna. Photo: Franz Hubmann/Imagno/picturedesk.com

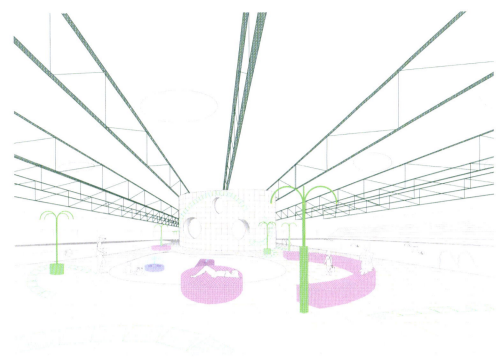

Doorzon, BALSANEO, Centre Aquatique Intercommunal Balsan'éo, Châteauroux, France, 2019. In collaboration with Mikou Studio, Paris, France. Study of the recreational pool with palm-like showers. Digital drawing.

Hans Hollein worked tirelessly to dissolve the boundaries between disciplines—
and especially between design, interior architecture, and architecture.
How do you reflect on this?

CL The answer is in a way very simple, because we're not architects, but interior architects, so our interest in interior architecture is a given. We tell ourselves this is a nice position to be in because we are not constrained by a lot of the issues that architects have to deal with.

SE The diploma we have is not considered a real diploma because we're not qualified to design a structure. But if we want to build something, it's really easy: we just invite an architect to our team.

CL So we're not held back by the fact that we're not architects.

SE In fact, the opposite applies. Rather than being a handicap, it frees us to operate across a broader spectrum. We can go from architecture, via scenography and interior design, to furniture design or even smaller details. This keeps our practice very interesting and alive, because we're not bound to perform the same kinds of tasks over and over.

You once gave a lecture on your work titled "Are We Attacking Architecture?" [1]
Is this a question that you posed yourselves, or was it proposed by your hosts?

SE An architect friend of ours, Lorenzo Bini from Studio Binocle in Milan,[2] asked us this question during a joint lecture that we were doing with him. It struck a chord, because there's something aggressive about it. Not necessarily in a negative sense—it's more like a passionate aggression. And we like to think of ourselves as passionate and a little bit aggressive in our questioning of architecture and the position of interior architecture in relation to architecture.

CL When we began working together with architecture offices in teams for big competitions, we noticed how we could bring a different perspective on the given situation or program, allowing a certain critical examination to take place. The difference has to do with scale and, of course, with seeing the building from the viewpoint of the people who are ultimately going to be using it.

SE What's also interesting is the way that architects often have a fixed idea of what we can contribute to the project. They're invariably surprised when we come up with something different. They expect us to sort out how the offices work or suggest some nice fabrics or materials, which is part of our remit, of course. But there is much more to it. We always try to notice and address other aspects, and in most cases architects welcome this engagement as they have so many other issues to deal with.

Hollein managed to escape a fixed idea of what is expected from an architect by referring to himself as an artist.

SE I think many important architects have questioned the limits of the profession, transgressing and testing the boundaries between art and scenography, as well as landscape, interiors, and buildings.

Hollein's time in the States had a lasting impact on his work, though he was also influenced more or less directly by historical Viennese references such as Johann Fischer von Erlach, Otto Wagner, and Adolf Loos. Are there influences that you can point to in your work? And what are your thoughts on the lack of female role models—something you've talked about in other contexts?

SE It's true that our world of references has a male and classical bias. We also have to admit that includes the references we discuss with our students. To be honest, it's something we've been aware of for some time, but are not yet actively doing enough about.

In terms of our personal references, there's no particular topic that we keep returning to. Of course we both worked at Maarten Van Severen, I started working in the furniture workshop in the late 1990s and Caroline worked in the office in the early 2000s. If we're speaking of the most important reference for Doorzon, that's where we have to go. Other references, such as Philippe Starck, also came to us through Maarten. We learned a lot from him that still informs the way we work today.

CL It wasn't just about the finished work, but about the process— the pleasure he took in making objects and drawings and in taking the necessary time to develop ideas, even if it didn't make economic sense.

SE His approach was thoroughly unacademic as well. Rather than drawing on textual references, his source of inspiration was always his life.

Did you ever talk with Maarten Van Severen about Hans Hollein? As you know, Hollein also designed plenty of furniture.

SE I think at the time we were working there, Maarten was concealing certain references—with a smile, of course. Hollein, Bořek Šípek, or even Philippe Starck, who was a great example for him, we only

76

discovered afterwards. Minimalism was very much the new thing in those years, meaning other issues were off the table, so to speak.

How exactly do you work with references?

SE We use direct visual references when we're choosing a piece of furniture or a particular color, for example. And these loose references vary a lot. But we also have more specific references that are particular to a project, and this kind of reference can be anything. Like almost every architect, we take a lot of pictures when we travel, which often serve as references for our projects.

What is so fascinating about Hollein is the way he works with references, transforming a precedent, such as the shop fronts of Otto Wagner or Adolf Loos, into something unexpected. One can recognize the "original" but the outcome is completely new.

SE We actually have a project where we clearly referenced a Hollein design. Unusually for us, the reference is very direct. Some of our friends refer to it as our "little Hans Hollein project."

And which project is this?

SE It's a small Japanese tea house and photography bookshop, Zoff, in a leftover space of a big house in Antwerp. I think this reference could be called quite direct—but visually direct, as we don't know exactly what Hollein's way of working would have been in a similar situation.

Hollein was very attentive to how his work was published and took great care in selecting images for books and magazines. You published a monograph on your work, *Doorzon–Vlees & Beton*, some time ago.[3] In comparison with your website, which is quite dynamic and associative in the way images are displayed, the book seems more conventional in its structure. Do you think this is a fair description?

SE We like to give maximum freedom to whoever is collaborating with us. For the book, we worked together with a publisher and a graphic designer, and of course they both had a hand in how it turned out. But I would say that in terms of how it is structured the book is also very intuitive. This was also the case with the website, where our webdesigner, Atelier Haegeman-Tem, after having studied our work, suggested we work with overlaps and developed a loose way of showing our projects—something we are very enthusiastic about.

CL For the book, we decided to structure it by introducing themed chapters. It was a way of organizing the amount of material we'd accumulated by that time.

SE After eight years, this was the first moment of reflection of our practice.

Doorzon, ZOFF, interior design for Zoff Books, Berchem, Belgium, 2020. Tea counter. Photo: Filip Dujardin

77

We've had the chance to explore the archive of Atelier Hans Hollein.
It's incredible how much material he and his office produced. The archive
has been organized in the meantime by the Az W, but we were told that
his office was a creative mix.

CL I can imagine. There was also a moment at the office of Maarten
Van Severen, towards the end of his life, when the question of archiving
his material and drawings came up. It was such chaos, and almost
impossible to bring into order, because everything related to everything
else, with copies of the same drawing cropping up in different piles.
And that brings me to the starting point of our first book, where we had
almost the same experience. Stefanie had printed out a lot of material,
drawings and also pictures of models and references, and we spread
it all over the floor. Looking at this mass of images, we had the intuitive
idea of not showing our work project by project, but rather starting
from what "a kitchen" is to us, or "a bathroom," and where do we see
interesting connections between inside and outside. I still find it
a very interesting way of representing or looking back at our own work.

SE To me, it's much more interesting than looking at the projects
separately, in a chronological way, because that's actually what you
do in any case when you're working in the office. You're behind
your computer the whole time, always busy with project after project
after project, trying to make some money. Rather than looking at
these projects separately, it's more interesting for us, as a reflective
action, to find the connections between them.

A recurrent theme in Hollein's oeuvre was the creation of complex spatial
experiences. This was to a large extent related to the public and representative
character of most of the projects he worked on.

Similarly, in your work you also strive for unusually exalted spatial qualities,
even if you are mostly making domestic settings for private clients. How do you
manage to persuade your clients to pursue unconventional spatial solutions?

SE Unfortunately we don't manage to convince clients as often as we'd
like! Regardless of the scale of the project, we begin by considering the
spatial situation and the bigger picture. Often, we're asked to do some
small unconnected interventions in a house. The client asks us, "Can you
do the bathroom and maybe the kitchen and we need some storage there
or a cupboard, and we think that room is a little too dark." We'll always
try to conceptually tie those issues together because most of the time
one thing has an impact on the other. Removing a wall or creating
a new opening or connection can completely change the dynamics of
the space. What we also like to do is to add something visual in these
places. Take, for example, the connection between the dining space and
the kitchen, a fundamentally common situation: if sometimes there is
a mirror involved, or a different material, or something happening with
the floor, it emphasizes new connections or relations between spaces.

Doorzon, HEM, interior conversion of terraced house, Ghent, Belgium, 2016, in collaboration with B5 architecten. View from back extension towards kitchen with serving hatch. Photo: Filip Dujardin

And how do you convince the client that connecting disparate parts of the dwelling is a good idea?

CL The client has to be open to ideas that depart from their original expectations, even if this creates a little moment of friction or conflict. A good client might be surprised, but they will still recognize the advantages of what we're proposing. It also allows us to introduce an added value, making the clients see their own house in a new way.

Stefanie, when you took part in the Seven Questions series of the Chair of Jan De Vylder at the ETH, you mentioned a research project about the status of interior architecture in relation to architecture.[4] Is this still going ahead?

SE Yes, we're still working on it. The project is mainly about the relevance of interior architecture and the role it plays in the wider context of architecture. Architecture is changing very rapidly today and we've noticed that architects are beginning to address many of the same topics that interior architects have been dealing with for a very long time—yet architects act as if these issues are new, and they are ones who have discovered them. Our aim is to address themes that other types of practices have already engaged with, and to show ways of making architecture more inviting and closer to the people.

CL We believe that addressing architectural design from the perspective of an interior architect can add value to a project.

SE Yes, in Belgium we have a very good competition system, but there is a lack of awareness of the added value interior architects bring.

It's other, more powerful project partners that bring us into play—we could never initiate a competition entry ourselves. To be honest, having to wait by the phone is quite a stupid situation to be in.

In the case of Hollein this issue is quite interesting. On the one hand he was the powerful male architect dominating the local discourse. On the other, many of the things that he was preoccupied with, especially interior architecture, were traditionally considered a female domain.

SE And no one asked him about this contradiction while he was still alive?

No, but indirectly we can point to a recent comment by Peter Noever, who knew him very well.[5] He said of Hollein that "he occupied everything" (*er hat alles besetzt*) in Vienna. Due to his powerful standing, also as the main curator of the Austrian Pavilion in Venice, he had a huge influence on Austrian culture at the time. In a way, this allowed him to transgress professional boundaries.

The range of his work is evident in the Hollein archive, which is full of design variants and options. During the design process he kept making changes and keeping his options open as long as possible. How do you work in this regard?

Doorzon, FRIANT, interior design for a house in Ghent, Belgium, 2020, in collaboration with architecten de vylder vinck tallieu, Ghent. Model photo: Doorzon

SE We often hear the same story about the genius architects—of course, only the male architects, because they have a lot of time. The so-called geniuses, such as Le Corbusier or Hans Hollein, and also Jan De Vylder, a famous architect from Ghent that we like to work with, they always say the same thing: "Everything has to remain open until the end." But we think this isn't so. At the beginning we have an open phase where everything is possible. The two of us are very good at imagining beforehand what it will be like. But then, when the project is being built, we never change anything unless there's a problem on site. Everything is executed as it was planned on the drawing table. And we've never had difficulties or regrets doing things this way. The process is quite closed in our practice.

CL It's something that we learned in Maarten Van Severen's atelier. The freedom is in the drawing, not in the process of deciding things on site.

Your interior models are very close to the final result.

CL Yes, for us it's a positive thing if the built project is very close in appearance to the model. But when you're aware of what goes into the process, or sometimes even just of the time that elapses between the design and realization, the resemblance is almost shocking.

We'd like to finish by talking about teaching. Hollein taught throughout his professional career, first at the academy in Düsseldorf and then later for many years at the University of Applied Arts, where he led the studio for industrial design. Hermann Czech, who was his teaching assistant for many years, told us about Hollein's open-minded and discursive approach to teaching. We know that you also teach a studio at the KU Leuven, but couldn't find that much information about what you do. Could you tell us about it?

SE The lack of information is scandalous, really. Unfortunately our university doesn't have the same tradition of publishing student work that you find in other schools.

But the setup, which was defined by the former programme director of Interior Architecture at KU Leuven, Faculty of Architecture Ghent, Prof. Ir. Arch. Fredie Floré is interesting.

She felt the master's studios did not engage enough with the realities of practice, so she decided to invite practicing duos to teach. The first semester is taught by two of our colleagues Koen Pauwels & Wim Van der Vurst (ISM Architecten) and we teach the second semester. The program is called "Interieur van de architectuur van het interieur", which of course indicates something very pragmatic. But our approach is to teach our students how to develop a relevant idea of their own. So they all work on different master theses—we have 20 students working on 20 different subjects.

CL Relevant to us means that the project should be related to the world we're living in and tackle some of the major issues facing society.

SE ... Society as linked to the city and the needs of particular groups of people. The projects are underpinned by the ideas of functionality and practicability, which are of course very important to us, but then we try to guide our students towards a project that really appeals to the imagination, that is inviting, contains surprises, and so on. It should be something that people can recognize and relate to. We try to teach students to preserve this tension between the idea and the actual object or architecture that they make. In that sense, Hans Hollein would have been a great student.

Endnotes

1 Doorzon Interieurarchitecten, "*Are We Attacking Architecture?*", lecture in the "Slow Space" Architecture, Urbanism and Design 2021/2022 series organized by Stad en Architectuur, KU Leuven, November 17, 2021.

2 Milan, founded by architect Lorenzo Bini.

3 Christophe Van Gerrewey and Halewijn Lievens, eds., *Doorzon Interieurarchitecten— Vlees & Beton* (Ghent: WZW Editions, 2013).

4 Jan De Vylder, Annamaria Prandi, ETH Studio, eds., *Seven Questions* (Berlin: Ruby Press, 2022).

5 Peter Noever (b. 1941), Austrian designer and curator, director of the Austrian Museum of Applied Arts, MAK, 1986–2011.

This Dialogue on Hans Hollein took place on April 29, 2022 online.

Doorzon

Doorzon interior architects were founded in 2005 by Stefanie Everaert and Caroline Lateur in Ghent. Focusing on interior design for private and institutional projects, their multidisciplinary work, often made in collaboration with other design studios, is driven by a complex and playful assemblage of materials and textures. In addition to their building projects, they also teach interior design at the KU Leuven (Ghent) and were recently appointed guest professors at the EPFL in Lausanne.

Andreas Rumpfhuber
Expanded Design

What is your personal relationship to Hollein's work?

AR My interest in Hollein's work is rather limited to his early projects and relates to my research on the transformation of labor. In the postwar years "immaterial labor" became the dominant productive force in Western industrialized countries, and some of Hollein's projects mirror this transformation. The key question for me is the extent to which architecture alters in relation to the sphere of work. The starting point of my engagement with Hollein was the Mobile Office project, where he presents himself as a globally networked, Cessna-flying entrepreneur, designing an architecture for work—a transparent bubble in which he then sits down and works.

What is it in particular that interests you about this project?

AR There are several interesting aspects to the Mobile Office. On a general level, it's astonishing how much the project mirrors and condenses discourses around the postwar transformation of labor. For example, there is the performative aspect of work, which had been important since the 1950s. The project was produced for a TV series, *Das österreichische Portrait* (Portrait of Austria) and aired some time in December 1969.[1] So I read it not as an "installation" or an object—which is how it has been presented in the collection of the Generali Foundation in Vienna and in many exhibitions—but rather as a singular performance by the architect, recorded for television. In this respect it is obvious that architecture, that is, the bubble which wraps around Hollein and protects him from the elements, is transparent: performative work requires the workplace to be a stage.

But it is perhaps also interesting, from today's perspective, that a public broadcasting service would devote an entire program to such a young architect. Hollein was thirty-four at the time. It could be seen as a kind of "nation building" for the still young state of Austria. For Hollein, and for many of his generation, it created a freedom, a space for action, which they used for projects.

Hans Hollein sitting in his inflatable Mobile Office, 1969. Photographed on the Aspern air field, Vienna. Archive Hans Hollein, Az W and MAK, Vienna. Photo: Gino Molin-Pradel

What other Hollein projects from that time interested you?

AR The 1966 collage, Proposal for an Extension of the University of Vienna, for example, was the starting point for a text I wrote about

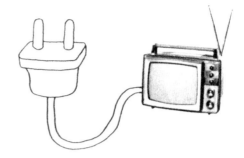

Hans Hollein, proposal for an Extension of the University of Vienna, Austria, 1966.
Collage from *BAU*, no. 2–3 (1969): 32.

the architecture of knowledge spaces and their transformation into the so-called "edu-factory." Another time, I looked at the museum in Mönchengladbach in relation to the role of the creative industry in the reinvention of the European city.

What's so special about the collage for the extension of the university?

AR The collage consists of two halves. On the left-hand side you can see an image of the University of Vienna. It was obviously taken from the Burgtheater, with the focus not on the famous theater stage, but turning around to look on the stage of knowledge production. On the right side you can see the planned extension of the university: a portable TV with an oversized, hand-drawn power plug—a plug that can be connected at any time to the university and its lecture halls, ready to transmit all the content produced in the university into living rooms across the city and indeed the nation.

As with the Mobile Office, one can read this quick collage project as an ironic or cynical commentary on the status of architecture at that time. In Mobile Office Hollein reduced architecture to a transparent, inflated placeholder. In the university extension architecture is replaced by a technical device. I see Hollein here more as an observer who uses the means of architecture to exemplify the shifts and changes happening in society, without offering a solution.

Why are you interested in this today?

AR For me, projects like the university extension or the Mobile Office mirror popular discouses that are still relevant for understanding contemporary society: the idea of leisure society, or the promise of the end of labor. These projects bear witness to a time when a new order was starting to emerge but the old order was still visible. Looking closely, the changes and shifts become very clear. The collage of the university extension, for example, can be understood as a commentary on social democratic education policy, as it was discussed all over Europe. Everyone and anyone, regardless of their background or class, should have the opportunity for higher education. To put Hollein's project into context: the competition for the Free University in Berlin was in 1967, the Open University in Britain was founded in 1969, and the Bergische Universität in Wuppertal in 1972.

Hollein also deliberately staged himself using the media of film or television…

AR Great hopes were invested in television, a nascent technology at the time. Hollein amplifies this, saying: let's not build anything anymore, but use the new media channels to broadcast the lectures. I'm sure Hollein meant this ironically: he clearly wanted to build. In retrospect, however, the project was prophetic, encapsulating the evolution of the university into an edu-factory. The Open University would begin course-based television broadcasts three years after the project.

Austria was trying, after World War II, to reconstruct a society. In addition to politics and economics, the Church also played a not unimportant role. Hollein was a key protagonist during this period, with exhibitions, publications, and his first realized works.

Can the paradigm shift that is happening around this time also be seen in Hollein's works?

AR I would say that in Austria the Roman Catholic Church is both part of the political establishment and a hugely important player in the economy. At that time, it was probably still one of the largest landowners in the country. The Second Vatican Council between 1962 and 1965 promoted a fairly progressive understanding of the doctrine of the faith. This renewal of the relationship between Church and society gave a fillip to art, design, and architecture. The Austrian avant-garde was born in the Galerie nächst St. Stephan with the help of the Roman Catholic Church. There are several churches built around this time that are still fascinating today, but the Church was also involved in participatory housing initiatives.

How would you situate Hollein in this social context?

AR I've never seen Hollein as being particularly close to the Church. For me, Hollein, like any other architect, is part of the local economy. The projects emerge from this economy. For Hollein, in Vienna, it was small shops, but also commissions for a manufacturer of office furniture. Oswald Mathias Ungers in Germany, James Stirling in Britain—each had to work within a different economy.

Where else is this "economic" aspect, as you describe it, visible in Hollein's architecture?

AR The Abteiberg Museum comes to mind. Mönchengladbach was a small city of about 150,000 inhabitants. Up until the postwar period, it had a flourishing textile industry, but in the 1960s the city's economy was massively affected by the crisis in European textile production, which is usually framed as a structural economic change. I would argue that the idea of building the museum became a means for Mönchengladbach to reinvent itself. Here, the topping-out ceremony (*Gleichenfeier*) of the museum is significant. The ceremony is traditionally a gathering of all the people involved in the construction. In the case of the museum, it became an urban event attended by a large number of the city's inhabitants. I find the pictures and descriptions of the topping-out ceremony intriguing. It seems as if the whole city was mobilized and set into a common rhythm—the rhythm of the new cultural economy represented by the Abteiberg Museum.

The museum is also a good example of the ties between the Church and
the cultural sphere. There was already a sense of great optimism, the feeling
of a new beginning.

AR Yes, that's true, but this wasn't just down to the Church. The welfare state and tax revenues also made things possible. A building like the Abteiberg Museum would be unthinkable today, when savings are being made at every turn and global corporations no longer pay taxes.

You describe the associations that certain phenomena—images, texts, films—
elicit in you. Is that something typically Viennese, something that connects you
as an architect and a theoretician with Vienna?

Hans Hollein, *Traum und Wirklichkeit: Wien 1870–1930*, exhibition at the Künstlerhaus, Vienna, Austria, 1984–1985, sketch of Sigmund Freud's couch. Slide. Archive Hans Hollein, Az W and MAK, Vienna.

AR I'm not from Vienna, but I live here. And I've been doing psychoanalysis for years. That's perhaps something Viennese. Psychoanalytic work mainly consists of the process of associating and interpreting structures in these associations. That's how I would describe it. You circle around a problem and describe how you see it from different angles. As you do so, you become conscious of certain aspects and with this the initial problem also changes. It's a permanent process of finding and analyzing.

Finding was something Hollein also did a lot of: I am interested, for example, in his observations and analyses of the pueblos in New Mexico, which for me are very strongly associated with a particular idea of dwelling. Hollein works on and repeats this "finding" over and over again. Through this constant repetition something happens—the repeated thing begins to change and to distinguish itself from the original.

We don't know if Hollein ever underwent psychoanalysis himself, but you could
say his whole architecture is psychoanalytical.

AR He did design an analyst's couch, after all. And we know his assistant at the time, Hermann Czech, has done psychoanalysis. Hollein also designed the exhibition *Wien: Traum und Wirklichkeit* (*Vienna: Dream and Reality*, 1985), which has many psychoanalytical components. So psychoanalysis was not a completely alien concept for Hollein. I don't think it matters whether he did psychoanalysis or not. The repetitions in his works are still interesting.

Is repetition something negative or positive for you?

AR All of us repeat ourselves constantly. The question is, how do we deal with this repetition? You always repeat the behavior your parents instilled in you in childhood. Your children then repeat you...

In his exhibition, *Werk und Verhalten—Leben und Tod* (*Work and Behavior—Life
and Death*, Venice Biennale, 1972), Hollein made symbolic use of a rectangular
raft holding a white chair with two palm trees behind it, linking the installation
to a childhood memory—a boat trip he took with his father.[2] Is making something
like this typically "Viennese"?

AR Perhaps... perhaps the narrative is strange for us today, or out of step with the times. I can't imagine one of today's architectural superstars talking about their childhood. At most, that kind of memory might be used strategically, as we've seen with Rem Koolhaas when he talks about his time in Indonesia. Hollein's relationship to Joseph Beuys comes to mind here. Autobiographical narratives were integral to Beuys's art. And today we know that a large part of his "autobiographical" stories were freely invented…

Would you say autobiographical narratives have no place in the conceptual development of architecture today?

AR They're not exactly zeitgeisty…

And yet they're somehow appealing, right?

AR Totally appealing, yes! But using an autobiographical narrative as a starting point for the development of a project also opens you to criticism. I guess that's another difference between art and architecture. In architecture, emphasizing authorship through autobiographical details is rather suspect—architecture is supposed to be for the many, not for the individual. At the same time, we all have a history that we cannot cast off.

In your book, *Wunschmaschine Wohnanlage*, you've talked about the oppressive forms of governance that are reflected in housing and proposed a future model of participatory coexistence that is not controlled or predetermined, but allows the individual to activate their own "desiring-production" (*Wunschmaschine* in German, referring to the Deleuze and Guattari term, *machine désirante*).[3] Hollein, as you mentioned earlier, was interested in the pueblos of New Mexico. Do you see a connection between these two projects?

A pueblo in New Mexico, United States, photographed by Hans Hollein in the early 1960s. *Der Aufbau,* no. 9 (September 1964): 377.

AR Hollein's engagement with the pueblos of New Mexico is important for understanding his approach to the structuring of space. His interest in this vernacular architecture was ahead of the times (1964). He visited the pueblos himself and wrote a substantial text about them. However, it could also be alleged that this engagement later telescoped into an image of their fascinating structure—an image that could be disposed of as required.

Whereas Hollein was fascinated by the form of the structures, I am more interested in the spatial, economic, and sociological realities of the people who inhabit them. You can see this already in the first paragraphs of *Wunschmaschine Wohnanlage*, where I insist on the need to update the *Gemeinnützigkeitsgesetz*, the Non-Profit Act regulating the business model for all non-profit housing developers. I see in Hollein a formal and symbolic approach to architecture that is still able to ignore questions of how people live. Ethnographic issues only became popular in the 1970s, with the structuralists.

Does the *Wunschmaschine Wohnanlage* project also have a formal component?

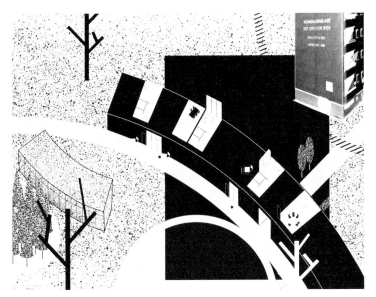

Expanded Design, *Wunschmaschine Wohnanlage*, Vienna, Austria, 2014–2016.

AR Of course, the *Wunschmaschine Wohnanlage* also has a formal component. Architecture is always also formal. The project is ultimately based on a formal principle that I argue can be applied to all mass housing built in the city of Vienna between 1950 and 1980. The *Wunschmaschine* is an abstract machine. The circle I use, much like the transparent bubble in the Mobile Office, is a placeholder. The extent to which the chosen shape is implemented formally is undecided. What is shown is a system that can be applied flexibly. The *Wunschmaschine* is thus also a reaction to the specific reality of housing production in Vienna.

And this *Wunschmaschine* has also taken on a life of its own, in some respects?

AR One could say so, yes. Even though it is so abstract, I have the feeling that some people understand it very well. The project has been shown in numerous exhibitions. Most recently it was included in the CCA exhibition, *A Section of Now*, in 2022.

You also did an interview with Hollein. What did you talk about?

What I had with Hollein was more of a conversation than an interview. It was back in 2011, I think, a few years before his death, and before the publication of my book *Architektur immaterieller Arbeit* (Architecture of Immaterial Labor).[4] In the course of my research, I'd come across the Austrian Pavilion Hollein designed for the 1968 Triennale in Milan. The Triennale opened at the end of May and was almost immediately overshadowed by student protests.[5] The students criticized the content of the exhibition and demanded a complete rethink. At the same time, they occupied—and vandalized—the venue, shutting down the Triennale for several weeks. An article in *Die Presse* described how Hollein's contribution—the glasses factory—had been destroyed during the protests.[6] Reading this irritated me, because I'd only ever been aware of all the wonderful photos showing visitors engaging with the installation. These pictures were published very prominently in the *A+U* on Hollein in 1985.

But when I asked Hollein about the protests, he obviously didn't want to talk about it: "There were no protests! I don't remember any!" And that was the end of the conversation.

I don't understand why Hollein didn't want to talk about it. The project itself is not degraded or enhanced by mentioning the protests. In fact, it's a great project, despite and because of the related history of student protests.

Hollein placed great importance on how his persona and his projects were perceived by the public.

He curated himself and his work and kept everything permanently under his control. In his ironizing way, he simply performed this architecture. In the Austrian TV program I mentioned earlier, there is a scene where he stands in a telephone booth and raises his hat. The staging is self-deprecating. His whole architecture is ironic and self-critical and at the same time deadly serious.

Where in his work can this still be seen?

There's a moment in the catalog for the 1974 *MAN transFORMS* exhibition that I think is really important.[7] It's the last but one page, and it brings together all these elements—the irony, the self-criticism, and the total seriousness. On the left is a historic drawing from the Austrian National Library showing a group of twelve male scholars arguing about the representation of stars in the galaxy. On the right is a comment by Hollein: "There are one hundred billion stars in the Milky Way and not one is star-shaped."

Hollein had invited some male colleagues to produce contributions to the exhibition, which are also included in the catalog. Eleven of them in total, with him making up the twelve. So I read this double-page spread as an ironic commentary on the architectural discourse that he himself had promoted in the exhibition. He is poking fun at the fact that these learned architects are arguing about a particular representation, a particular form. The twelve scholars are arguing about seven stars. Yet in 1974 they knew there were one hundred billion stars and that not one of them looked like the symbol of a star. So everything is relative… This contribution to the catalog is a good example of Hollein's sense of humor. From this perspective, he could sometimes be subtle, and not the in-your-face character of his general reputation. He was a very complex, often inscrutable architect with different facets in his projects as well.

Endnotes

1 Directed by Dieter O. Holzinger (1941–2006), Austrian author, filmmaker, and theater director.

2 *Work and Behavior – Life and Death. Everyday Situations* (German: *Werk und Verhalten – Leben und Tod. Alltägliche Situationen),* exhibition at the 36th Venice Art Biennale, Italy, 1971–1972.

3 Andreas Rumpfhuber, *Wunschmaschine Wohnanlage: Eine Studie zur funktionalen Nachverdichtung von 46 Großwohnanlagen der Stadt Wien* (Vienna: Sonderzahl Verlag, 2016).

4 Andreas Rumpfhuber, *Architektur immaterieller Arbeit* (Vienna: Turia & Kant, 2013).

5 *Austriennale* was Austria's national contribution to the ill-fated fourteenth Milan Triennale in 1968. Already on the opening day at the end of May, the installation was damaged during student protests and forced to close. It would only reopen to the public at the end of June.

6 Manfred Sack, "Triennale-Tod auf italienisch. Nach der Eröffnung von Studenten und Künstlern okkupiert*," Die Zeit,* June 7, 1968, http://www.zeit.de/1968/23/triennale-tod-auf-italienisch.

7 Hans Hollein, George Nelson, Lisa Taylor, et al., *MAN transFORMS: An International Exhibition of Aspects of Design* (New York: Cooper-Hewitt Museum, 1976).

This Dialogue on Hans Hollein took place on October 7, 2022 in Vienna.

Expanded Design / Andreas Rumpfhuber

Andreas Rumpfhuber founded his interdisciplinary practice Expanded Design in 2011, after studying architecture at TU Graz, the Bartlett, and Sci-Arc and completing a PhD at the Royal Academy of Fine Arts in Copenhagen and Goldsmiths College, London. His work is divided between critical research projects dealing with labor, politics, and space, on which he has published several books and essays, and residential architectural projects at various scales. In addition to his research and built work, he has held several professorships at different schools of architecture.

Wilfried Kuehn
Kuehn Malvezzi

Can you tell us about your personal connection to Hans Hollein?

WK Frankly, I've always leaned more towards Czech and Krischanitz than Hollein. But there is a point where their orbits overlap, namely Hans Hollein's groundbreaking *MAN transFORMS* exhibition in New York (1976), for which Hermann Czech was the project architect. Hollein did not always make it easy for him in Vienna, but Czech is of course not one of his disciples, either age-wise, or in terms of the content of his work. Those who did study with Hollein are, like all students, a little traumatized by the experience. In this respect, Hollein cast a large shadow, and his legacy should not be entrusted to his followers alone.

Some of us studied here in Vienna in the mid- to late 1990s. At that time, we were quite clear that we did not want to study in Hans Hollein's masterclass.

WK By then, Hollein had already passed his peak. It's interesting that we don't know of any outstanding students—his architecture has remained a one-off. That's quite different from Rossi, who had prominent students like Jacques Herzog and Pierre de Meuron, or O.M. Ungers, who taught Hans Kollhoff and Rem Koolhaas. My generation has engaged much more intensely with those younger figures, and with architects like Alvaro Siza, and largely rejected their postmodern predecessors.

What aspect of Hollein's work would you define as a central moment?

WK I always use a lot of Hollein material to tell my students stories that are important to me. Hollein is fundamental, especially in his exploration of curatorial and art-related aspects in architecture. This bears fruit in his museum projects, like the one in Mönchengladbach. These Hollein museums have small fan base, admittedly, but contemporary artists appreciate them because they have spaces they can engage with as an artist: they're based on a strong attitude. Personally, however, I sometimes find Hans Hollein's formal language difficult. It doesn't always attract me—it has repelled me as well.

The museums are spatially very complex and not easy to read from the floor plans.

WK The museums display a level of spatial mastery and complexity that is very rare in architecture. And if you actually visit them, you find the spaces much easier to read than the drawings and plans. The approach is not schematic, but corporeal. Hollein is a spatial artist, designing the experience of the space. For me, this spatial principle has its origins in the baroque. Rather than first designing the core, he begins with certain spatial situations, for example, a staircase opening up to all sides. The staircase is like a nerve center of the building—the point at which

89

it begins to live. It is not an object, but neither is it hidden away, treated as a repeatable core, as it is with the neo-rationalist architects. It's conceived almost in biological terms, as an organ: before Hollein even begins to draw, there is a real sense of the physical experience of the space. This approach is a testament to Hollein's design ability. It's also unrepeatable, and very hard to teach.

One could argue that the staging of the staircase is something typically Viennese; it can also be seen in the work of Adolf Loos, Josef Frank, or Hermann Czech.

WK Hermann Czech, however, works with different scales.

Exactly, what Czech produces are more like miniatures. But wasn't it also in his large-scale works that Hollein ultimately came unstuck?

WK There's an ambivalence with Hollein, as seen, characteristically, in the Haas Haus. I remember thinking it was a dubious project, but when I came to Vienna in the mid-1990s and saw it for myself I was impressed by the experience of the space. Its quality lay not in its surfaces, but in its spatiality. Later, in the course of a refurbishment, the whole interior got ripped out, destroying the integrity and the central value of the building. But a museum like the MMK in Frankfurt remains an outstanding space on a large scale, and if Hollein had built the museum at Salzburg's Mönchsberg (1989) or Disney Hall in LA (1988), they would be outstanding spaces too.

When Hollein was designing a building, he had a very strong perception of the space that was difficult to convey in plans at that stage. For this reason, working models and photos were important for his way of working.

Hans Hollein, Abteiberg Municipal Museum, Mönchengladbach, Germany, 1972–1982. Working model of the so-called "cloverleaf principle" gallery spaces. Archive Hans Hollein, Az W and MAK, Vienna. Photo: Elmar Bertsch

WK I became aware of how intensively Hollein worked with models and photographs when I was preparing the double exhibition at the MAK and the Abteiberg Museum. He used all scales and also photographed the models in order to generate spatial views or test a space in relation to the hanging of specific paintings in a museum collection. Hollein's office produced some huge models; they probably needed them to avoid the pitfalls of the floor plan. But many architects today are trapped, especially when they're designing on the computer, because CAD soon imposes a very systematic approach—something that didn't fit with Hollein at all.

You referred to Hollein in relation to other architects—Alvaro Siza, Rem Koolhaas?

WK There are not only contrasts, but also parallels between Hollein and Siza. If you try to understand Siza's work from the floor plans, you soon find yourself thinking, "I can't make sense of it. It's just not logical." But spatially, Siza's projects are fantastic. Siza's office also worked a lot (and still does) with models, and Siza, like Hollein, sketches brilliantly. Siza and Hollein could be real role models here, for all those architects

Kuehn Malvezzi, *HOLLEIN*, exhibition design, MAK, Vienna, Austria, 2014.
View of installation including a scale model of the Feigen Gallery and
the Kohlmarkt lamps. MAK, Photo: Mika J. Wißkirchen

who think mainly from the floor plan and who can't draw freehand.
On the other hand you have Koolhaas, not known for his drawings,
but whose *Delirious New York* is in line with Hollein's artistic and
publishing work of the 1960s, reconnecting architecture to societal
transformation at all levels and expressions.

How is this Holleinian spatial approach expressed in your work at Kuehn Malvezzi?

WK Not long after those exhibitions at the MAK and Abteiberg, where
I engaged strongly with the content of Hollein's work, we did a competition where we worked in a completely different way from before.
It wasn't a conscious decision, and I only thought about it afterwards.
We made a working model that was several square meters, even though
we don't usually build such large models. The forms were also different
from our previous designs, which was perhaps down to my exposure
to Hollein. It was a museum competition, and we won it. Half of the
museum is underground, and the spaces are not orthogonal but organic—
effectively Hollein themes.

Which project is this?

WK It's the Montreal Insectarium, which opened in 2022.[1] It was liber-
ating and very satisfying to work in a different way. In a sense, Hollein
helped me to develop in a direction I might not otherwise have taken,
even though I'd made a conscious decision to study in Portugal and had

always been very interested in Siza. This corporeal mode of perception was always something that had interested me, but working on the Hollein exhibition was probably the catalyst for applying this principle more organically in combination with the kind of temporally structured museum architecture that we'd developed with our projects for Okwui Enwezor's Documenta 11 (2002) and Rieckhallen Berlin (2004).

Kuehn Malvezzi, Insectarium, Montreal, Canada, 2014–2022, with Pelletier De Fontenay, Jodoin Lamarre Pratte, Atelier Le Balto (Landscape). Model from the competition stage. Photo: Kuehn Malvezzi

Kuehn Malvezzi, *Documenta 11*, Kassel, Germany, 2002. Intersection of exhibition spaces with bench. Photo: ULRICH SCHWARZ, BERLIN

Another project that Kuehn Malvezzi is currently involved with is the "House of One." In terms of the process of planning and construction, can you see parallels to the Haas Haus situation? There, Hollein went on producing model studies even after he'd submitted the design.

WK In the House of One project, we also built models after the competition, in this long phase of planning before construction, when everything is often in flux. As the planning drags on, it's helpful to build new models and modify the existing ones. The House of One is not influenced by Hollein, but the themes it deals with are akin to Hollein's principles: how do you translate urban space into the space of the building? This question has always moved me, and it underpins the work of our practice in general. How can you do urban planning, whatever the scale you're working at? Whether you're planning an exhibition, doing just one room, or designing a large building, each space is in the first instance an urban space. The House of One can be seen as a paradigmatic example: it's a building like a city, condensing in one place three buildings—a synagogue, a church, a mosque—a model city. There's an interesting publication about squares that Hollein did with his students at the University of Applied Arts.[2] This kind of analysis of urban morphology based on public space rather than buildings interests me a lot. I worked with Adolf Krischanitz and he is much less concerned with these questions—his thinking revolves around typology, which I share of course. Krischanitz's architecture is conceptually rigorous and very beautiful, but when I was working at his office I found myself missing this space-oriented, sculptural-morphological approach.

In the House of One, the interior has little to do with the external appearance.
One could see a connection with Hollein's Retti project, where the facade plays
a major role in mediating the public space.

WK In general I think the inner structure and the facade are two
different things. They can coincide, but I don't see any compelling need
for them to do so. You can also have this tension in architecture, which
arises when the interior form completely contradicts the exterior. That's
often the case with Hollein. He also said that architecture should first
be seen as if it were underground. He referred to the Frankfurt Museum
as a mine, although it's hardly subterranean. He saw digging and piling
up as the basic principles of architectural forming, whereby space is
generated through the processes of excavation and sculpting; that's how
I've always imagined architecture, too. The House of One is also a good
example of this idea of hollowing out.

The House of One will be a spiritual place. What was Hollein's relationship to religion?

WK There were some interesting points of contact between Hollein
and the Church in the beginning. The Galerie nächst St. Stephan,[3] where
Hollein and Pichler had their 1963 exhibition, was founded by the priest
(and art connoisseur), Monsignor Otto Mauer.[4] There's also a crypto-
Catholic dimension to the Retti candle shop of course, and you can see
other Catholic references in Hollein's work, in his relationship to Beuys
and to the director of the Abteiberg Museum, Johannes Cladders, both
of whom were indebted to Paul Wember, Rhineland's equivalent of Otto
Mauer. Hollein's work looked for the sacred within the secular. He was
not a church-going person, but as a young architect he did projects for
churches and also designed ideal churches that resembled sexualized
representations of women. The decisive transfer from religion into
Hollein's architecture, however, was surely the way rituals and ceremonies
formed the starting point for his understanding of spatial relations.

Kuehn Malvezzi, House of One, Berlin, Germany, 2012–(under construction). Model of the negative
spaces. The project is included in the ifa (Institut für Auslandsbeziehungen) touring exhibition
An Atlas of Commoning, Places of Collective Production. Model: Martin Edelmann (ifa). Photo:
Simone Gilges

And while we're on an existential theme, you contributed a text to the last issue of *San Rocco* on "Muerte."[5]

WK I'm interested in the subject. I also found points of reference in Hollein's work: the exhibition presenting his work in Mönchengladbach in 1970 was called *Everything is Architecture–An Exhibition about Death*. Architecture is very closely connected with the theme of death. I wrote the *San Rocco* text with Plan Común, while we were working together on a project for the central cemetery in Santiago de Chile. The cemetery is an interesting subject in every way–architecturally, politically. The article we wrote is also about politics and how the way our society is organized in life is then expressed in death as well.

Which is also a very Viennese theme.

WK Of course, these rituals in art–death and the body–apply to Vienna. Actionism could be interpreted in this way, and Hollein's work also fits in very well.

If we're talking about particular Viennese atmospheres and this connection between Church and society, something changes–disappears–between the 1980s and the 1990s, perhaps because you had a new generation that was no longer predominantly brought up in the Catholic faith. How do you see this question of faith today, and how is it expressed in your work?

WK Ritual and sacred spaces are important, even if fewer and fewer people today are believers. I don't think we either can or would want to live without these spaces. I understand the turn to the sacred as not just a religious practice, but as a cultural practice that can evolve and be taken up by younger people. If we think about the many Muslim migrants in Vienna today, some of them very devout, this also raises questions about the spatial order and hierarchy of the European city, which is based on Christian traditions. Now that our cities are multicultural, what form should the place for ritual gatherings take? The House of One is an important project because it brings a mosque into the center of Berlin for the first time in the city's history and addresses the question of a contemporary place of worship as a space of cultural encounter.

One of the first issues of the magazine you founded, *Displayer*,[6] has an article by Stephan Trüby hypothesizing a close link between Hollein's exhibition projects and his architecture. Trüby describes the former as an experimental setup that builds up a tension. Do you also see exhibition design in this sense, as a testing ground for your buildings?

WK Yes, though exhibitions are more closely related to urban design than they are to building, as you're developing a structure that has to allow for other things to happen. With an architectural project, the idea would be to work out every last detail, but you can't do that in an exhibition because there are always other authors involved–curators, artists, the exhibits themselves. Making an exhibition is urban design in the best sense of the word: there are clear forms, clear spaces, clear edges, clear ideas, but the final objects or surfaces are not prescribed. Documenta was a challenge for us, on account of its scale. We actually broached the exhibition layout in terms of urban design: with axes, rings, and labyrinthine paths. Then we had the input from the artists, and the space again changed a great deal, with passageways being moved, for example. It was a testing ground for our approach, where the question was: how far is this a fixture, and how far can it be moved? Our commercial and residential buildings are also based on principles of urbanism, and the House of One has evolved as an urban idea. It's an evolution of this in-between spatial typology, from a central space that acts as the main means of circulation for the sacred spaces, towards a central space that becomes an important gathering place, like a square. I found that again in Hollein. With him, everything was about these lived in-between spaces, these nerve centers. Exhibitions are a testing ground. Their ephemeral character gives you great freedom in the design, and we've been able to realize typologically specific floor plans in them.

According to Hollein, his museum in Mönchengladbach was itself a work of art.
Is this different from your approach?

WK You can't deny that element of artistic narcissism in Hollein, which can be traced back to his beginnings. In the 1960s, he wasn't sure whether he wanted to be an architect or an artist. He ultimately chose architecture in the early 1970s. Perhaps it was a mistake for him to let go of art. His friend Claes Oldenburg, for example, was very much influenced by him. As were Walter Pichler and others.

Our generation is in a different place today. I don't know if any of the architects in this exhibition would identify with the idea of the artist-architect, never mind lay claim to this kind of artistic autonomy. Hollein got really upset when the new director of the Frankfurt Museum had the artist Günther Förg create murals for the two large walls by the staircase. Hollein didn't want another artist to rework his art. He had conceived the room as a white space and was horrified at the thought that it now had four colors, thanks to Förg's permanent installation. I came to understand it wasn't even the colors themselves that irritated Hollein so much as the fact that another artist was becoming part of his own work. That attitude appears somewhat outdated to me. Isn't it the most beautiful thing if the intervention of an artist amplifies, develops further, the thinking of your own architecture?

There is also this question of authorship. Hollein takes himself very seriously as a person; he puts himself to the fore as the protagonist of his buildings.

WK This may also depend on whether you're working as an individual or as part of a group. The strategies you develop will be different if you're in a collective as opposed to working on your own. But it's also the case that you can work as an individual without drawing attention to yourself as the protagonist of the architecture. There are also many architects who give their practice their own name, but who approach day-to-day office life as a dialogue with others, giving their collaborators space to develop as well as public recognition. Hollein had some long-standing, structurally important collaborators, but there is virtually no trace of them in the public record. I find that a bit problematic.

We're interested in the format of the dialogue. You can also have a dialogue across the ages, as *San Rocco* has impressively shown. We'll be very happy if we succeed in doing something similar in Vienna.

WK The topic is a good one for Vienna, for the very reason that Hollein was active here, but this differentiated perception of Hollein is somewhat submerged in the current Viennese discourse. What appears to interest you about Hollein, and interests me too, is not part of the mainstream discourse here. As far as his university affiliations are concerned, Hollein is also not a "product" of the Technical University of Vienna, but trained at the Academy of Fine Arts and was a professor at the University of Applied Arts. In this respect, we are sitting here today, at the TU Wien, in precisely the right place to be talking about Hollein in an unbiased way.

Endnotes

1 The Montreal Insectarium is part of Space for Life, science museum district.

2 *Ort und Platz: Stadträumliche Architektur-analysen*, (Vienna: Hochschule für angewandte Kunst Wien, 1989).

3 An art gallery funded by the archdiocese of Vienna that acted as a nexus between the postwar avant-garde and the Catholic Church, through exhibitions and lectures.

4 (1907–1973), Roman Catholic priest, publisher, and co-founder in 1964 of the Galerie nächst St. Stephan.

5 Wilfried Kuehn, Kim Courrèges, and Felipe De Ferrari, "Life After Death," *Muerte, San Rocco,* no. 15 (2019): 132–140.

6 *Displayer* (issues 1–4) is a magazine about exhibition design and curatorial practice, edited by Wilfried Kuehn during his professorship at the HFG Karlsruhe (2007–2012).

This Dialogue on Hans Hollein took place on December 11, 2019 in Vienna.

Kuehn Malvezzi / Wilfried Kuehn

Kuehn Malvezzi Architects was founded by Simona Malvezzi, Wilfried Kuehn, and Johannes Kuehn in Berlin in 2001. The work of the practice spans from public buildings, museums, and exhibitions, to residential projects and office buildings. Their strong interest in contemporary art and curatorial practice has led them to pursue architecture that forms a robust spatial framework for the content and uses it houses.

Wilfried Kuehn studied architecture at the Politecnico di Milano and ESBAL Lisboa. In addition to the built work with Kuehn Malvezzi, he has co-curated several exhibitions, including the large double show on Hans Hollein in Vienna and Mönchengladbach 2014. He has also published several essays on twentieth-century architecture and was the founder and editor of the magazine *Displayer*, published at the Chair of Exhibition Design at the HfG Karlsruhe, where he taught before becoming a professor at the Technical University of Vienna.

Oliver Lütjens and Thomas Padmanabhan
Lütjens Padmanabhan Architekt*innen

What is your relationship to Hans Hollein's work and ideas?

OL I'd describe it as very fragmentary. That applies to our relation to all architects, but particularly to Hollein. As a student, I was very impressed by the artistic aspect of his work, the drawings, collages, and conceptual projects like the Mobile Office (1969), an inflatable plastic wrap structure he set up in a field. Over time, Hollein has become less and less important in our work, but we still value the small things very much—Hollein can create a whole world full of meaning in these small projects, which are complex and subtle. You really get a sense from them of the Hollein who put out feelers everywhere and brought everything into the work.

TP I grew up in southern Germany, in Stuttgart. I was twelve or thirteen years old when James Stirling's Staatsgalerie (1984) opened. I also remember an early visit to Hollein's Frankfurt Museum and Abteiberg Museum. I saw the Abteiberg Museum again during my studies and it made a deep impression on me then, so I would exclude it from our criticism of Hollein's large projects. This museum is a wonder, an unsolvable riddle, a fascinating thing.

Also, before I started studying, I saw the Haas Haus when I was visiting friends in Vienna. Although I made a conscious effort to look at it, it ricocheted off me. Hollein is an inspirational character—especially if you're looking out of the corner of your eye, or at a point just beyond the work, you can really gain something. Hans Hollein's Austrian Travel Agencies are currently serving as our inspiration for the interior design of an office floor. They are a world unto themselves.

It's interesting that you make a distinction between the large and small projects.

TP The Abteiberg Museum embodies a tension between modernism and history, just like James Stirling's best projects from his middle creative period. This inner tension and conflict is present in Hollein's work from his first collages. When it's removed, as in the Frankfurt Museum, for example, or the Haas Haus, it pretty much takes away our point of connection.

How is Hollein seen in Switzerland?

TP As a one-off, larger-than-life figure. We don't have anyone like him in Switzerland. For us, Hermann Czech and Hans Hollein belong to Vienna, their work is a special expression of a Central European culture that is deeply rooted in the city. The idea of urban culture as a total project inspires us. It's how we want to do architecture, too.

Hollein grew up in the fourth district, next to the Belvedere and Fischer von Erlach's Karlskirche.[1] He went to a kindergarten designed by a student of Loos. As he described it, these essential spatial experiences would influence him both consciously and subconsciously. What influence does Zurich exert on you?

OL We work in Zurich, but we met in Basel at Diener & Diener, which was an incredibly formative time for both of us. Working there was almost more important than our studies. At Diener, architecture could be experienced as an extended intellectual adventure. The content is foregrounded. The basis of the working process is the exploration of new things, though this state of flux is no longer visible in the finished building. It's an inspiration, but also a method: things develop through conversation.

TP This imprinting at Diener & Diener and also at Meili Peter is something we often talk about. The work of both offices, how they conceive of themselves and how they are received, is strongly rooted in European culture. This embedding in a cultural geography—the sense of connection and elective affinity—interests us a lot. We see Zurich as neutral territory, a base for operation even if it's not a source of great inspiration: we have work here, and also a lot of architect friends.

OL In Vienna these oversized figures like Hans Hollein or Wolf Prix have a left a vacuum—a state of paralysis. It's similar with our friends in Portugal, with this monumental figure of Alvaro Siza. How do you get away from that? The young people there are trying to strike a blow for freedom with a pop architecture that breaks with Siza's earnestness.

In this series of photos of the Wetscher House (1985–1986), an unrealized design by Hans Hollein, we're not seeing the same model over and over. Instead, the model was built anew for each shot, with infinite variations on this little tower, for example, or on the position of the windows. What do you think of this kind of process, and what is your opinion of working with models in general?

TP Our working models really are working models. They are a means of concretizing ideas, for each other as well as for other collaborators. When we're working on a competition or a commission we build a shell construction at 1:50, which is the best scale for evaluating many things. We stick facades on this shell, tear them off, stick them back on again. Out of this emerges something essential, which is shared, rather than existing in the imagination of just one of us. 1:50 is a peculiar scale: it allows you to decide whether or not to build certain constructive details that are important for the expression of the building. You can also determine whether a window sill is architecturally significant for the facade. This kind of model forms a link between the overall idea of the building and a structural plan on a scale of 1:50, 1:20, 1:10, or 1:5. It's a way to quickly check certain things. For us, architecture is above all a communicative art that can be judged by eye.

Lütjens Padmanabhan Architekt*innen, Residence of the Swiss Ambassador in Algiers, Algeria, 2017–2023. 1:50 model. Photo: Lütjens Padmanabhan

OL Unlike Hollein, we don't study any variants. We always work with just one version of the design, which we're continually changing. We look for a resistance within the architecture. Variants—where you see things side by side—are not productive for us at all. It's only when you're focused on the one thing that you see the conflicts that arise, or the forces that begin to operate when different ideas coalesce within the same object. We almost never start with a bright idea or a burst of creativity. Instead, we begin the project quite pragmatically: with the building regulations, maximizing the volume, making full use of surface areas, building an ugly model. Then we try to wrest the architecture from this framework and to understand what we have and what is still possible.

Do your models also have a representative function? Are they shown to the clients?

OL We build the models for others as well as for ourselves, as an expression of our way of making architecture. We photograph them and place them as a counter-proposal next to the renderings required by the market. The model stands, alongside the drawing, for everything. We take the model to client meetings, then it's in our office for two to three years while we're working on the project. Whenever we have questions about the project, we go to the 1:50 model.

In Hans Hollein's work there is the idea that architecture has its origins in ritual. Do you think this idea is still relevant today?

TP We love architecture that eludes a specific interpretation. Our way of looking is detached from any fixed sense of cultural ritual. What interests us most about architecture is its power to articulate, its permanence, the experience of the context, the figural elements and what these can achieve.

OL Ritual is a difficult word. When we talk about our buildings, we're talking more about a specific attitude towards life. Each building has a strong character that derives from what is there, from the perception of the urban situation. And what is there is usually fragmented, requiring interpretation. This approach leads to an "overall feeling" which we think the building should express. It's made up of many different aspects, from the construction to the facade, and these details are important to us.

TP We worked on a project for a site in Zurich opposite a slaughterhouse and a soccer stadium. Initially we wanted to design the building as a book end to the incomplete perimeter block. But we got nowhere with the design until we came up with a new understanding: the building in total isolation, as a lone, heroic house looking at dying animals and an arena. A Corbusian house, for sure, not Corbu with a Mediterranean accent, but rather a very dark Russian version of a Corbusian modernism. Once we got a clear sense of this character, of the loneliness and existential detachment, we found our way into the project. The narrative developed out of the particular place.

For the apartment building on Waldmeisterweg, we struggled for a long time with the facade. Our reference in the competition was Brunelleschi and we used light gray and dark gray pilasters. A good friend came by the office to pick us up for lunch and said, "Ah, you're doing a Venturi

Lütjens Padmanabhan Architekt*innen, Herdernstrasse apartment building, Zurich, Switzerland, 2011–2016. Street elevation. Photo: Walter Mair

Beach House?" Suddenly, the scales fell from our eyes. There before us was this garden city world with its laidback way of life, an eternal summertime with people in shorts washing their cars while the kids play outside. That was the world of our house and that narrative defined the entire project and indeed has stayed with us, to the point where we now even have the feeling that we've lived in this house.

So not rituals, but narratives?

OL We've designed smaller things that have to do with rituals. The mailbox in Binningen, for example. It's an object somewhere between architecture and sculpture, and which looks like a cat. Actually, it's more architecture, because it has many functions—mailbox, intercom (there's a speaker system in the cat's ears)... The act of arriving, the letters, they're always the same, they're already rituals. We want to bring all these elements of everyday life into the architecture in an open form. In this respect, we feel very close to Hollein, but he went much further.

In 2014 there were two major exhibitions on Hollein at the museum in Mönchengladbach and the MAK in Vienna.[2] New photographs were taken for the catalog, and they show the projects in use, the wear and tear, and also their decay. Hollein did not understand the purpose of doing this, rather than using the historical iconic photos of these projects that he himself had commissioned. Can you relate to his reaction, and how do you document and photograph your projects?

TP It's a dilemma, for sure. Our first buildings were documented by a Swiss photographer, Walter Mair, who we worked very closely with. How do you photograph a building that is finished but empty? At one point we built cardboard furniture that stood around the interior like ghosts. For the photos of another project, we looked for objects that would serve like props in a play. When you look at the photographs that came out of Armin Linke's revisiting of Hollein's projects, however, you see a great historical distance from the work.

OL Sometimes it's a matter of luck—of knowing the person who lives in your house and of them being willing to let you in to take pictures at a later date. At Waldmeisterweg there was this sunny "beach house" narrative. But then we had to photograph the house in early December, when there was not a blade of grass to be seen and the sky was not blue, but full of fog. So now we have these beautiful cold images by Hélène Binet that show a different mood of the house than the one we'd imagined. We love these pictures, but they have nothing to do with our narrative and they are not at all good for promotional purposes.

You also use the term "squatting" to refer to the inhabitation of your houses?

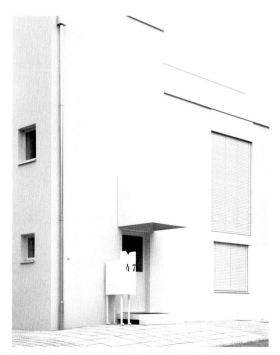

Lütjens Padmanabhan Architekt*innen, Binningen II, apartment building, Binningen, Switzerland, 2011–2014. Main entrance with cat-like element. Photo: Walter Mair

TP Yes, that's true, but we're on an equal footing with the inhabitants, we don't look down from on high. There should also be room for flat screen TVs and plastic toys—in fact, being able to accommodate such things is a gauge of the resilience of a home. We don't have that idea of the interior defining a neutral space anymore. The building has to do almost everything because we're surrounding ourselves with fewer objects. This dramatically shifts the boundary between building and user, making the question of the character of a space important. When someone says "I want a neutral space where I can unwind!" we think "They don't know what they're saying, what do they want to unwind with, a sofa and a TV?"

OL When we showed the house in Binningen in a lecture, someone asked us towards the end: "But space doesn't interest you, does it?" That made us think, because we are concerned with space and function, and we think about where to put the cupboards, too—but we don't think of space in pictorial terms, or as a volume. Instead, we talk about particular ideas that contribute to this space. We can talk at great length about a support, a window, and how the frame meets the wall, or about different floor coverings. These are architectural ideas and architectural conversations that ultimately add up to something that can be called space. For the photos, we end up giving the photographer free rein, because we know they have better ideas about how to go about it than we do. Commissioning these photographs allows us to revisit the buildings, to see them from a different, outsider's perspective. Which is very refreshing!

There are some aspects of your work that we also associate with Hans Hollein: a certain humor and a playful approach to materialization and dematerialization. In Hollein's work the theme of the column is really chewed over and interpreted in different ways.

We also see in your work an interest in a very specific form of expression drawing on historical references. In this respect, would you say there's a connection with Hans Hollein?

TP The starting point in our projects is the mid-range reality of Swiss construction. The norm is a middling budget and rental housing. In Switzerland, there's a certain standard, but also an economic cap. That's the dough we have to knead. We never start with notions of ideal types—it's always about trying to tease architecture out of this dough. The question is more: so if there is already a downpipe, what can you do with it? This is perhaps also the opposite of Hollein, where the quotation of the ideal type, detached from the context, plays the main role. This kind of staging of the ideal type creates a distance. What remains are symbols, metaphors, iconography in the art-historical sense, none of which interests us. We are serious about the things we do, even if we have a sense of humor. We're humorous, but not ironic. Irony is a kind of a distancing, a deflection from what you really mean. We mean what we say. We're also on a moral search for architectural truth. The truth that shaped the generation before us in Switzerland comes down to: monolithic appearance and unity of structure, form, and expression in the silent building. There's too much pathos in that for us. We see it as a completely impossible basis for a contemporary architectural language.

This is a picture of Schullin II, a jewelry store in Vienna that Hollein designed.

OL What is the structure of those floor lamps? Is it marble?

It's metal, carefully lacquered to look like marble, but it's not a "real material."

OL I think it's excellent. The classic, the super modern, and the old decorative tradition all collide in this nostalgic modern lamp. The energy and tension in this collision is something we could feel close to.

The palm trees that Hollein uses in the Austrian Travel Agencies are caught in an in-between world, as half-sculpture and half-architecture. In the main branch in Opernringhof they're arranged very picturesquely, but in the smallest branch here, they're set in a straight line. The last one bends towards a picture.

TP But they also represent a narrative architecture that is quite hermetic. Loos is a quarry of architecture. You can go there, help yourself, and immediately make it your own. There are no hidden meanings attached to his architecture—it's universal. That's not the case with Hollein; it's something you could criticize him for.

OL Someday we'll make a palm tree, Thomas?

Kersten Geers wrote in *San Rocco* about the Austrian Travel Agencies,
which unfortunately have been destroyed.[3]

OL For me the best thing about the article was its timing. There had
been a pall of silence over Hollein, but I'm sure this text triggered a lot
of discussion. How was it received in Vienna?

What's clearly impressive about the article is the freedom with which
Kersten Geers approaches the subject—but in Vienna this baggage-free
distance to Hollein will perhaps take a bit longer to develop.

OL I'm intrigued by these surrealistic moments with Hollein, like
in the cinema auditorium of the Mönchengladbach museum, where
the red wall suddenly spills over the floor to form the base of the
column. In the Waldmeisterweg house, we incorporated an imaginary
shadow of the pillar into the materiality of the floor, a detail related
to Hollein's. It's a detail that is hard to justify on financial grounds,
but that's also the beauty of it.

TP The problem with Hollein is that you don't always know whether
the references are actually about Egypt, or more about Elizabeth Taylor

Lütjens Padmanabhan Architekt*innen, Waldmeisterweg apartment building, Zurich,
Switzerland, 2013-2018. Column with wood inlay "shadow" in the floor surface.
Photo: Hélène Binet

as Cleopatra. You have to penetrate these multiple layers to find out whether there's something behind them. Hollein works with volume, intellectually, culturally. He is a volume guy who occupies many worlds. From this bird's-eye view, I think he's brilliant, but when I get up close, his work crumbles before my eyes. Most of it dissolves, as if I can't focus properly. I feel the same way about the column.

OL Oh, you are harsh! I also like, for example, those sunglasses he designed. He goes into this fashion world, but it remains clear that he's doing it as an architect, not a designer. Conceptual and sharp, a Super Fox, hoovering everything up, and giving his all.

Hans Hollein, Abteiberg Municipal Museum, Mönchengladbach, Germany, 1972–1982. Column in the cinema space, 2014.
Photo: Aglaia Konrad

Endnotes

1 Karlskirche (St. Charles Church) is a baroque church in Vienna designed by Johann Bernhard Fischer von Erlach (1656–1723) and consecrated in 1737.

2 Hans Hollein, Aglaia Konrad, Armin Linke, Wilfried Kuehn, Städtisches Museum Abteiberg, Österreichisches Museum für Angewandte Kunst, and Kunstmuseum, eds., *Hans Hollein Photographed by Aglaia Konrad and Armin Linke,* published to accompany the exhibitions *Hans Hollein: Alles ist Architektur,* Museum Abteiberg, Mönchengladbach (Aprll 12 to September 28, 2014), *HOLLEIN*, MAK–Austrian Museum of Applied Arts/Contemporary Art, Vienna (June 25 to October 5, 2014).

3 Kersten Geers, "Model Architecture," *Innocence, San Rocco*, no. 0 (2010): 66–70.

This Dialogue on Hans Hollein took place on May 27, 2020 online.

Lütjens Padmanabhan Architekt*innen

Oliver Lütjens and Thomas Padmanabhan established their office in 2007 in Zurich. Their work, primarily focused on residential architecture, is characterized by an interest in historical references from both the Renaissance and twentieth-century modernism. They have taught at various architecture schools in Europe and are Kenzo Tange Design Critics at the Harvard GSD. In addition, they have published several essays on the work of other contemporary offices, including baukuh.

Beate Hølmebakk
Manthey Kula

What is your relationship to the work and the ideas of Hans Hollein?

BH I began studying architecture in Oslo in 1984. Hans Hollein was known to us as a prominent postmodernist, but we didn't really relate to him or his work. Within the Norwegian tradition, postmodernism was not well regarded. We were taught that the architectural idea was closely connected to construction and therefore the structure itself was central to architectural expression. The figurative and the use of historical references were considered problematic by many of my teachers, among them Sverre Fehn and Wenche Selmer. There were some exceptions, however, such as Christian Norberg-Schulz,[1] who was an advocate of the postmodern movement in Norway. After my first three years in Oslo, I spent some time in New York, first studying at the Cooper Union and then returning to work for Raimund Abraham[2] after I'd completed my diploma back home. Through Abraham there was a connection with Austria and Vienna, and Hans Hollein was talked about, but I never developed a close connection with his work. I have to admit that up until now I'd always judged it quite super-ficially. From the collection of images of his work that you sent me, it seems obvious that he engaged with architecture on many different levels. And I see an energy in his work that I can relate to.

After his studies in Vienna in the 1950s, Hollein received a scholarship to go to study at UC Berkeley. In a lecture Hollein gave at the Architectural Association in 1981 he talks about his experience of going to the States and mentions that one of the most important things he brought back was the sense of space – the sense of the infinity of the flat and empty space of the landscape.

BH It's interesting to hear that Hollein was taken with the openness of the American landscape because, as I understand him, his work is about cultivation and the urban situation—the qualities in his work are very much manmade. So, it's surprising that the horizon and these empty spaces were important to him. It makes me curious about his way of thinking about space.

What role does America play in your architectural thinking?

BH One of the reasons I went to study at the Cooper Union was my curiosity about John Hejduk and his work. It was reassuring to discover architects who produced paper projects, as I too felt this was a way to develop the discipline. It was radically different from what was the norm in Norway—especially back then. Even today the prevailing opinion is that architecture has to be built in order to have value.

However, I found it very hard to concentrate in New York, to formulate a position. I'm more at home with the empty road and the open landscape on the Hollein slide you showed me. There's something very potent in that, which I couldn't find in New York. I had to go back to Norway to develop my own approach.

One aspect that we appreciate about Hans Hollein is how he worked extensively with architectural models as a way of testing his spatial ideas. How do you work with models in your office? How do they drive forward the overall design process?

BH I think it's fair to say that we work a lot with models. There's something fantastic about them. They're a direct way to study space and to speculate about form, proportions, dimensions, and materials, but they're also as close as you can get to a building before anything is built. We start with models very early in the design process. Many of our projects to date have been in a landscape context, so landscape models have been crucial for understanding the site. The next step is then to work with construction models. Here we often end up with quite large models, at scales of 1:25 or 1:20—even 1:10 or 1:5.

We remember a sculptural model in your exhibition at Betts Project in London in spring 2020. Is that something that you do often—build a model of one specific aspect of a project after it's finished?

Manthey Kula, *Postludes*, Betts Project, London, United Kingdom, 2020. Photo: Manthey Kula

BH We find models the best way to discuss our projects with clients, including at a very late stage of the design development, which is when we would be focusing on a specific part of the project in a model. And for paper projects, the model, together with drawings and sometimes text, is the project. The final outcome.

The little cake-like model you saw at Betts Project came out of our work on the permanent exhibitions at the new Munch Museum in Oslo.[3] One of the early ideas was to have freestanding panels, which we built as models. At some point, I just started to stack these panels together and it became this structure. It was never intended as a model of something. It was just a stack of panels. But I really liked the shape. It's not really an architectural model—more like an offshoot of an architectural model.

This is a nice connection to the notion of the "sculptural" in an architectural object, in the light of Hollein's interest in reversing the relationship between form and function. You also make reference to the idea of the sculptural quality of an architectural form. This of course has made us very curious, because even fifty years on from Hollein's explorations, it's still a topic that polarizes.

BH For some people sculptural quality is never okay; an aspect of architecture not worth talking about. We have a very intuitive approach to our work and often start with a formal response to a site, a position, or a function—even though our buildings are mostly so simple they hardly have more than one function.

106

Manthey Kula, Forvik ferry port, Norway, 2015. View of ferry port building with inverted steel vault roof structure. Photo: Manthey Kula

We can say two things about our work when it comes to sculptural form. On the one hand, if a form that we really like appears early, we go for it. In that sense, it's actually a bit like what you said—it is not that form follows function, but function, or rather architecture, follows from the form. For instance, we have this ferry port with an upside-down vault. That's a good example of a design where we believed strongly in the form. We were intrigued by the spatial and technical consequences of the upturned vault, which seemed to have a structural potential. It all came from a feeling for the form, and it was a big challenge for us to make it work as a building.

On the other hand, we're very interested in structure and constructions. Most often the form is a result of a structure or otherwise derived from a structural aspect.

I would say we have a problem with form if it's just applied like an ornament or something that is added later. Ideally, it has to be an integral part of the architectural idea.

Your office has made several exhibition designs. Hans Hollein also worked extensively in this field: one could say that the exhibitions were like testbeds for his building projects. What is the relationship between your buildings and your exhibition designs?

BH We feel slightly ambiguous towards exhibition design. We like this kind of work a lot, but we struggle with the temporary nature of exhibitions. Architecturally, they are very much part of our work, because we treat exhibition design in the same way as a building or an infrastructure project. But something happens when a structure is only built for a short period of time. The craftsmanship is different, the use of material is different. Generally, when we work on projects, we like to think they will last. There is something about time that is very important, we want our projects to outlive us. Added to this, the practical issues—the fact, for example, that you can rarely use bronze or similar fantastic materials—automatically make exhibitions much more superficial.

107

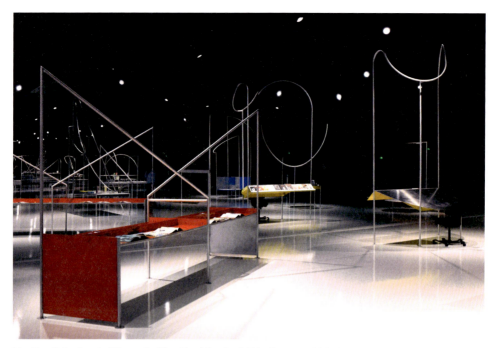

Manthey Kula, Guest of Honor Pavilion, Frankfurt Book Fair, Germany, 2019, in collaboration with
LCLA. View of installation showing aluminum furniture. Photo: Manthey Kula

Spatially, however, they are very much part of our work and thinking.
We often begin projects by interpreting situations, sites, and programs
to give them meaning. And that element of interpretation, either of
the curator's ideas or of the art itself, is also present in our exhibition
design. So there's definitely a connection between the exhibition work
and the rest of what we do.

Thinking about the ephemeral aspect of an exhibition and—despite this—
the beautifully made pavilion for the Frankfurt book fair, are you concerned
about what happens to the pieces of the installation and whether the exhibition
design has an afterlife?

BH Yes, that was very important to us with this project, which was won
through an open competition that we did together with Luis Callejas
and Charlotte Hansson (LCLA).[4] Already in the competition we suggested
that the furniture should last longer than the exhibition itself, and that
it should be possible to use the materials afterwards. And thankfully
that's what has happened. The beautifully made aluminum furniture
has been dispersed, given away to institutions around Germany and
Norway, where it has an afterlife. It's a real shame to think of the many
exhibitions that are produced worldwide, and of how millions and
millions of euros are spent on things intended to last only a few months
before they're thrown away.

Hans Hollein considered himself an artist and he worked intensively in an art
context. You also work on the border between art, architecture, and landscape
architecture. Would you regard yourself as an artist in the sense that Hollein did?

BH I would like to say yes, because I think architecture is an art—though
today, architecture is many other things as well, many of which I'm not
interested in. It's so hard to make good architecture—it really is very,
very, very difficult. There needs to be an intention and a will behind it,

someone who really has ambitions with the project. This is rare. Also, I don't think that good architecture necessarily is the result of a democratic process. I try to teach my students to believe in architecture, to believe in its possibilities, but at the same time I know how hard that is. I think that if art were to disappear from architecture, there would be very little left. I know this sounds pathetic, but it's really about the soul of the discipline. I think if there is no art left in what is built, then it's not architecture.

What is your relationship with artists from other disciplines? Do you enjoy collaborations of this kind?

BH That's a very good question. Given our belief that architecture is an art, it would be logical to think that we would seek collaborations or do installations together with other artists, but actually we're quite restrained. I know it sounds terrible, but realizing one's ideas is already a struggle and collaborations just make things harder. We're currently working on a couple of projects that could have been done by artists, and I'm sure many artists are frustrated that they're not doing them. But we never thought about involving collaborators in these projects.

But architecture is still very much based on teamwork.

BH Yes, of course. And naturally we've collaborated with others. The Frankfurt project we were just talking about is an example of teamwork that went really well. Yet, as I said, I don't necessarily believe that making architecture is a democratic process. A will and a direction are necessary to create something specific, and with many voices that can be difficult to find. But of course, we have to be able to collaborate because we're a small office. So we do it, it's possible, but it's always hard.

Hans Hollein started his lecture at the AA by defining his position on the basis of two opposing concepts.[5] One was an inflatable sphere—a synthetic environment—the other a Roman funerary monument—the Tomb of Eurysaces the Baker—which for Hollein stood for the ritual, the cultic. Manthey Kula works on memorials and monuments. What kind of role can this arcane topic play in the contemporary discourse?

BH I think the concept of ritual is still relevant today. In the case of a memorial, it's clear that the function is related to ritual. But one could also talk about this concept in relation to meaning, and to the existential dimension of architecture. Whatever program or project you're working on, it can be related in some way to life. It can have an emotional character that makes it feel connected to your existence. These kinds of profound issues are hard to talk about, but I think that at its best architecture relates to truth and to a fundamental experience of reality. It has to do with us existing for a short while in the world, with some things lasting longer and being handed down to us and later to those who come after us. One goal for me is when architecture manages to remind us of this point. These issues seem meaningful and can be connected to the notion of ritual.

One can also think about ritual in a more everyday sense. Paraguayan architect Solano Benítez has talked about the special dish his mother makes every Saturday, and how "what it is repeated, endures; and what

Manthey Kula, Utøyakaia National Memorial, Norway, 2022. In collaboration with Bureau Bas Smets, Brussels. Seventy-seven individually formed, solid bronze columns are placed on the first step of a stone stair by the water: each column carries the name of a victim, each name is a unique relief. Photo: Karin Björkquist & Sébastien Corbari

endures is eternal, and because it is eternal, it is sacred." It's a very beautiful statement about something simple and pragmatic. I think it's wonderful, because it's about the need to make things important in life. Many of us have this need, and some of us become architects, so then that need is expressed through architecture. This could be another link to ritual. Again, it has to do with time.

Hans Hollein was also a teacher, but he didn't really establish a school of thought through his teaching, nor did he leave very strong traces compared to figures like Ungers or Rossi. Hollein's teaching lives on through his students, but not really as a project on its own. How do you approach teaching, and do you see your involvement as a "project"?

BH Teaching is a big responsibility. It can also be at odds with the office work, because it's time-consuming and you get involved with so many people and their projects. And I enjoy teaching because I enjoy talking to students about architecture. But I've never had the ambition to develop a project with students that would feed directly into our own work. I have been asked if I'd like to exhibit our work alongside my students' work, but that's not something I want to do because to me my work as an architect and my teaching are two different worlds. On a certain level, however, I'm sure that my teaching is influenced by what we do in the office.

Our last question concerns photography and image-making?

BH That's also an interesting topic because it ties up with the earlier question about form. I don't know where you want us to go with this question, but I was looking at these photographs of Hollein's work and many of them are strong images. They are formally very clear and I recognize that quality as something we also work with. What I find interesting in these images is that they can be considered as solitary entities. They show complex motifs, but there is something self-contained in every image. We try to work in the same way to create images that are clear and speak for themselves.

Hollein stated that Franz Hubmann, the photographer who took these images of the Retti candle shop, was able to capture not just what was there, but the idea behind it.

BH Yes, one can see that—it is really evident and very powerful.

You take many of the pictures of your projects yourselves. How do you approach image production in connection with your work?

BH This is something we care about. For us, every part of the project—the photographs, even the working drawings—should express the character of the project. Going back to the notion of form, we consider form to be very important and this also applies to the photographic documentation and drawings. An image serves to confirm your intentions, ambitions, and even your doubts.

Hans Hollein, Retti candle shop, Vienna, Austria, 1964–1965. Working model. Front display space with entrance door and wall mirror. Archive Hans Hollein, Az W and MAK, Vienna. Photo: Elmar Bertsch

Endnotes

1 Christian Norberg-Schulz (1926–2000), Norwegian architect, educator, architectural theorist, and author of many books including: *Genius Loci, Towards a Phenomenology of Architecture* (New York: Rizzoli, 1980).

2 Raimund Abraham (1933–2010), Austrian architect and educator. Professor at the Cooper Union, New York (1971–2002) and SCI-Arc, Los Angeles (2003–2010).

3 *Edward Munch Infinite*, exhibition of the permanent collection in the new Munch Museum, Oslo, Norway, 2021.

4 Guest of Honor Pavilion, Frankfurt Book Fair, Germany, 2019.

5 Lecture entitled "Viennese Blood" at the *Architectural Association*, October 26, 1981.

   This Dialogue on Hans Hollein took place on February 24, 2021 online.

Manthey Kula

Manthey Kula was founded in Oslo in 2004 by Beate Hølmebakk, who studied at the Oslo School of Architecture and Design as well as the Cooper Union in New York, and Per Tamsen, who graduated from Lund University. Manthey Kula works at the intersection of architecture, art, and landscape architecture. Their projects are characterized by distinctively sculptural qualities and special attention to site, form, construction, and narrative. The work spans from private houses and exhibition design to public commissions. Beate Hølmebakk is a professor of architecture at the Oslo School of Architecture and Design.

Martin Feiersinger

What is your relationship to Hans Hollein?

MF My first contact with Hans Hollein was in 1980, when I came to Vienna to study and scoped out the master classes at the University of Applied Arts. From the very beginning, I was certain that I didn't want to study with Hollein, because I associated him with industrial design and furnishings rather than with architecture. The students I talked to in his studio reported that his classes involved extensive analyses and model building that could go on for months. What I wanted, on the other hand, was to get going on design problems as quickly as possible, which is why I went with Wilhelm Holzbauer, who took a more pragmatic approach.[1]

While I was a student, Hollein wasn't around that much. But when he did come to the university, students from other classes would attend his crits. He seemed to take a long time to comprehend a project and he didn't comment much. If you didn't show a model, you couldn't get any response whatsoever.

A few years later, I encountered Hollein again. I was studying in America, getting ready to strike out on my own. He took part in a panel discussion at the Museum of Fine Arts in Houston, alongside other important architects. The topic was the future expansion of the museum. Charles Moore, who was sat next to Hollein, remarked: "Oh Hans, you spend way more time on a single room than others do on an entire complex. I guess in Vienna it's possible to work so slowly."

How do you see Hollein today?

After my initial rejection of Hollein, I now look at my own projects and see that in many respects I'm very close to his way of working, his way of thinking, his notion of being an architect. Now, like Hollein, I find myself working on a small-scale project for a whole two years.

What interests us about Hollein's work are the different scales on the one hand, but also the particular archetypes. What interests you?

MF Different scales and archetypes also interest me, although I would approach them more subtly than he did. In Hollein's view, a silver bowl could incorporate an architecture in miniature, or, conversely, a building could metamorphose into a miniature. I remember hearing Claes Oldenburg speak of Hollein's influence on his work. I was amazed to learn that Hollein had contributed to pop art's leaps of scale.

I sometimes find myself in situations where I might look at a stool, for example, and think it could also work as a building. But then

I generally take a step back. Unlike Hollein, who had an office with many employees, I usually work alone, devoting myself to one project at a time.

But do you see working at these different scales as a kind of experiment?

MF Yes, and that also has to do with the timeframe of architecture in general. With exhibitions, you can get a lot done in a short period of time. But with buildings, many more factors come into play. Some of my concepts that had to be discarded for whatever reason have resurfaced in other contexts and the theme evolves and becomes something else. That dynamic often happens.

With Hollein, there was the shiny double-column, for example, as seen in the Feigen Gallery in New York. This motif appears again and again, its form mutating on occasion into a handrail that is actually much too thick. In the architectural scene, everyone was watching what everyone else was doing—and having looked at the work of Italian architects of the period, I know of several other instances of overly thick, shiny polished handrails. Hollein was very well connected.

What role did art play in Hollein's work?

For the *Follies* exhibition at the Leo Castelli Gallery in New York in 1983, a select group of architects were invited to submit proposals for a pavilion.[2] The only one who stepped out of line was Hans Hollein, who presented his concept in written form, inscribing panels with wordplays such as "Holly Folly" or "Folly Follows," or puns on famous dictums of architecture: "Form, Follies, Function," "Folless is more."

You mentioned two things, namely this claim to art and then "form follies function."
But Hollein attached great importance to architectural form, once even insisting
"function follows form." Do you have a similar view?

Hans Hollein, Holly Folly, 1983, from B.J. Archer and Anthony Vidler, eds., *Follies: Architecture for the Late-Twentieth-Century Landscape* (New York: Rizzoli, 1983), 67. Archive Martin Feiersinger.

MF Here I am closer to Hermann Czech's approach, "Less or more. It depends." When I work on a new project, I try to approach the task without preconceptions. So for me, form is rarely the starting point. But there are exceptions. For example, I was recently commissioned to design a tomb in Stumm for a Tyrolean family. Here, the task is reduced to the elementary. There are no structural demands, no complicated spatial program. It is a design problem that calls for a pared down solution, in this instance, a block of white marble to which nothing has been added, only taken away.

Another recent project is a library in South Tyrol for a family of art collectors.[3] The clients at first asked me to design a set of bookcases for a vaulted space. A bookshelf has to work, it has to have reasonable dimensions—but it should also somehow interact with its setting, in this case a medieval building. It's a balancing act, weighing the symbolic potential of such an intervention against the need to be practical. As the project progressed, the clients asked me to design every single piece of furnishing for the library.

Hollein always emphasized the new in his architecture. What about you?
Do you see reference, rather than invention, as the source of form?

MF For me the idea of inventing architecture from scratch is a myth.
I've studied the 1960s, particularly in Italy, very intensively. If you
compare all these projects, you'll see that almost everything has been
done before—in the north, in the south, in Asia, in the American sphere.
Hollein was an international figure and he wanted to be "in the mix."
As I see it, he was very good at myth-making.

Hollein polarized opinions, and still does today. Some say Hollein's architecture
is not real architecture. Is that something you're familiar with?

MF Yes, I've heard that criticism, and it was certainly a problem for
Hollein. He was very concerned with how he was portrayed in the media.
He didn't like to be perceived as an industrial or interior designer.
When he declared "everything is architecture," what he really meant,
in my opinion, was "everything I make is architecture." If Hollein
designed a bowl, it was also architecture, because he, as an architect,
had conceived it.

We also spoke with Hermann Czech, who sees Hollein's greatest achievement
as the dissolution of the concept of design. Where do you stand on this?

MF Everything *is* architecture. Hollein used his own dictum to free
himself of the discipline's limitations. At a conceptual level, it was and
is architecture in the expanded field.

You do many of your projects together with your brother, who is an artist.
How do you see the collaboration between the different disciplines, and also
their autonomy? Would Hollein be taken seriously as an artist?

MF What are the first projects that you might get built as a young
architect? Mine was a walk-in sculpture, an art installation. The invitation
had originally been extended to Werner, but he didn't have the time,

Martin and Werner Feiersinger, Folly, Königsbrunn, Austria, 2013–2014. The open-air
stage located on the Wagram plateau acts as a viewing platform and landmark.
Photo: Werner Feiersinger

so I took the job. The result was a small theater, a folly in aluminum. I would never call Hollein an artist, any more than I would call myself one. Only another architect would view me as an artist. I am the architect, and my brother is the artist. Nevertheless, we work well together because we complement each other. Although I am the architect, it's my brother who is more involved in the implementation of the joint projects because he always works and thinks at a scale of one to one. I can work well with pencil and paper, and prefer the abstract realm of the drafting table to the workshop.

Are you saying that Hollein was never really taken seriously as an artist? He was invited to contribute as an artist to the Austrian Pavilion at the 1972 Venice Biennale (*Work and Behavior–Life and Death. Everyday Situations*).[4]

Hans Hollein, *Work and Behavior - Life and Death. Everyday Situations,* exhibition at the 36th Venice Biennale, Italy, 1972. View of the garden space with tiled chair. Archive Hans Hollein, Az W and MAK, Vienna.

MF He may have been invited as an artist, but what he produced was architecture. For me, that's elementary, it's how my world operates too. In his installation for Venice, Hollein made it clear: you can call a building into existence with nothing more than a few poles, in the same way you can build a chair out of just a few tiles. For me, that's architecture. By the way, this predated the architecture biennale. Hollein's work with the artist Walter Pichler[5] (on the *Architektur* exhibition at Galerie nächst St. Stephan in 1963, for example)[6] tested the boundaries of the disciplines, but I suspect the backstory was similar to the way my brother and I work.

Hollein had an intense urge to present his ideas in public. Walter Pichler was probably the right partner for him in the development of urban models and utopias.

We've discussed Hollein in terms of references. When you work with references in your own design process, is your approach more intuitive or systematic?

MF I see references as purely a means to an end. Their presence should not be intrusive—in fact, you should hardly notice them. And once you've found a solution that works, you don't need the references anymore. Even the most superficial reference might become a catalyst.

Perhaps the current preoccupation with references has something to do with the question of how we want to represent architectural history today?

MF Hollein engaged intensively with architectural history in his teaching at the University of Applied Arts. For him, it was a means of understanding his profession, not a source of quotations. But during my time as a student, architectural history was almost entirely about quotation. Postmodernism was at its height! My understanding of architectural history rejects the notion of a closed system, i.e., that you only refer to modernism. I see my work as part of a continuum, taking into account all of history as it is known to us.

When we spoke to Claudia Cavallar, she told us that when she was a student of Hollein's, she found the palm trees in the travel agencies over the top. Today she looks at it in a more nuanced way: the palm tree motif could even become a brooch.

MF It's a trick he borrowed from Josef Hoffmann, of subordinating everything to a symbol. The headquarters of the Austrian Travel Agency across from the opera house was real overkill.

You told us that you avert your eyes from the Haas Haus when you walk past it. Why is that? We've learned to almost love it.

MF When the Haas Haus was finished, Holzbauer and I walked past the green stone facade on Goldschmiedgasse, and he said to me: "The bar was set high, he's done a good job." To me, however, it was like looking at a freeze frame from the process of development—as if the building had taken form before Hollein had finished his design. Structural glazing was seen as a kind of magic formula at the time, and Hollein wanted to apply it artistically, in a way not typically associated with commercial buildings. The project was deliberately complex in every phase, starting with the design of the construction-site fence and culminating in the intricate roofscape.

Is the Haas Haus perhaps a relic from another time when it was still economically feasible to build like this?

MF Yes, the economic situation was different then. But it was interesting to see how various architects approached this. Holzbauer always wanted to have just a few themes clearly expressed in a building. He would pare back the design, because he assumed the commissions would keep on coming and that he would have the opportunity to try out other things

Hans Hollein, Haas Haus, Vienna, Austria, 1985–1990. Detail of rooftop canopy and aedicula. Archive Hans Hollein, Az W and MAK, Vienna.

Martin and Werner Feiersinger, *Italomodern*, traveling exhibition showcasing postwar architecture in northern Italy, 2014. Installation view in Bergamo, Italy. Photo: Werner Feiersinger

in subsequent projects. By contrast, Rice University professor Peter Waldman told me, "You have to treat every project as if it's the only commission you'll ever get. You have to pour everything into it." During my time in Waldman's office in Houston, the design's narrative was of primary importance. We put in everything that was good and that we held dear. Hollein also put in absolutely everything the client could afford–he pulled out all the stops.

Hollein wrote texts about Schindler, which were published in the magazine *BAU*. Do you write as well?

MF No, not really. But I have put in writing some observations on postwar architecture. In my *Italomodern* publications, I explored the ambivalence of the Italian architecture scene.[7] Unlike Hollein, I don't find it necessary to explain my ideas through text. When I write, it's mostly about questions I'm trying to answer related to my work. Why does something look the way it does? How does it work? Has it stood the test of time? Over the course of a decade my brother Werner and I made several trips to northern Italy to document buildings. As an artist, he thinks in terms of exhibitions. So that changed the nature of the project. In fact, sometimes it's good to have the input of an artist who is willing to mediate. Hollein probably combined both in one person.

What access do you have to means of communication?

MF Drawing is still at the top of my list.

Italomodern started out as texts of just a few pages. That was the original concept, which then evolved.

MF Yes exactly. My very first publication, named *Detours*, documented ten buildings in northern Italy. Its ingredients—Werner's photos and my drawings and brief texts—were to become the basis for *Italomodern*.

117

Looking back now, do you think you would have been happy in Hollein's class?

MF Not at the beginning. While I've since taken to heart topics and analyses he pursued, I was closer then to Holzbauer's way of thinking. Back then I didn't have the patience for an extensive analysis—a few weeks, perhaps, but no way could I have devoted a year or more to it, as a fellow student did with a Piero della Francesca painting. He spent endless hours turning a two-dimensional work into a very large model. As a student, my understanding of the discipline was focused on the design of new, large buildings. Of course, my attitude has changed over time. I was also shaped by my stay in the US. It was in Houston that I encountered other takes on "everything is architecture," for example, that even a poem might be architecture.

Although Hollein was an international player, it turns out there were lapses. There's a group photo in the publication *Team 10: In Search of a Utopia of the Present 1953–81*.[8] The caption lists him as "unknown," his identity apparently eluding the publisher.

Endnotes

1 Wilhelm Holzbauer (1930–2019), Austrian architect and professor of architecture.

2 B.J. Archer and Anthony Vidler, eds., *Follies: Architecture for the Late-Twentieth-Century Landscape* (New York: Rizzoli, 1983), 67.

3 Transformation and restoration of the ringwall wing, Gandegg castle, Eppan, Italy, 2019–2022.

4 Hans Hollein, *Werk und Verhalten – Leben und Tod. Alltägliche Situationen*, catalog to accompany exhibition at 36th Venice Biennale (Vienna: Bundesministerium für Unterricht und Kunst, 1972).

5 Hans Hollein and Walter Pichler, *Architektur: Work in Progress*, in Galerie nächst St. Stephan, Vienna, May 1963.

6 Werner Feiersinger (b. 1966), Austrian sculptor and photographer.

7 Martin Feiersinger, Werner Feiersinger, *Italomodern 1 & 2: Architecture in Northern Italy 1946–1976* (Zurich: Park Books, 2016).

8 Max Risselada, *Team 10: 1953–81: In Search of a Utopia of the Present* (Rotterdam: nai Publishers, 2006).

This Dialogue on Hans Hollein took place on October 26, 2022 in Vienna.

Martin Feiersinger

Martin Feiersinger studied architecture at the University of Applied Arts in Vienna and Rice University in Houston. In 1989, he established his architecture practice in Vienna. His varied oeuvre includes apartment buildings and private residences, urban design concepts and renovations, exhibition designs and follies. Martin and his brother Werner, a sculptor and photographer, are the authors of *Italomodern*, a two-volume work on postwar architecture in Northern Italy.

Job Floris
Monadnock

What is your relationship to Hans Hollein's work?

Hans Hollein, Schullin I jewelry store, Vienna, Austria,
1972–1974. Interior looking back towards the entrance.
Archive Hans Hollein, Az W and MAK, Vienna.
Photo: Franz Hubmann/Imagno/picturedesk.com

JF There are two connections to the work of Hans Hollein that are important for us in our practice. The first one comes from studying early modern Viennese architecture, a period that has always intrigued us. There was an urge to define modernity through the reinterpretation of classical elements of architecture: Otto Wagner, Josef Hoffmann, Adolf Loos, and of course Josef Frank—each, in their own way, was concerned with this. Extending that line of inquiry, we began looking at Hans Hollein's work in relation to this strand of Viennese modernism. At first, we couldn't establish a very clear connection between them, but we did notice a combination of thoroughness and refinement in Hollein's work, especially in the small shops. It was not a completely different vocabulary or approach, but slightly different—like a sequel, more contemporary and playful. That interested us.

And what about the other connection?

JF That is a more personal one. I worked for a long time in the office of Christian Rapp, a pupil of Hans Kollhoff. The ideas and attitude of Kollhoff were all around. It was there that I learned that Kollhoff had in turn worked in Hollein's atelier.[1] This gave me a slightly different perspective on the frivolity, the looseness of Hollein, because I understood that when Kollhoff was working for Hollein he spent half a year researching the type of leather and how this leather should be curved exactly around a sales counter. It made me understand there was more to the work than the visual aspects, the symbols and signs which have to do with direct experience.

One important aspect of Hollein's work that we've been discussing throughout our research is the importance of models for his architectural practice. How do architectural models inform your work?

JF I do see parallels, because we're very fond of making models for different purposes—sometimes we also continue making models after the project is finished and presented. During the development of

119

the design, we do quick and dirty models to assess the form and articulation of the building. And this in several scales. Firstly, we work on the scale of the volume and then on the expression of the window reliefs or the proportions of the window frames, studying how these come together in detail in the interior. Even as the use of digital representations is increasing, and offering a lot, I remain strongly in favor of making models. We're not nostalgic about this, but see models as a parallel tool for the development of a project. We use models as a valuable source of information, as a means to understand—and play around with—the spatial performance of an idea.

Has the role of the model in the design process changed since the start of your office?

JF Yes, there is a development in this. For example, we're currently working on a project in Hanover where we just make large boxes and attach prints of the facades to them and then take a picture. These pictures come very close to the built reality. It's a technique that is relatively new to us. Of course, a practice evolves: when we first started, we needed more proof, we really needed to make a series of models to be certain about what we were doing before we felt able to present our ideas to the outside world. The need to convince ourselves did not change, but the route to get there evolved.

As part of your work you make temporary structures that have an object-like character where you can sense the idea of a model built at 1:1 scale. Your installation, "Make No Little Plans," is one example of this.[2] What potential do you see in this notion of the scale model?

JF It's nice that you make that connection, because the installation was made from very basic scaffolding material. When working on this proposal, we decided the best thing to do was to fully engage with the rough grain of a temporary structure, because there was just not enough time, money, or space for refined detailing. In that sense, the situation was indeed comparable to the abstraction, or low-resolution, of building a scale model.

Initially, we seriously considered turning down the commission that led to "Make No Little Plans." But once we started reflecting on the topic, we realized could follow a daring route because the installation was going to be there for just ten days. During its short lifespan it would constantly interact with public life, as it was positioned on a square in the middle of the city. The temporary character of the installation, combined with the setting, allowed us to be provocative and polemical. In the end we were very happy with how it worked out, and these types of settings have proved to be fertile ground for our practice.

In his article "'Everything is Architecture' versus 'Absolute Architecture': On Hans Hollein" (2009), Stephan Trüby reflects on Hans Hollein's architectural practice in the 1970s and 1980s in an interesting way.[3] He argues that Hollein's exhibition design and installations could be regarded as the perfect testbed for his architecture. How would you describe the relation between your exhibition designs and your architectural projects?

JF When we set up our practice we assumed we would be starting to make robust, urban buildings right away, because this was the scale of the projects we had worked on in previous practices. But since no commission of this kind immediately came our way, we started making models of buildings, or solidified ideas, and we found that these explorations gave us a lot, in terms of generating new ideas that we then continued to develop and to recycle into new interpretations and directions for projects. Later, when we got invited to take part in an exhibition or to design temporary installations, we began to see these projects as laboratories for further testing our ideas. They provided an opportunity for experiments, allowing us to build up knowledge about articulation and expression that we could later translate into building designs—not in a very literal and direct way, but more as a resonance, as part of a conceptual and formal understanding.

We see the work of Hollein as rooted in a Viennese tradition of the baroque, where the interior space and the facade of a building are two separate entities: they don't mirror each other. Several of Monadnock's recent buildings clearly display a tension between the exterior and the interior volume. In a lecture where you talked about the Park Pavilion, you specifically described the relationship between inside and outside in terms of the "baroque." Is this something that could be seen as a general current in your recent work?

Monadnock, Landmark Nieuw Bergen, Netherlands, 2015. View from main square.
Photo: Stijn Bollaert

JF I think a building such as the Landmark Nieuw Bergen, for example, is much more related to a figurative approach than it is to baroque ideas. Our spatial approach here is not comparable. It is a strong volume, apart from a generous high ceiling; the interior mainly confirms the clarity of the diagram. On the other hand, in our most recent building, the Park Pavilion, we literally engaged with the disconnection of the interior from the exterior because we had the feeling that both elements had to perform in a completely different setting and respond to completely different questions.

This brought us back to Borromini[4] and also to forgotten architects from the Netherlands who were dealing with these pre-modernist issues—people such as Frits Eschauzier and Sybold Van Ravesteyn. Eschauzier was heavily inspired by, and in contact with, Josef Frank. Van Ravesteyn designed numerous train stations and a zoo but was disliked by other architects of his time, who saw him as too frivolous—as you might imagine, during the high-tide of functionalism.

With the Park Pavilion, however, it has become clear that detaching the interior from the exterior actually turns out to be quite efficient because it gives you a lot of poché space to solve all the technical installations you don't want to see, but do want to have for reasons of comfort.

121

To be honest, I'd never made that direct connection with Hollein up to now, as I was not aware of his preference for the baroque. Then again, looking at the Museum for Modern Art in Frankfurt, this building clearly does not want to connect to the modernist canon—it wants to connect to times before that. Once you start digging in the eras before modernism, you quickly end up in the Renaissance, mannerism, and of course the baroque, so it makes absolute sense.

Monadnock, Royal Tichelaar Offices, Makkum, Netherlands, 2013–2015. Office space with textile ceiling.
Photo: Stijn Bollaert

Right from the beginning of his practice, Hollein was interested in the origins of architecture in ritual. With your Landmark Nieuw Bergen you describe the historic importance of church towers as markers of an urban settlement. Does this project relate to religion or the ritual origins of architecture in the broadest sense? Is this a topic that interests you at all and if so, in what way?

JF In principle, I do think this aspect enriches architecture, but we don't use it in a very conscious way in our practice. On the other hand, we do make use of conventions. I would not immediately call the entering of a building a ritual; rather, it's an act that relates to a set of conventions established by particular elements—a door and an announcement of the door and the entrance. A ritual is really a whole construct involving time, religion, social conventions, traditions. Although we were both raised in a Catholic region, which means it probably runs quietly through our veins, ritual or religion is not something that actively relates to our designing of buildings. The word ritual is rather out of our league, but the person who immediately comes to mind in this regard is the much-admired Alvaro Siza. He seems very aware of these (religious) rituals.

Looking at Hans Hollein's realized projects in detail we became interested in his ambiguous and playful approach towards the materialization of his architectural visions.

In the built work of Monadnock we also see a strong interest in the qualities of materials. The textile ceiling in the Royal Tichelaar Factory or the colored brick wall of the Landmark building suggest a similar search for ambiguity and playfulness in the use of materials. How would you describe your approach to the "final material layer" during the design and realization process?

JF Well, keep in mind that we studied at the Academy of Fine Arts during the Super Dutch era, but at the same time we had a lot of Flemish architects coming by to give lectures. Although we speak the same language, the two cultures are quite distinct. These Belgian architects, such as Luc Deleu, Marie-Jose Van Hee, Bob Van Reeth, Wim Cuyvers, Paul Robbrecht & Hilde Daem, provided perspectives that were completely novel to us. And then there was Christian Kieckens, herald of the good news, talking about Swiss architecture and how the Swiss were dealing with the issues of craftsmanship and truth to materials like concrete and wood. We were completely flabbergasted by this careful and precise treatment of materials and started embracing this type of precision ourselves. It opened up a new world for us. The early works of Peter Zumthor, Jacques Herzog and Pierre de Meuron as well as Peter Märkli fascinated us immensely, and we went on trips to Switzerland to visit all of these buildings. In a way this "Belgo-Swiss" experience became the foundation of our thinking.

And how did this approach to materialization evolve over time?

JF After a while, we began to get a bit fed up with the rather dogmatic aspect of this approach—the idea that you have at all times to be true to the material is also rather limiting. It's not helpful in every situation, especially when you want to build up a spatial narrative. Sometimes you have to develop stories, and the material should confirm and support this story, even overruling the constructive logic. So, we gradually started to find other grounds, which is what brought us to the narratives of postmodernism and pre-modern architecture.

Adding to the mix there were encounters with kindred spirits such as Oliver Lütjens and Thomas Padmanabhan, for example. They were heading towards making their buildings as thin as possible, which left us wondering: Why are we making our buildings heavy, expressing only robustness, when they are in fact completely assembled? Could we keep the sense of cohesion while at the same time questioning the hard-wired choice of solidity? I think our more recent projects, such as the Park Pavilion, have gradually moved closer towards a new type of cohesion, infused with a decent dose of baroque and irony. We're embracing more tools leading to the possibility of ambiguity: resonating collage and assemblage.

Monadnock, Park Pavilion, Park de Hoge Veluwe, Netherlands, 2012–2019.
Digital collage showing the entrance and restaurant.

Was your participation in the *Designing the Surface*[5] exhibition another one of those encounters?

Monadnock, *Designing the Surface*, Het Nieuwe Instituut, Rotterdam, Netherlands, 2017. View from within a display case. Photo: Stijn Bollaert

JF Yes, this was a rather significant event for us. Working on the spatial design for the exhibition had a major influence on our thinking about surface, cladding, and the final material layer. For this we collaborated with the curators, product designers and graphic designers Koehorst in t' Veld and the designer Chris Kabel, who appeared to be pleasantly open, having a non-dogmatic spirit towards dealing with cladding and surface. They stated: "Nowadays, a lot of objects around us that have the appearance of steel actually just have a thin layer of coating. And this clever coating is made in such a way that it feels a bit cold, and is really convincing in performing as steel. But it's really just coating on plastic—and it's beautiful, isn't it?" At first, this perspective quite surprised us: "Beautiful?" But after proper reflection we were able to empathize and recognize the attraction and the possibilities it offered. And we realized once again that architecture is much slower and more conventional than some related design disciplines. It got us much more interested in using different technologies to shape appearances and to build up narratives.

Like Hollein's famous Kohlmarkt floor lamp with the "marble" shaft that is not really marble but a steel pipe painted with a marble effect.

JF Yes exactly, and this brings us back to different times where it was quite common to do this. By taking part in this exhibition, we got more familiar with the moment in time when it was more expensive to use "faux" painting techniques. People preferred not to buy the real material, a type of marble, but to hire painters to mimic it because this was a way to display their wealth. Nowadays, technology offers an inspiring variety of (much cheaper) techniques for creating a finish.

Hollein was the editor of *BAU* magazine and wrote quite a few texts.[6] You've worked as an editor as well. Was this before you were actively building, or was it done in parallel? In your case, did writing and building influence each other?

JF Yes, this was absolutely influential. There were earlier attempts, but the point at which writing really took off for me came when Mechthild Stuhlmacher, a German architect practicing in the Netherlands, invited me to contribute an article to an issue of *OASE Journal for Architecture* on "Context."[7] This was the moment when I experienced that writing is a part of the architectural project, and one that is at least as difficult as designing architecture. Actually, it's even harder: writing requires a completely different toolbox of expression, compared to designing a building. Ever since then, I've felt the necessity to formulate ideas that we consider and discuss with each other. This also allows us to define more precisely what we do in our practice—and so share it with others. Besides, it's good for architects to find their own words instead of outsourcing this to others.

For Hollein writing was also a way to establish a discourse and define a framework for issues he was interested in.

JF Yes, that is a recognizable motive. One of my reasons for joining the editorial board of *OASE* was to find a vehicle for reflecting on and exploring interests. Although writing was already included in my idea of working on architecture, *OASE* offered a serious platform for developing this further. It had an inspiring editorial board consisting of a rather specific constellation of people—a mix of Flemish and Dutch engaging with very outspoken interests. So, yes, my involvement in *OASE* was important for building up a discourse.

For us, there was also a slight feeling of disappointment in the development of the Dutch discourse in the years of the economic crisis. All notions of the cultural dimension of architecture seemed to swiftly dissipate, with entrepreneurship becoming the sole driver. Of course, it's a balancing act, but we noticed that previous generations, also the Super Dutch, deserve credit for establishing a discourse. There used to be a lot of discussion and debate, with architects taking a position and bringing it out into the world. In general—with some notable exceptions—this is something that seems to have faded away in the Netherlands. It's noticeable that when you travel to countries such as Belgium or Switzerland you can discuss architecture with colleagues in a more thorough and precise way. As the cultural dimension of architecture in the Netherlands has changed so much in relation to two decades ago, we're aiming for the wider fertile grounds of Europe as a platform and framework for building up a discourse.

Endnotes

1 Amsterdam-based architect, professor of architecture, and city architect (*Bouwmeester*) of Antwerp.

2 Main sign for the *Festival aan de Werf*, an annual theater and visual arts festival in Utrecht, Netherlands. The title is a quote attributed to the architect and urban planner Daniel Burnham (1846–1912), a protagonist of the Chicago School.

3 Stephan Trüby: "'Everything is Architecture' Versus 'Absolute Architecture,'" *Displayer*, no. 3, ed. Wilfried Kuehn and Stephan Trüby/Staatliche Hochschule für Gestaltung Karlsruhe (Karlsruhe: Hfg Karlsruhe, Ausstellungsdesign und Kuratorische Praxis, 2009): 136–140.

4 Francesco Borromini (1599–1667).

5 Chris Kabel with Jannetje in 't Veld and Toon Koehorst (Koehorst in 't Veld), *Designing the Surface*, exhibition at Het Nieuwe Instituut, Rotterdam, Netherlands, January–August 2017. Exhibition design by Monadnock.

6 From 1965 to 1970, Hollein was first co-editor and then chief editor of the magazine *BAU Schrift für Architektur und Umwelt* (BAU Magazine for Architecture and Environment) published by the Association of Architects in Austria.

7 Job Floris, "On Monadnock: A Reflection on the Work of Monadnock," *Specificity*, *OASE*, no. 76 (September 2008): 121–126.

This Dialogue on Hans Hollein took place on January 16, 2020 in Vienna.

Monadnock

Monadnock was founded in 2006 in Rotterdam and is run by Job Floris and Sandor Naus. Both were trained as interior and furniture designers at the Academy of Fine Arts St. Joost in Breda. They subsequently received their master's degree in architecture at the Academy of Architecture and Urbanism in Rotterdam and Tilburg University. The work of Monadnock explores themes such as contemporaneity and tradition, convention and banality, constructive logic and illusionary representation. In addition to the built work, Monadnock is engaged in teaching and writing about architecture.

Job Floris has lectured and taught at several architecture schools in Europe and North America.

Kersten Geers
OFFICE Kersten Geers David Van Severen

Our first question concerns your relationship to the oeuvre and ideas of Hans Hollein?

KG The two images you show here, the Austrian Travel Agency in the Ringturm and the museum in Mönchengladbach, explain well my relationship to Hans Hollein (though of course this cannot be reduced to a few images). They show aspects of his work that have fascinated me for a long time. When I visit some of Hollein's later buildings or see the collages he made early in his career, they don't interest me in the same fundamental way.

Hans Hollein, Abteiberg Municipal Museum, Mönchengladbach, Germany, 1972–1982. Lower open plan gallery space with stair. Archive Hans Hollein, Az W and MAK, Vienna.

The heterogeneity of his oeuvre allows you to define your specific focus?

KG I started looking carefully at Hans Hollein's work in the context of us starting *San Rocco* magazine.[1] We thought of it as giving ourselves a kind of *laissez-passer* that would allow us to go places that otherwise would remain off limits. With a press pass, you can write about architects in the way you want to, you don't have to care about what they said on a specific subject or consider the evolution of their career. Instead, you're able to appropriate. If you see something you like, you can say: "What I see here is beautiful, this travel agency could be a David Hockney painting." I mean, it's a very simplistic approach, but that was somehow the special power we invented for ourselves when we started *San Rocco*—the ability to say, "Look, Hans Hollein is cool, not in all circumstances, admittedly, but here specifically he is cool."

And Mönchengladbach, what exactly fascinates you about this work?

KG This building has always intrigued me. Today, the museum in Mönchengladbach is seen as cool again, but for a very long time it was considered bad. I visited it years ago with some artist friends of mine. They have an amazing art collection from the 1960s and 1970s which is an integral part of the Mönchengladbach museum. This means that the art and the building—what they show and how they show it—form a natural biotope. The fact that I liked much of the art on show made me look at the building from another perspective. If you look at the glazed cafeteria, the benches, the various stairs, the auditorium, this little classroom through the experience of the art you see another building. And I think this is very strong.

Does this apply to other experiences of Hollein buildings?

KG I wrote about the travel agencies for the first issue of *San Rocco*, which was on Innocence,[2] as in my opinion they have an innocent kind of expression. Innocence is about formulating your ideas without you realizing they are your ideas. To a certain extent I had the feeling that everything I could see in the Mönchengladbach museum was in the Austrian Travel Agency too, only more explicit, clumsier, perhaps over-eager in its desire to say everything. In a way it was like a concentrated narrative.

And how do the travel bureaus set themselves apart from the rest of his oeuvre?

KG I think what counts in both of the projects we've talked about is that the typical distinctions between architecture and furniture, and between interior and exterior, do not apply. I'm quite fascinated, too, with the idea that you can make a building which represents an accumulation of thoughts, ideas, and elements in the grand tradition of the "museum of everything." Of course, it's a very bourgeois idea, to show everything you know and have—the whole world. But this is the reason why Hollein became interesting for me. He's perhaps the most explicit proponent in architecture—at least in my understanding— of this notion. Ettore Sottsass Jr. is another example of someone who worked with the theme of furniture as archi- tecture. But he's a furniture designer and his architecture is terrible. Or you have architects from the same era, like James Stirling or Robert Venturi, who embrace a similar complexity, but in a way they're less skilled in this kind of "object as architecture," where the painting becomes the screen, which becomes the bench, and so forth. I've never drawn this parallel before, and I'm not certain it's a helpful one, but this is also what makes Carlo Scarpa unique. I don't know whether Hollein would have liked to be compared to Scarpa, but in terms of technique—the accumulation of an endless number of figures as a means to make architecture—I think this is very powerful.

Hans Hollein, Austrian Travel Agency, Ringturm branch, Vienna, Austria, 1978–1979. Sales counter and screen with Formica laminate ornamentation. Archive Hans Hollein, Az W and MAK, Vienna. Photo: Jerzy Surwillo

Does this aspect also relate to your own work?

In our work it is always more complicated. I see myself as a discoverer, someone who looks around and brings themes back to the office. And of course, through the dialogue I have with David Van Severen, some of them enter the mix of our work and others don't. Also, some themes are implicit and others explicit, which is okay because in the end we are a different practice from the ones that we've looked at. For me, it is fundamental to bring these themes into our discussions.

A question related to this objectlike attitude to architecture is the relationship between architecture and art. Hollein saw himself as not just an architect, but also an artist.

KG Absolutely, he always said he'd started out as an artist, and then somehow become an architect.

I think it's interesting that he cultivated a manifold relationship to art and the art world right up to the end of his career. And we could argue that he used art, with its scale, size, and materiality, as a testbed to put forward his architectural ideas.

KG I'm sure you're right about this. But at the same time it confirms one of the things I liked very much about *San Rocco*: it was never about figuring out what our subjects, the people we were talking about, thought themselves. As an architect, I know how much we manipulate our own storytelling.

Still, with Hollein I do see this total embrace of the art practice, especially of course the art practice of the 1960s and 1970s, maybe even up to the early 1980s. It's a particular kind of art, very much concerned with metaphorical objects—a conceptual art that in many ways is also very formalist. Despite the evident parallels with this art practice, personally I can only see Hollein as an architect. As much as I can understand his affinity with art and perhaps also the initial desire to be an artist, for me the work is only interesting when it is the work of an architect, and that's also why I have more trouble with his early projects.

Yet in 2014 Wilfried Kuehn and Susanne Titz curated a show at the Abteiberg Museum in Mönchengladbach that focused on the artistic dimension in Hollein's work.[3]

KG I was at the opening and also part of a panel with Suzanne Titz, Wilfried Kuehn, Rita McBride, and Max Hollein. I was happy to be there, and it was a great exchange. But at the same time, and as much as I liked the exhibition, the works didn't really speak to me as I walked through the show. These are works that are very much aware of their own artistic value.

Of course, I know that Hollein first got involved in the museum project as an artist making architecture, and perhaps that's the reason why it turned out the way it did. But ultimately, I'm only able to judge the work in terms of an architect making a building which houses an art collection. I simply cannot look at one of Hollein's benches and think it is done by an artist. When I look at the strange green auditorium I can only think of it as architecture.

At the same time, you also have a close connection to art.

KG Of course, I'm close to a fair number of artists. I often appreciate people who make work that is not so far removed from what our practice stands for. For example, Richard Venlet is a very important person for our dialogues with art. He's an artist, and we often collaborate on specific architectural projects, but I am still totally aware that he is there as an artist, and we are the architects. And that applies also to Rita McBride or Koenraad Dedobbeleer or others.

When some of us were studying here in Vienna, Hans Hollein was a well-known architect and an important cultural figure, and yet we were not interested in joining his masterclass. It is quite revealing for us to revisit and reclaim Hans Hollein's work twenty years later.

KG I understand that very well because I've had similar experiences with quite a few architects who have become important figures for my writing or in our work in the last ten to fifteen years—from Robert Venturi, to Aldo Rossi, Hans Hollein, and James Stirling, or even Rem Koolhaas, just to name the most obvious ones. All of them are architects, which I disliked when I was a student.

San Rocco became a vehicle to explicitly revisit them. An important motive for starting the magazine was to find a place where you had the freedom to reclaim their ideas, without having to like everything or know too much about them. I remember before *San Rocco*, Pier Paolo Tamburelli and I did an issue on James Stirling for *OASE*.[4] Weirdly, that coincided with the first iteration of the CCA Stirling show curated by Anthony Vidler at Tate Britain, and I was asked to go there and present our project.[5] Vidler became upset when I made all kinds of bizarre claims about Stirling. He said, "That's not possible because I once talked to Jim about it and Jim said something different." And I replied, "I'm sorry, but you know, if people talk to me, I don't always say what's going on in the back of my mind." Even if my position is naive, I think it's very healthy to have some distance. And I think it's the same for you guys. I mean, I can totally understand that you could only embrace Hollein after having first dismissed him. It's the Hollein you create yourself. And I think that is significant. That's also what I wanted to say before: "This is my interpretation of Hollein."

As you know, the first project Hans Hollein built in Vienna was this little candle shop. It was photographed by Franz Hubmann, who became a good friend of his. Hubmann's photographs really jump-started Hollein's career. The project was shown to Angelo Mangiarotti, who published it in *Domus*, and then Hollein submitted it for the Reynolds Memorial Award, which he won. The photographs, and the attention generated by the award, also launched his American career. You and your office also have this strong relationship to your photographer Bas Princen. How does your collaboration work?

KG I don't know about the relationship Hubmann had with Hollein, but I think the relationships between architects and photographers are often based on serendipity. I can almost tell a parallel story to the one you told about Hubmann and Hollein. I met Bas Princen in Rotterdam when he

OFFICE Kersten Geers David Van Severen, Notary's Office, Antwerp, Belgium, 2002–2003.
Entrance space. Photo: Bas Princen

was working on a documentation of what he called "Artificial Arcadia"—places without people or places which are artificially made.[6] Our professional relationship started not long afterwards, when I convinced him to photograph our first built project, the notary's office in Antwerp that I designed with David Van Severen.

The Japanese magazine *A+U* was publishing a special issue on Belgian architecture,[7] and somehow they'd heard about this project. I can't imagine how—we were nobodies at the time, we didn't even have an office. So, I asked Bas if he would be interested in photographing the notary's office for that publication. My pitch was that our space was a kind of non-functional space, and somehow in the mindset of his work—I knew Bas would otherwise never photograph architecture, as he wasn't interested in commercial work. Luckily, he thought this was compelling. He took the pictures and for that occasion we invented the name for our office. We invented our office for *A+U*, so to speak—that is absolutely a fact. And we also invented a collaboration with Bas Princen because there was *A+U*.

How did the collaboration evolve after that?

KG The collaboration after that became an evident one. But I think it had more to do—and maybe with Hollein it was the same—with an acceptance of the autonomy of the artist. In other words, if you invite Bas Princen, he has to be able to do what he wants. And in the dialogue—

our shared world—you build up this kind of ongoing conversation about his images. I do believe that our relationship with artists, where we embrace them and their work, is similar to the one Hollein had with artists, at least in the 1970s and 1980s. I have many colleagues, without naming names, who think that photographers just exist to take pictures of their work and that artists are there to decorate their buildings.

For the catalog of the two exhibitions in 2014 in Mönchengladbach and at the MAK in Vienna, iconic projects like the Retti or Media Lines were rephotographed by Armin Linke and Aglaia Konrad. Hollein was still alive and when he was told about this he could not understand why they would want to rephotograph the projects. He did not see the need for these new pictures, as he thought the iconic images—the ones that represented perfectly the expression of his buildings— already existed. Have you ever had a project rephotographed?

KG Yes, Bas Princen recently went back to rephotograph some of our buildings, and I found it fascinating. In the catalog you mentioned I particularly like the photographs Aglaia Konrad made—there are a couple of very beautiful ones. At the same time, I understand Hollein's viewpoint, especially with his shops in Vienna. They're a good example because not so long ago I went to see the few that still exist. Some of them are still beautiful today, but others are kind of mutilated.

For example, the Retti candle shop was a complex composition of elements, where even the candles played a role. Now they sell terrible jewelry there.

With some of our projects I'm very intrigued and happy that they were temporary. Essentially all that remains of our Biennale pavilions in 2008[8] and 2010[9] are Bas's pictures along with a couple of films or snapshots people took. I think the tradition of mythical projects which have a certain status because of what you can and cannot know about them is an integral part of architecture— some projects become tautological. It makes these buildings similar to the paper architecture from the 1960s and 1970s and I think that's impressive. Those works were certainly part of our cultural production.

Hans Hollein, Retti candle shop, Vienna, Austria, 1964–1965. Front display space with entrance door and wall mirror. Archive Hans Hollein, Az W and MAK, Vienna. Photo: Franz Hubmann/Imagno/picturedesk.com

There's another side to Hollein, which is teaching. For three decades he was a professor at the University of Applied Arts in Vienna.[10] As a teacher, he also pursued the idea of architecture as continuity and cultural production. Still, it makes us wonder how, after decades of teaching, there isn't a Hollein school of thought. You've taught successfully at many different schools.

Do you think this issue of not establishing a school of thought is a common one, or is it specific to Hollein? Was he such a strong figure that he could not produce successful followers?

KG I find it a very interesting question, and I don't know if there's an easy answer. I would say it's interesting from a bigger perspective, rather than just in relation to Hollein. Having seen how things work in various schools in the States and Europe, I have a feeling that fundamentally there have always been two different kinds of teachers. One is the teacher as a catalyst, who assists in finding ideas, rather than with the actual project—Rem Koolhaas, say, whose actual teaching has not had such a big impact, despite the books he's made. The same goes for James Stirling, who taught forever. Even Venturi's teaching—we don't know much about it. Beyond Hollein, there are quite a few of these cases where you would say that the teaching didn't do that much, compared to the big influence they had through their offices. It has often been said that many of the people who worked for OMA in the 1980s went on to set up quite successful practices themselves. In that sense, the office was probably a better place to be than Delft or Harvard, when Koolhaas was teaching there.

The other model, which I think is rarer, with O.M. Ungers being perhaps the most obvious example, is teaching as a project. That approach requires a lot of discipline. I'm sure there are people who think that Ungers the teacher was important because he was also a successful architect. But I'm not so sure. Ungers' important years as a teacher—

OFFICE Kersten Geers David Van Severen, *After the Party*, Belgian Pavilion, Venice Architecture Biennale, Italy, 2008. A 7m-high metal enclosure wraps around the historical pavilion. Photo: Bas Princen

his oeuvre as teacher, if you like—lasted only about a decade and is a closed chapter.[11] Hans Kollhoff, who briefly worked for Hans Hollein, is another intriguing example. He taught at the ETH in Zurich for a long time and I think people who went to study with him also hoped to get an invitation to his office. The teaching studio and the office were interrelated. So, I think it's a super interesting topic, where "founding a school" as a teacher is more the exception to the rule. Seen from that perspective, it's difficult to accuse Hollein of failing to have founded a school. He is more the norm in that sense.

Endnotes

1 *San Rocco* magazine 2010–2019. Editor: Matteo Ghidoni; Editorial Board: Matteo Costanzo, Francesca Pellicciari, Giovanni Piovene, Giovanna Silva, Pier Paolo Tamburelli. Founded by 2A+P/A, baukuh, Stefano Graziani, OFFICE Kersten Geers David Van Severen, pupilla grafik, Salottobuono, Giovanna Silva.

2 Kersten Geers, "Model Architecture," *Innocence, San Rocco,* no. 0 (Summer 2010), 66–70.

3 *Hans Hollein. Alles Ist Architektur*, Museum Abteiberg, Mönchengladbach, Germany, April 12 to September 28, 2014, Concept: Wilfried Kuehn und Susanne Titz.

4 Christoph Grafe, Joachim Declerck, Kersten Geers, Pier Paolo Tamburelli, Ruben Molendijk, Tom Vandeputte, eds., *The Architecture of James Stirling 1964–1992. A Non-Dogmatic Accumulation of Formal Knowledge, OASE,* no. 79, (November 2009).

5 *James Stirling: Notes from the Archive* curated by Anthony Vidler, Tate Britain April 5 to August 21, 2011, and conference "Rethinking James Stirling" at the Clore Gallery, Tate Britain.

6 Photo project and publication (010 Publishers, 2004) about outdoor subculture hobbies such as kite surfing, RC-cars, and motocross bike racing picturing people in vast, mostly manmade landscapes.

7 A+U, no. 392–393 (2003).

8 OFFICE Kersten Geers David Van Severen, *After The Party*, Venice Architecture Biennale, Italy, 2008.

9 OFFICE Kersten Geers David Van Severen, *Garden Pavilion: 7 Rooms/21 Perspectives*, Venice Architecture Biennale, Italy, 2010.

10 At the University of Applied Arts in Vienna Hans Hollein was head of the masterclass for industrial design and head of the Institute for Design from 1976 until 1979, as well as head of a masterclass for architecture from 1979 until 2002 and head of the Department of Architecture from 1995 until 1999.

11 O.M. Ungers was Professor at TU Berlin from 1963 to 1969 and Cornell University, Ithaca (NY) from 1969 to 1975.

This Dialogue on Hans Hollein took place on June 17, 2020 online.

OFFICE Kersten Geers David Van Severen / Kersten Geers

OFFICE is an architectural practice founded by Kersten Geers and David Van Severen, who both studied at the University of Ghent and ETSAM in Madrid. Since it was set up in 2002 in Brussels, OFFICE has been working on a wide variety of projects, ranging from small-scale interventions and residential projects to large public buildings. Their work is rooted in a profound interest in architectural histories, especially from the second half of the twentieth century.

Kersten Geers has taught extensively at architecture schools in Europe and North America and is a full professor at the Accademia in Mendrisio and visiting professor at Harvard GSD. He was a founding member of *San Rocco* magazine and has published several essays on, amongst other things, the intersection of architecture and contemporary art.

considerations

How can we comprehend and make accessible an architectural universe as complex and seemingly hermetic as Hans Hollein's? To tackle this challenge, the Dialogues on Hans Hollein project identified various themes that run through his body of work. In the subsequent interviews with contemporary architects, a number of these topics emerged as particularly valuable for understanding Hollein's work. Here, these concepts are distilled into concise considerations on Hans Hollein's practice that open up diverse interpretative approaches to his intricate world of ideas. The same themes prove to be equally relevant to the ongoing discourse around architectural design today.

exhibiting

The making of exhibitions was an overarching, constantly evolving element of Hollein's conception of architecture: a means he used to analyze both functional and aesthetic issues related to the emerging consumer culture. A coming together of the themes of exhibiting and mass consumption is already evident in Hollein's diploma thesis (1956), a design for a World's Fair pavilion shaped by the beginnings of the postwar economic boom. This project would be followed by others that applied the same combination of elements to a wide variety of uses—shopping mall, department store, shops, exhibitions, gallery spaces, commercial buildings, and large museum complexes. Conceptually, the connecting of these themes brought questions of display, staging, and spectacle to the fore. Hollein's pop-glamorous designs, oscillating between display and architecture, staged and directed a heightened experience of both commodities and space. A prototypical example is his early design for the Austrian contribution to the 14th Triennale in Milan (1968), an intimate panopticon of consumer goods that visitors could access via narrow, precisely designed corridors and view through special spectacles manufactured on site.

In Hollein's work, the means of display became a direct means of communication. Rather than a reserved, documentary framework, they created an inclusive show that directly appealed to the viewers/consumers, challenging and involving them in both active and passive ways. The focus, however, remained primarily on the personal experience of the individual, rather than that of the collective or the masses.

photography

An inveterate photographer himself, Hollein recognized early on the importance of "cool images" for the promotion and dissemination of contemporary architecture. Even before he established his own practice, he came into contact with established architectural photographers such as Walter Peterhans and Julius Shulman during his time studying in America (1958–1960). Back in Vienna, the media's lavish attention to Hollein's debut work, the Retti candle shop (1965), owed much to the iconic photographs by Austrian photographer and photojournalist Franz Hubmann. Nor did the importance that Hollein assigned to the role of photographers in the world of architecture diminish over time. As curator of the 1996 Venice Architecture Biennale, he gave twelve selected photographers their own exhibition in the Giardini under the rubric *Photographers of Architecture*. Hubmann and Shulman were among those invited.

Photography was always an integral part of the everyday life of Hollein's studio, used to constantly document and reflect on the process of developing the work and the many variants of the model that were produced. Design decisions would be based on a comparison of series of images. In contrast to others, Hollein was only marginally interested in documenting how his buildings were appropriated and used. If there were iconic photographs that presented an ideal image of his architecture, he saw no need to photograph the work again at a later date. In his mind's eye, his architecture remained eternally young.

furniture

In the 1960s, Hollein addressed the performative quality of furniture with designs such as the revolving Roto Desk (1966). In Mobile Office (1969), the performer was Hollein himself, wrapped in a transparent plastic bubble furnished only with the tools of his trade–drafting table, pen, and telephone. For the MAK in Vienna in 1966 he designed an exhibition, *Selection 66*, that transformed well-known pieces of furniture into novel sculptures using audiovisual techniques. Rather than being set on a pedestal, the items could be actively experienced.

Beginning with the Retti candle shop (1965), Hollein approached furniture as an integral part of his architectural projects. In the most interesting of his interiors, such as the Austrian Travel Agencies (1979) or the small Viennese shops, the boundaries between architecture, furniture, decor, and sculpture are blurred. All the objects in the space are charged with meaning and linked in a chain of association. Hollein developed an obsession with certain kinds of objects such as palm trees, temples, pagodas, ritual tables, or columns, which resurfaced in his projects in many different guises, like the protagonists of a narrative. For Hollein, everyday objects harbored the essence of all architecture. In the Schullin II jewelry store (1982), for example, three of his so-called Kohlmarkt floor lamps stand in a row, like triplets, their head-like uplighters set onto marble-effect columns. Hollein also designed stand-alone pieces of furniture charged with associative meaning, such as the Marilyn sofa, the Sigmund Freud couch, or the "Vanity" dressing table adorned with feathers. Only a few of these went into small-scale serial production, and they are mostly sold today as collector's items.

materiality

The question of materiality plays a subordinate role at the outset of Hollein's design process, only being considered after form and space have been defined. As the project is elaborated further, however, materials become an increasingly important element of the finished design. Hollein's treatment of materials can be seen as emblematic of his way of thinking as a whole, in that the symbolic, associative, and technical connotations of the chosen materials are brought together—amalgamated—to create a multivalent spatial structure. The juxtaposition of contrasting materials, such as plastic and stone, or metal and textile, creates a material tension that is important for the architectural concept as a whole.

This is particularly evident in the small shops he designed in Vienna like the Retti candle shop (1965) or Schullin I jewelry store (1974). In one, the candles are inserted as artifacts into a display of brushed aluminum and burnt-orange fabric. In the other, a dark stone facade conceals a golden room lined with velvet and granite.

Hollein's idiosyncratic understanding of materiality is best seen, however, in the interiors for the Austrian Travel Agency, which employ four radically different palettes of materials.

The principle of synthesizing opposites is also evident in his approach to building technology, which brings together his interest in craftsmanship and his use of the most up-to-date production techniques.

For Hollein, urbanity encompassed both the city and the countryside. As he described it, the city was the focal point of the human spirit, whereas the countryside constituted the tension area between urban settlements ("Architektur, Inhalt und Form," 1964). Hollein's collages evoking a utopian urbanity soon gained a certain fame: an aircraft carrier in the landscape became a city (1967), a car chassis became a superstructure above Manhattan (1963). Hollein was also fascinated with the pueblos built by the indigenous peoples of the American Southwest and Mexico, which he visited in the 1960s. These vernacular urban settlements, constructed in adobe and stone, were for him "an architectural form of great complexity," "a development of architecture par excellence" ("Pueblos," 1964).

Some of Hollein's projects, such as the Abteiberg Museum in Mönchengladbach (1982) or the Köhlergasse elementary school in Vienna (1990), merge almost seamlessly into the existing urban fabric. A number of the architect's most significant works are concentrated within an area of around one square kilometer in the center of Vienna. Each of these buildings is carefully and thoughtfully integrated into the urban context and sets up a charged spatial relationship with the public space around it. The Haas Haus (1990), located next to Stephansplatz, and the relationship between building and square, explored in countless variations, take on a special significance in Hollein's work within an urban context.

models

Hollein built his first expressive and informal models, such as "The City" or the "Potemkin Hanging Sculpture," while he was still a student in the late 1950s. Later on, the building of models would become an important part of the daily working routine of Atelier Hollein as a means for him and his collaborators to communicate ideas to each other. Countless models showing variants of the design were produced in order to compare different solutions and maintain a tight control over the development of the design. A physical working model would be repeatedly adapted and rebuilt during the process of design. Hollein's designs, among them the Abteiberg Museum in Mönchengladbach (1982), Haas Haus (1990), and Vulcania (2002), were often based on complex spatial ideas that could not be easily grasped from a floor plan. Early on, with the museum in Mönchengladbach, Hollein developed a special technique of model building that allowed him to test interior effects, especially the effects of natural and artificial light, as well as the relations between spaces. The models could also conjure the atmosphere of a place. Beyond their role in the studio, they were used to facilitate a dialogue with the clients. Observing the model in three dimensions makes apparent both the conceptual arrangement and the architect's high degree of expertise. In the studio, similar models were used to explore spatial ideas in a concrete way and to develop them further.

Apart from the built projects, a unique body of work consisting of models in many different scales was created over the decades.

references

The brazen use of references, cutting and pasting elements from earlier, mainly classical architecture, is one of the most conspicuous traits of postmodern architecture. Hollein's work can also be placed in this category, but rather than explicitly quoting historical sources, as other architects did at the time, his approach is more to subtly transform and defamiliarize the models. Hollein's contribution to the iconic *Strada Novissima* installation at the first Venice Architecture Biennale in 1980 refers, among other things, to Adolf Loos's design for the Chicago Tribune Tower (1923) and can be seen as an example of a postmodern quotation, but also of its paraphrasing.

Hollein's interest in references is also evident from his slide collection, which covers a broad palette of subject categories, from historical architecture to contemporary buildings, alongside cars, design objects, and airplanes.

One example of a direct borrowing is the use of palm trees in the Austrian Travel Agencies, which Hollein took from the kitchen in John Nash's Royal Pavilion in Brighton. In addition, his early commercial spaces reference Viennese modernism, as represented in particular by Otto Wagner, Adolf Loos, and Josef Hoffmann, in various ways.

Hollein also used motifs from the fine arts as catalysts for his designs. For example, Andrea Mantegna's *Lamentation of Christ* was the basis of his installation *Werk und Verhalten— Leben und Tod* (*Work and Behavior—Life and Death*) at the 1972 Venice Biennale, while Édouard Riou's and Gustave Doré's etchings for Dante's *Divine Comedy* formed the starting point for the Vulcania project in Auvergne, France (2002).

Hollein saw himself as both an architect and an artist, and his work reveals a multi-faceted and complex engagement with the meaning and conception of art. On one level, some of his most successful works are buildings for art. On another, he used associative strategies that are more commonly found in art than in architecture. His close friendships with artists such as Walter Pichler, Joseph Beuys, and Claes Oldenburg were also formative for his thinking and left concrete traces in his work.

What lies at the core of Hollein's embrace of art is his self-perception as an "Ideas Man." In his work the idea, the way of thinking, has primacy as the generator of form, as evinced most clearly by the many exhibition projects and installations in which he deliberately dissolves the boundary between architecture and art.

With the exhibition *Tod* (*Death*, 1970), Hollein created an early allegorical installation that fuses the elements of space, artifact, and performance into a total concept. Here, too, the line between architecture and art is intentionally blurred. Hollein further developed this format in *Werk und Verhalten—Leben und Tod* (*Work and Behavior—Life and Death*, 1972) at the Venice Biennale and in *Turnstunde* (Gym Lesson, 1984) for the Abteiberg Museum, among others.

At the other end of the spectrum, Hollein also created stand-alone sculptural pieces that can be more clearly described as artworks, such as *Das goldene Kalb* (Golden Calf, Genoa 2004/Graz 2011) and *Car Building* (Karlsruhe 2011). Here, elements of pop art are combined with the readymade.

Teaching

From early on, Hollein's work as a practicing architect was accompanied by teaching activities at various universities in Austria and abroad, including the University of Applied Arts in Vienna, where he led the masterclass for architecture from 1979 to 2002. In the first semester of the course, students undertook an analysis of an exemplary urban situation. The point of the exercise—an essential component of his teaching—was to open up fundamental questions of architecture. It is striking that Hollein's teaching activities did not produce a stylistically recognizable "Hollein school," in contrast to other architects teaching at the time. A point of reference for understanding Hollein's approach is his own experience as a student in Clemens Holzmeister's master-class (1953–1956). There, Holzmeister's goal was not to train a multitude of "stylistic" successors, but rather to support the student's independent search for a position through a modern form of teaching oriented towards dialogue. This interpretation of role of the teacher, in which the presence of the master did not loom large, was received positively in Vienna and served as a model for later generations. Hollein's early project for the Extension of the University of Vienna (1966) suggests an interest in critically examining the future of institutions of higher education. When it was his turn to be in charge, however, there was no further development or questioning of the principle of the masterclass, with all its dependencies, power imbalances, and rituals.

teamwork

In his essay "Zurück zur Architektur" (Back to Architecture, 1962), Hollein describes architecture as the "transformation of an idea through building," a process totally dependent on "the powers of the single personality." Unfettered individual creativity was for him, as it was for many architects of his generation at the time, the only legitimate means of reclaiming architecture. Contrary to the lone struggle postulated in his manifesto, however, cooperation and teamwork were part of everyday life for Hollein. New projects in Hollein's studio tended to begin not with a solitary, heroic act of creation, but with an exchange of ideas.

The hierarchies, however, were always clearly observed, within Hollein retaining overall control of the design process as well as the content of the projects. The studio's daily working routine was defined by a design development process that produced multiple variations of a scheme and constantly moved forward in repeating loops, with changes often being made under huge pressure right up to the last possible moment. In sketches signed by Hollein, many of them made after the fact, this laborious and time-consuming process was sometimes transfigured into a readymade design concept. Hollein's enduring success was enabled by an extremely productive team of collaborators—some of them very creative and interesting architects in their own right—and by the well-rehearsed teamwork of Hollein's clients and supporters from the worlds of business, politics, and culture, along with friends and family, and in particular his wife, Helene Hollein. Towards the end of his life, in 2010, he would establish a limited company, Hans Hollein & Partner ZT, with his colleague Christoph Monschein.

publishing

The majority of Hollein's written reflections on architecture were published while he was still a young architect. In 1964, a young team (including Hollein as editor) took over the journal of Austria's Central Association of Architects, *BAU*, and made it one of the most essential architectural publications in the country. In addition to presenting contemporary Austrian architecture—as well as fashion and art—the magazine revisited historical models such as Adolf Loos, Rudolph M. Schindler, and Friedrich Kiesler. One issue in 1968 was devoted exclusively to Hollein's oft-quoted motto "everything is architecture": the cover showed Hollein's collage of a huge piece of Emmental cheese behind a panoramic photo of Vienna. Hollein contributed to the magazine as editor, graphic designer, and author of numerous texts up to 1970. Some of Hollein's early writings—for example, "Architecture in Exile" (1960)—had something of the fragmentary character of the concrete poetry of the Vienna Group, as represented by Friedrich Achleitner or Gerhard Rühm. Among the most interesting of his texts are a description of Pueblo architecture in North America and Mexico (1964) and a rediscovery of Schindler's architecture (1961, 1966). While Hollein did not produce a major theoretical work akin to Aldo Rossi's *Architecture of the City* or Robert Venturi's *Complexity and Contradiction in Architecture*, he did attach particular importance to the editing and publication of catalogs for exhibition projects such as the *Austriennale* (1968) or *MAN transFORMS* (1974).

gestalt

The investigation of object, form, and *gestalt* is a constant theme in Hollein's work. In his early texts, he frequently uses the term *gebilde* and places it above form and function. The architectural object can occur at all scales: as a building, a building component, a column, an item of furnishing, a lamp or a chair, but also as a design object, a ring, say, or a pair of sunglasses, or a silver bowl.

Hollein's work is characterized by a juxtaposition of a geometric form and irregularly shaped bodies, crevices, and fissures, which in their interplay form an unstable whole.

The configuration of the facade as a *gestalt*—where it takes on qualities that are more than the sum of all its parts—plays an important role in Hollein's designs for the shops in Vienna. Here, technical installations and conduits are integrated into the design, as seen in the arrangement of brass pipes over the entrance to the Schullin I jewelry store, which also serves as a cover for the air conditioning, light fixtures, and entrance sign.

At the Abteiberg Museum in Mönchengladbach, geometric volumes and architectural fragments are combined in a careful composition of varied, independent forms. In the large buildings, such as the Museum of Modern Art in Frankfurt am Main or the Haas Haus in Vienna, a great deal of effort is invested in bringing secondary elements, such as the housing for ventilation units, into the form. In sum, Hollein's work can be understood as an engagement with the concept of design as a phenomenon: everything is architecture—architecture is *gestalt*.

Selected Hans Hollein Projects

Retti Candle Shop
1964–1965

01

This candle shop from the early 1960s was Hollein's first commission in Vienna. Though small, and built to a limited budget, it gained instant international recognition when it won the prestigious R.S. Reynolds Award. It is located on one of the city's most exclusive shopping streets in the immediate vicinity of two later projects by Atelier Hollein—the Schullin II jewelry store (1982) and the archaeological grounds at Michaelerplatz (1992). At the time, Kohlmarkt was a busy road with a narrow sidewalk. In response to this spatially difficult situation, the two small display windows are turned sideways towards passers-by.

The whole candle shop is squeezed into the former portal to the building, which is barely 4m wide, and structured as a sequence of three separate elements: a sign-like facade, octagonal display space, and rear sales room. During the design process, Hollein explored several facade variants that alternated between the archaic and the technoid. The final effect is somewhere between an abstract mask and the entrance to a cave. At the same time, the choice

of aluminum for the facade alludes to aeronautics and space travel, lending it a strong futuristic note.

The atmosphere of the main room, with its orange textiles and niches filled with many candles, is reminiscent of a chapel. Mirrors placed on the side walls create the illusion that the geometrically nondirectional space expands infinitely in a transverse direction. The innermost room, where the sales counter is located, is dominated by diffuse light glowing through backlit textile panels.

Threaded throughout this remarkably innovative project are numerous motifs referring to historic Viennese commercial premises, such as Otto Wagner's dispatch bureau for the daily newspaper, *Die Zeit*, or Adolf Loos's Kniže & Co. Already here Hollein's "amalgamating" design method is brought into play.

Location Kohlmarkt 8–10, 1010 Vienna, Austria
Type Shop
Client Marius Retti

148

02

03

Hans Hollein, Retti candle shop, Vienna, Austria, 1964–1965.
All: Archive Hans Hollein, Az W and MAK, Vienna.

01   Shop front after completion.

02   Interior perspective.
      Pencil on translucent paper.

03   Study of shop front, working model in cardboard
      and metallic paper, alternative proposal. Model photo.

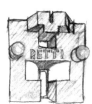

04

05

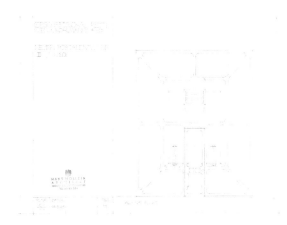

06

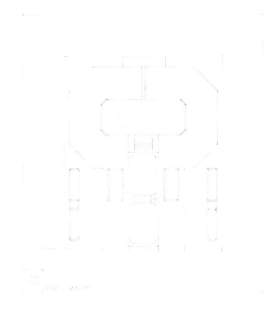

07

04   Alternative design for shop front, perspective sketch.
     Charcoal on translucent paper.

05   Alternative design for shop front, perspective sketch.
     Pencil on translucent paper.

06   "New portal design II" (Neuer Portalentwurf II),
     elevation and section. Pencil on translucent paper.

07   Alternative design for shop front, elevation.
     Pencil on translucent paper.

08

09

08   Candle holders, detail. Pencil on translucent paper.

09   Study of lighting object, working model.
Watercolor on card and wood. Photo: Elmar Bertsch

Richard Feigen Gallery
1967–1969

01

On the back of the extraordinary success of the Retti candle shop Hollein was commissioned to convert a townhouse on the Upper East Side of Manhattan. The client was Richard L. Feigen, a prominent gallerist and collector of contemporary and classical art. The building was to house Feigen's second gallery in New York, along with his private residence on the upper floors. At the opening, Hollein was fêted as a young avant-garde architect, but the client's euphoria waned as it gradually became apparent that the spatial concept, with its narrow section, did not lend itself to exhibiting art. However the space would find a new use as a fashion store and remain intact for many years until the entire townhouse was demolished to make way for a taller building.

The abstract, white-rendered facade of the gallery was pierced by a tall, narrow opening at street level. A mirror-polished stainless-steel double column in the entrance area brought reflections of the surroundings into the interior, acting as a hinge between inside and outside. The same reflective surfaces continued into the interior, in the form of mirror-polished handrails. The front exhibition space spanned two floors and allowed large-scale paintings to be viewed from both levels. Hollein designed a "media spine" element that ran along the ceiling to support light fixtures and air-conditioning pipes. This was a motif he would develop further in the Media Lines project in Munich (1972). At the back of the gallery, old master paintings were shown in a softly lit study-like room.

Location 27 East 79th Street, 10075 New York, United States
Type Art gallery
Client Richard L. Feigen & Co.

02

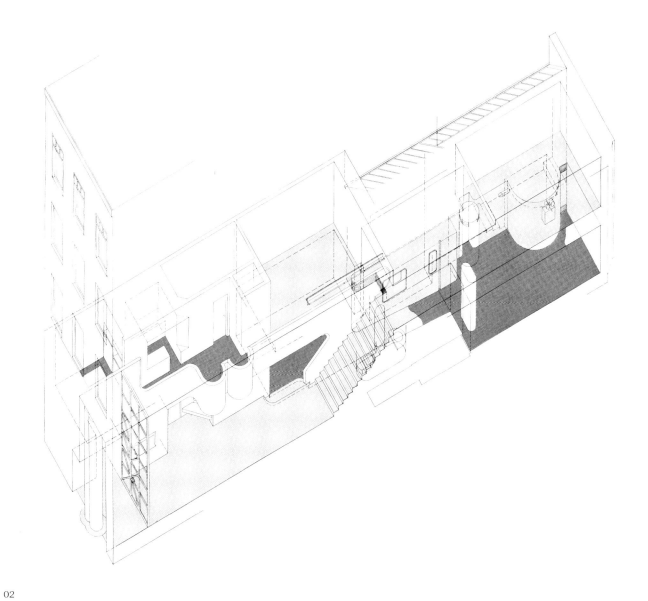

Hans Hollein, Richard Feigen Gallery, New York, United States, 1967–1969. All: Archive Hans Hollein, Az W and MAK, Vienna.

01   Street elevation. Photo: Estate of Evelyn Hofer

02   Axonometry. Dot screen foil on print.

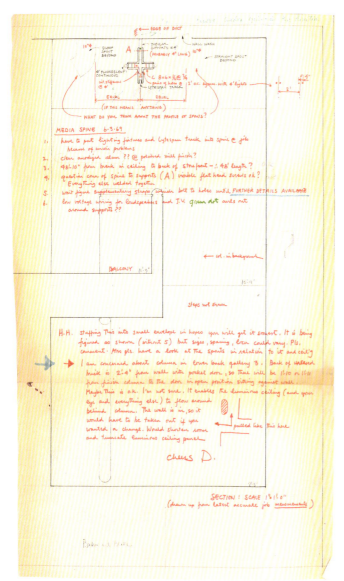

03

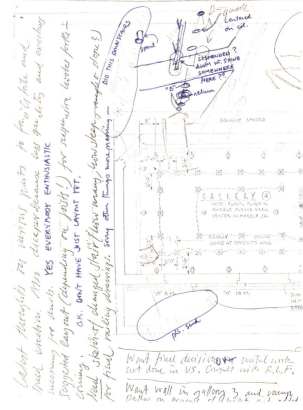

04

03   Cross section of the gallery showing the "Media Spine"
     with annotation concerning finishes and the column
     in the rear gallery space. Felt-tip and pencil on whiteprint.

04   Annotated first-floor construction plan used by Atelier Hollein
     to communicate with James Baker and Peter Blake Architects,
     the office overseeing the construction work in New York.
     Color pencil and felt-tip on photocopy.

05   View from the rear of the first-floor gallery towards main
     double-height space. Photo: Franz Hubmann/Imagno/
     picturedesk.com

05

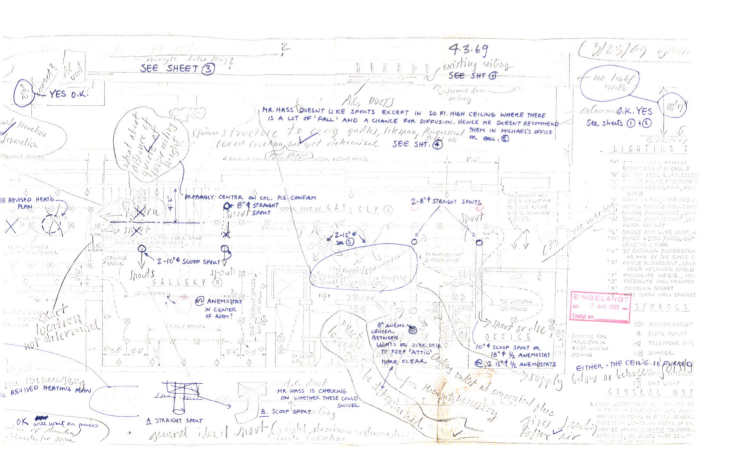

Austriennale – Austrian Contribution to the XIV Triennale di Milano
1968

01

Austriennale was Austria's national contribution to the ill-fated fourteenth Milan Triennale in 1968. Already on the opening day at the end of May, the installation was damaged during student protests and forced to close. It would only reopen to the public at the end of June.

The overarching theme of the Triennale was "The Greater Number" and, by extension, mass society. Hollein's response was to produce an associative allegory of consumer society. A fascination with the labyrinthine spatial structure as a place of disorientation is evident from the very first sketches for the project. In the final design, the labyrinth motif was distilled into a row of apparently identical aluminum doors, each inset with a pair of eye-level circular openings and giving onto a narrow corridor representing a specific theme, such as the supermarket, the "door of

frustration," the "passage of extreme confinement," or snow as a mass-produced commodity of Austria.

The corridors were set in parallel. All of them led to the same place: a yellow room that could only be entered through a single narrow pill-shaped opening. Here, visitors encountered a small amphitheater with an array of modern Austrian mass-produced goods. On leaving the installation, they were led past an injection molding machine that churned out red-white-red plastic glasses. These so-called "Austria glasses" could not be folded, they either had to be worn or thrown away.

Location Viale Emilio Alemagna 6, 20121 Milan, Italy
Type Exhibition
Client Federal Ministry of Trade, Commerce and Industry, Federal Ministry of Education, Federal Chamber of Commerce, City of Vienna

02

Hans Hollein, *Austriennale*, Austria's national contribution
to the fourteenth Milan Triennale, Milan, Italy, 1968.
All: Archive Hans Hollein, Az W and MAK, Vienna.

01   Exhibition view of the diagonal partition with aluminum doors.
       Photo: Franz Hubmann/Imagno/picturedesk.com

02   General layout, axonometry. Pencil on print.

03

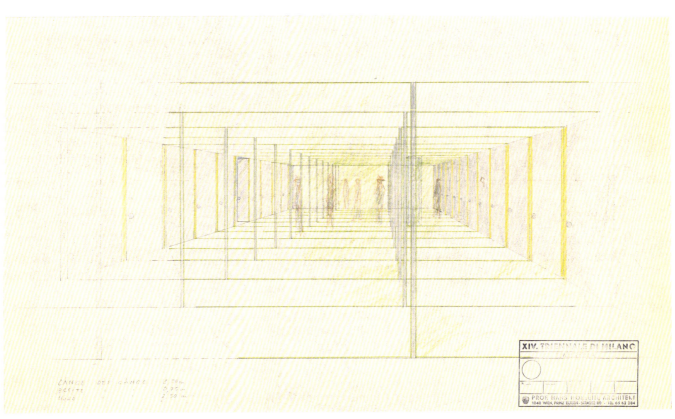

04

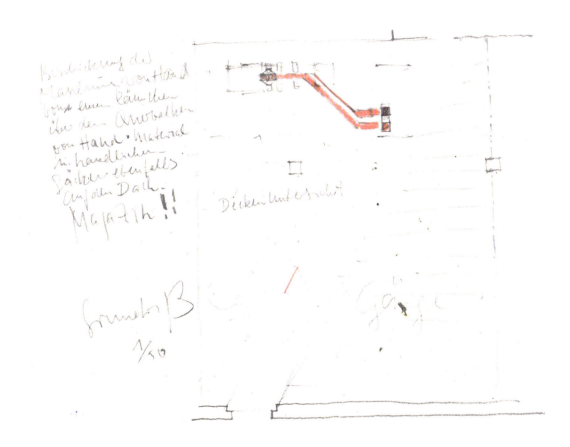

05

03 "Corridors to the great room," concept study showing corridors leading to the large space with product displays. Pencil and color pencil on translucent paper.

04 Perspective study of corridors. Color pencil on whiteprint.

05 General layout, sketch plan showing corridors and injection molding machine for the "Austria glasses". Pencil and color pencil on translucent paper.

Carl Friedrich von Siemens Foundation in Nymphenburg
1969–1972

01

In the early 1970s, Hollein took on two projects for the Siemens Group in Munich: the remodeling and extension of the Carl Friedrich von Siemens Foundation on the Südliches Schlossrondell, followed by the design of its administrative headquarters and a casino for staff and guests in the classicist Palais Ludwig Ferdinand on Wittelsbacherplatz.

At the time the Siemens Foundation was directed by Armin Mohler, who is today seen as one of the fathers of the New Right. Why a rightwing, conservative thinktank should have commissioned an unabashed modernist architect is a matter of debate. Hollein's reworking of the foundation's spaces, with its elements of pop art, projected an image which was hardly in tune with the program of the lecture series that Mohler oversaw.

Through a few artistic interventions, Hollein integrated the reception area of the Carl Friedrich von Siemens Foundation into the existing building. The mannerist double column and checkered stone floor are still in place today. The two parts of the column are joined by a distinctive capital. Behind their cladding of polished stainless steel are two structural H-beams in steel. The reception area served as a space of transition to the club rooms in the new extension designed by Hollein.

Location Südliches Schlossrondell 23, 80638 Munich, Germany
Type Club room
Client Siemens AG Munich

02

03

Hans Hollein, Carl Friedrich von Siemens Foundation,
Nymphenburg, Munich, Germany, 1969–1972.
All: Archive Hans Hollein, Az W and MAK, Vienna.

01   Entrance lobby. Photo: Franz Hubmann/Imagno/picturedesk.com

02   Entrance lobby, perspective study with wide column
and downlights, 1971. Pencil on translucent paper.

03   Entrance lobby, perspective study with twin column, 1971.
Pencil on translucent paper.

04

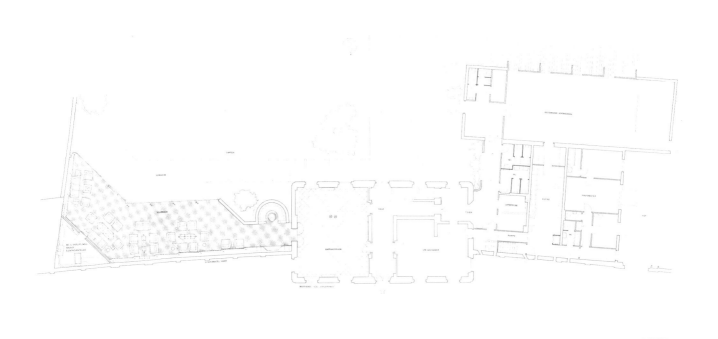

05

06

Media Lines — Olympic Village Munich
1971–1972

01

The Media Lines are a large-scale installation that served as an orientation system for the Olympic Village in Munich. Developed from Hollein's winning entry to an arts in public space competition, the project was realized over a period of a few months in 1972. The site, which was opposite the BMW factory on the northern edge of Munich, followed the principle of a car-oriented city, with a vertical separation of pedestrian and motorized traffic.

Hollein had already applied the basic idea of the "Media Line" in the Feigen Gallery in New York (1969) and his competition entry for the design of a public square in Ludwigshafen (1969). In Munich, the network of colored pipes that runs between and through the large terraced apartment blocks was primarily intended to give structure to the anonymous public space. With their bright colors, the pipes bear a resemblance to those in Pompidou Center in Paris, which was built around the same time. They originally carried water and air and provided environmental conditioning through nozzles that jetted warm or cold air. At the same time, the Media Lines supported technical equipment such as televisions, projectors, light fixtures, air-conditioning units, loudspeakers, and infrared heaters, as well as architectural elements such as roofs and textile walls. The project documentation also hints at floor heating. Today, however, the only technical infrastructure still in operation is a clock.

The pipes were modular and could be plugged into each other like toy train tracks. They converged at a central public square—the so-called forum, with its amphitheater and water curtain—which marked the transition between the housing podium and the green space.

Location Connollystraße, 80809 Munich, Germany
Type Public space design
Client Olympia-Dorf Maßnahmeträger-Gesellschaft (ODMG)

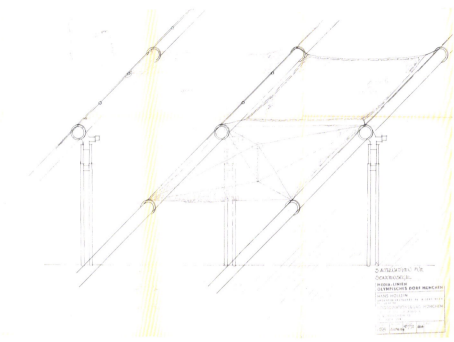

02

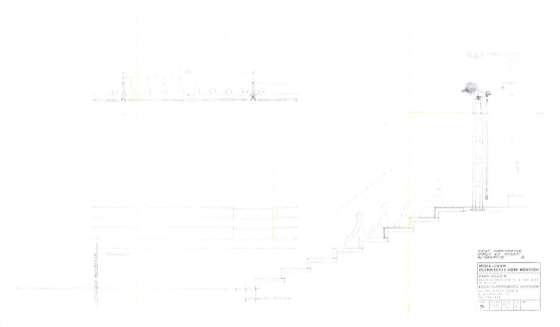

03

Hans Hollein, Media Lines, Olympic Village, Munich, Germany, 1971–1972. All: Archive Hans Hollein, Az W and MAK, Vienna.

01 Close-up of a Media Line.

02 Axonometry with three variations of the shade-sail. Whiteprint.

03 Section of amphitheater with column, "alternative 2." Whiteprint.

04

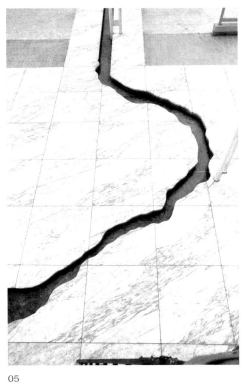

05

06

07

04 Close-up of a Media Line.
05 Detail of water feature.
06 Forum at night.
07 View from a terrace.

08 Close-up of a Media Line.
09 Amphitheater.
10 View towards canteen.
11 Water feature with amphitheater in the background.

09

10

08

11

Schullin I Jewelry Store
1972–1974

01

Chronologically, the small jewelry store on Graben still belongs to the early phase of those space-capsule-like stores in Vienna, such as the Retti candle shop (1965) and Christa Metek boutique (1967), or indeed the Feigen Gallery in New York (1969). In terms of the choice of materials and spatial atmosphere, however, Schullin I stands on its own. The Hollein motif of a free-form crevice inscribed into a gridded surface is applied prominently here as a guiding principle.

In the Archive Hans Hollein, Az W and MAK, Vienna, there are some drawings showing the lightweight facade substructure made of metal, which could be pushed into the opening in the wall with relative ease before it was clad with slabs of Baltic granite. The "crack," designed to conceal the air intake for the air-conditioning unit, contains brass tubes of varying cross-sections. A photographic record of the 1:1 model built and tested by Hollein's office is testimony to the many prototypes made during the meticulous design process.

The interior is an asymmetrical space with a stepped cross-section: on one side, the wall is partially covered with velvet panels; on the other, the wall is granite and lined with display cases. The lighting, consisting of a combination of bare bulbs and recessed spotlights, also underlines the asymmetry of the space.

Precisely positioned pill-shaped tables mediate between two formal worlds—between the grid and the organic form of the crack.

Location Graben 26, 1010 Vienna, Austria
Type Jewelry store
Client Herbert Schullin / Schullin & Söhne

NATURMASSE
NEHMEN

02

Hans Hollein, Schullin I jewelry store, Vienna, Austria, 1972–1974.
All: Archive Hans Hollein, Az W and MAK, Vienna.

01   Shop front, polished Baltic granite and brass.

02   Elevation, detail of shop front, outside face.
      Pencil on translucent paper.

NATURMASSE
NEHMEN

03

04

03 Elevation, detail of shop front, inside face.
    Pencil on translucent paper.

04 Facade studies, working models. Styrofoam, card, and pins.
    Photos: Elmar Bertsch

05

06

05   Installation of the steel support structure of the shop front.

06   Full-scale prototype of the detail above the entrance door,
      photographed at Atelier Hollein. Photo: Jerzy Surwillo

Abteiberg Municipal Museum
1972–1982

01

The Abteiberg Museum in Mönchengladbach stands on a hill in a historic neighborhood defined by a Benedictine abbey with cathedral, garden, and city wall. Partly built into the face of the hill, it thematizes the threshold space between city and museum. Access was originally from the main terrace, reached from a bridge leading directly from the city center. Today one enters from the street one story below. The new museum building opened in 1982, after an intensive ten-year process of planning and construction in which Hans Hollein worked closely with the then director Johannes Cladders. Their close relationship meant that the commission was not based on a competition-winning design but was awarded directly and "piecemeal" to Hollein. The initial focus of the project was the design of a new kind of ideal exhibition space. Alongside the display of the permanent collection, the museum also has spaces for temporary exhibitions, storerooms,

a cafeteria, lecture rooms, and educational facilities. The building was conceived as a counter-image to the conventional museum enfilade made up of a series of formally aligned rooms. The plan is organized according to the so-called "cloverleaf principle," with square exhibition spaces connected diagonally, from corner to corner. At the same time, the exhibition space extends into the areas between the clusters: interwoven with rooms of different sizes and functions, these areas also serve as zones of access and circulation. The staircases, conceived as sculptural forms, take on a special significance in Mönchengladbach.

Location Abteistraße 27/Johannes-Cladders-Platz, 41061 Mönchengladbach, Germany
Type Museum/cultural building
Client City of Mönchengladbach, Johannes Cladders (Director)

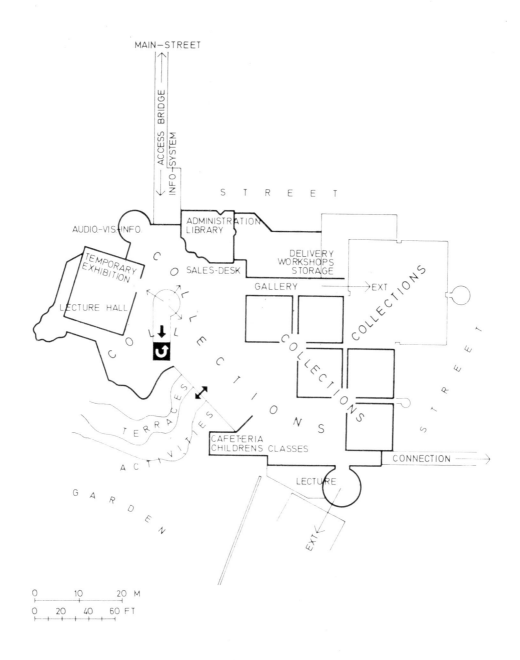

FUNCTIONAL SCHEME

02

Hans Hollein, Abteiberg Municipal Museum, Mönchengladbach, Germany, 1972–1982. All: Archive Hans Hollein, Az W and MAK, Vienna.

01 View from sculpture garden (Abteigarten).
    Photo: Franz Hubmann/Imagno/picturedesk.com

02 Functional scheme, plan. Photocopy.

03

04

05

06

03   Massing study, site model, variation E.

04   Massing study, site model, variation H.

05   Massing study, site model, variation G.

06   Massing study, site model, variation K.

All: Corrugated cardboard, card, straw, pins, wood, and paper. Photo: Elmar Bertsch

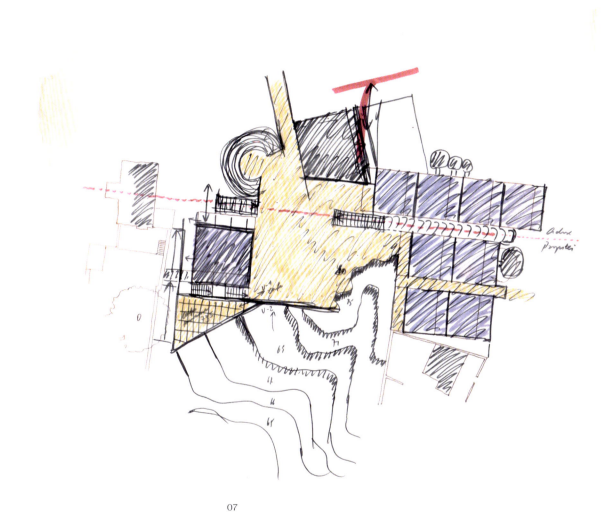

07

07 Study of general massing, variant "Axis Propstei, K,"
    sketch plan. Felt-tip on translucent paper.

MAN transFORMS—
Inaugural Exhibition of the Cooper Hewitt, Smithsonian Design Museum
1974–1976

01

Hollein, together with the museum director, Lisa Taylor, designed and curated the 1976 show that marked the opening of the Cooper Hewitt as the US's new national museum of design. Housed in a Georgian-style mansion with a total of sixty-four rooms, the museum has one of the most comprehensive design collections in the world. The groundbreaking exhibition of manmade artifacts filled every space over three floors of the building, including the area outside the entrance. Contributions by other architects such as Buckminster Fuller, Arata Isozaki, Richard Meier, and Oswald Mathias Ungers complemented Hollein's overall concept.

The essential idea behind the design was to create a total environment where the objects could be experienced directly, rather than being mediated by traditional means of museal display. Most of the exhibits were therefore not precious originals but were selected to support a narrative reading.

For the exhibition, Hollein developed a series of highly evocative, atmospherically charged spatial sequences and installations. Geometric figures and objects were inscribed into the historical spaces to create rooms with rooms. The focus of the narrative was on objects of everyday use. Anonymous objects such as hammers, loaves of bread, and textiles became reference points for design that is eternally valid, timeless.

The exhibition concept was assisted by Hermann Czech, who acted as project architect for Atelier Hollein on this commission.

Location 2 East 91st Street, 10128 New York, United States
Type Exhibition / curation
Client Cooper Hewitt, Smithsonian Design Museum; Lisa Taylor (Director)

02

03

Hans Hollein, *MAN transFORMS*, Cooper Hewitt,
Smithsonian Design Museum, New York, United States, 1974–1976.
All: Archive Hans Hollein, Az W and MAK, Vienna.

01 "Colored flags" installation, part of the "Metamorphosis
     of a Piece of Cloth" section on the second floor.
     Photo: Norman McGrath

02 General layout of first floor,
     axonometry with annotations. Collage.

03 General layout of second floor,
     axonometry with annotations. Collage.

04

05

04   "Stars" installation on the first floor.
      Photo: Norman McGrath

05   "Garments" installation, part of the "Metamorphosis
      of a Piece of Cloth" section on the second floor.
      Photo: Norman McGrath

06

07

06   "Bread" installation on the first floor, detail.
       Photo: Norman McGrath

07   "Bread" installation on the first floor.
       Photo: Norman McGrath

Austrian Travel Agency
1976–1979

01

In the late 1970s, Hollein designed several branches of the Austrian Travel Agency (Verkehrsbüro). In all, he created four new interiors, three in the center of Vienna and one, a shop fit out, in Shopping City Süd. With the exception of the City branch on Stephansplatz, very little remains today of these interiors, which could be seen as the built expression of Austria's postwar economic development and of a mass tourism that still had positive connotations at that time. The intertwining of functional areas and the artificial quality of the decor produced a staged atmosphere that signaled an escape from the banality of everyday life. Out of his typical interplay of irreconcilable opposites Hollein created an overall effect that was singularly melancholic-romantic. Palm trees, columns, screens, pavilions, birds, and other strange objects were charged with meaning as fragments of the exotic, encouraging free association.

Atelier Hollein developed a design manual—a kind of conceptual guide in catalog form—with the intention that others could design more branches in the spirit of the original. The special charm of the tourist offices lay in their claim to be at once architecture, interior, an exhibition of objects, and a worldly space.

Locations
Ringturm branch: Schottenring 30
Opernringhof branch: Opernring 3–5
City branch: Stephansplatz 10
All: 1010 Vienna, Austria

South branch: Shopping City Süd, Vösendorfer Südring, 2334 Vösendorf, Austria

Type Travel agency
Client Österreichisches Verkehrsbüro GmbH

02

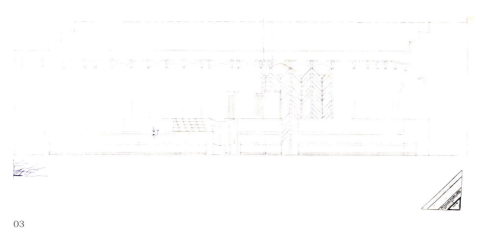

03

Hans Hollein, Austrian Travel Agency.
All: Archive Hans Hollein, Az W and MAK, Vienna.

01   Opernringhof branch, Vienna, Austria, 1976–1978.
      Main hall. Photo: Jerzy Surwillo

02   Opernringhof branch, Vienna, Austria, 1976–1978.
      Overall view, axonometry. Ink and color pencil on whiteprint.

03   Ringturm branch, Vienna, Austria, 1978–1979.
      Sales counter and folding screen with palms, elevation.
      Pencil and felt-tip on translucent paper.

04

05

06

07

04 Opernringhof branch, Vienna, Austria, 1976–1978.
Main hall with waiting "pavilion." Photo: Jerzy Surwillo

05 City branch, Vienna, Austria, 1978–1979.
Waiting area with palms and water feature.
Photo: Jerzy Surwillo

06 City branch, Vienna, Austria, 1978–1979.
Sales counter. Photo: Jerzy Surwillo

07 Ringturm branch, Vienna, Austria, 1978–1979.
Sales counter and folding screen. Photo: Jerzy Surwillo

08 South branch, Shopping City Süd, Vösendorfer Südring,
Vösendorf, Austria, 1976. Entrance with waiting pavilion.

08

Glassware and Ceramic Museum Tehran
1977–1978

01

In the 1970s, Atelier Hollein was commissioned to transform a small nineteenth-century palace into a museum of Persian glassware and ceramic art. The former two-story private residence was to be transformed into a public building without destroying the historical substance of the richly decorated interiors dating from the Qajar period. The museum Hollein designed is still largely preserved in its original condition. It stands between 30th Tir and Nowbahar streets in the historic center of Tehran, surrounded by a garden. The exterior of the decorative brick building gives no hint of the interventions inside. Only two round display cases inserted into the high garden wall indicate a public use, setting up a new relation between the wall and the palace and staging the view of the building, which was formerly shielded from the street. In this way, the building itself becomes a protected exhibit.

This play of multiple layers of staging continues inside the museum, where the carefully conceived exhibition architecture enters into a dialogue with the existing spaces in a variety of ways. The display cases and fixtures present and protect the fragile glass and ceramic artworks, use integrated lighting systems to highlight the historic features of the building, and, through their varied designs, become exhibits themselves. The Glass Museum, which was completed before the opening of the Abteiberg Museum (1982), was the first museum building realized by Atelier Hollein.

Location 30th Tir Street, District 12, Tehran, Iran
Type Museum / cultural building
Client Special Bureau of Her Imperial Majesty the Shahbanou of Iran Farah Pahlavi

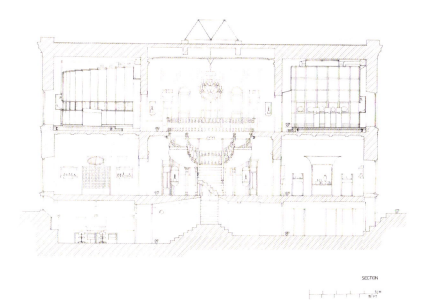

02

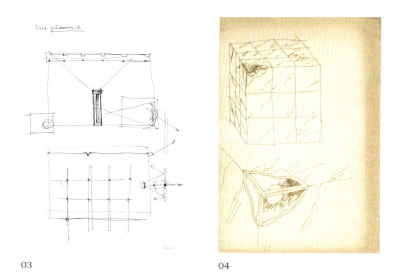

03   04

Hans Hollein, Glassware and Ceramic Museum, Tehran, Iran,
1977–1978. All: Archive Hans Hollein, Az W and MAK, Vienna.

01   Detail of display cases in Room 106. Photo: Peter Lehner

02   Section through central stair and exhibition spaces,
       presentation drawing. Ink, pencil, and dot screen foil
       on translucent paper, suspension tape.

03   Study of indirect lighting and suspended ceiling, sketch.
       Photocopy.

04   Study of a cubic display element with articulated corner.
       Whiteprint.

185

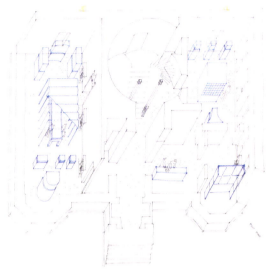

05

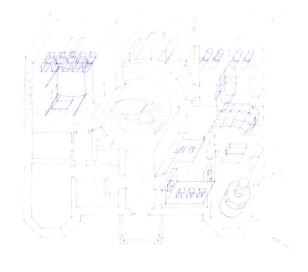

06

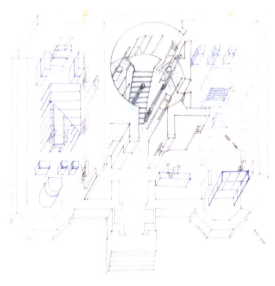

07

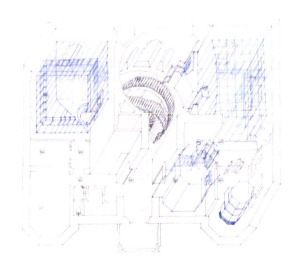

08

05　Study of display cases on first floor,
　　axonometric sketch. Felt-tip on translucent paper.

06　Study of display cases on second floor,
　　axonometric sketch. Felt-tip on translucent paper.

07　Study of display cases on first floor with overlay,
　　axonometric sketch. Felt-tip on translucent paper.

08　Study of display cases on second floor, variation,
　　axonometric sketch. Felt-tip on translucent paper.

09

Köhlergasse Elementary School
1979–1990

01

In parallel to the construction of the Abteiberg Museum, Atelier Hollein was awarded a direct commission for an elementary school in 1977 as part of Vienna's 2000 School Building Program. It was the practice's first school building and Hollein's first sizeable commission in Vienna. The school bears a similarity to the museum in Mönchengladbach, designed at the same time, in three essential respects: the overarching relation to the urban surroundings, the internal spatial organization, and the treatment of the roofscape. The corner site is characterized by the transition from a dense perimeter block structure to a loose development of villas and townhouses. Taking its cue from this heterogeneous urban context, the school complex is divided into seven buildings of different scales and design principles. The individual volumes

are held together by six connecting structures and by a system of internal circulation adapted to the topography. Given the density of construction and lack of open spaces on the site, the roof areas of three parts of the complex were designed to function as an outdoor classroom, sports field, and break terrace.

The school is laid out like a small city within the city. Individually designed architectural elements mediate between inside and outside, above and below. They connect the self-contained spatial experience of the school with the neighborhood around it.

Location Köhlergasse 9, 1180 Vienna, Austria
Type Public building
Client City of Vienna (MA 19), Hannes Swoboda, City Councilor for Urban Development and Urban Planning

02

Hans Hollein, Köhlergasse elementary school, Vienna, Austria,
1979-1990. All: Archive Hans Hollein, Az W and MAK, Vienna.

01 View towards roof terrace above the main entrance
and rotunda outdoor classroom. Photo: Georg Riha

02 Roofscape and facade towards Genzgasse,
isometry from northwest, 1981. Pencil on translucent paper.

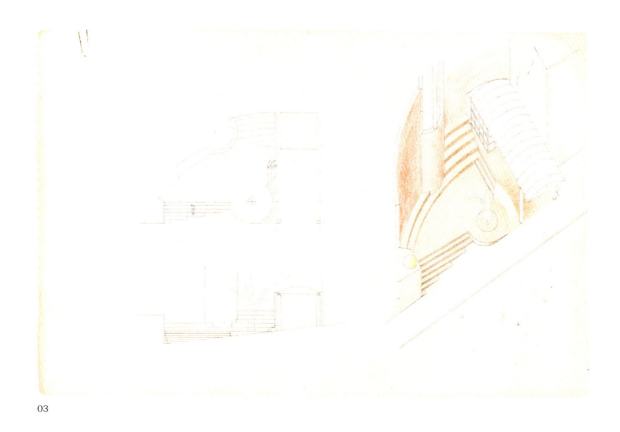

03

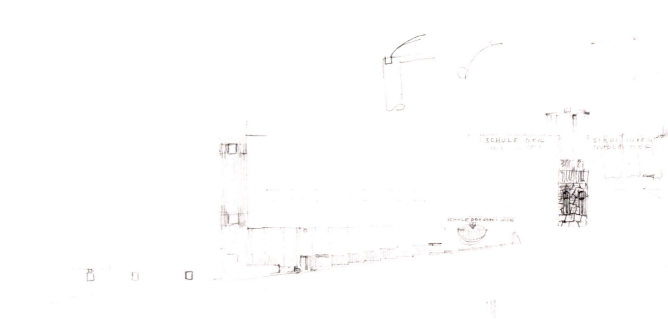

04

05

Schullin II Jewelry Store
1981–1982

01

The jewelry store on Kohlmarkt, realized by Hollein in the early 1980s, was the last in a series of conversions of small-scale commercial premises in central Vienna. The project encompassed the design of the facade and the remodeling of two sales rooms on the ground floor, along with the extension of the floor above, accessed via a small spiral staircase.

The two rectangular sales rooms, set one behind the other, are entered from a portal onto the street. The entrance to the second room is placed asymmetrically in relation to the front door, creating a more private zone in addition to the more public space at the front of the shop.

Jewelry is displayed along the walls either in cases or in niches furnished with a table and seating. The design appeals to several levels of association simultaneously. The portal has a symbolic charge, evoking an oversized archaic piece of jewelry. Uplighter floor lamps double as marble-effect columns. Viewed together, each individual architectural intervention accentuates the staging of the jewelry as almost sacred objects.

Location Kohlmarkt 7, 1010 Vienna, Austria
Type Jewelry store
Client Herbert Schullin/Schullin & Söhne

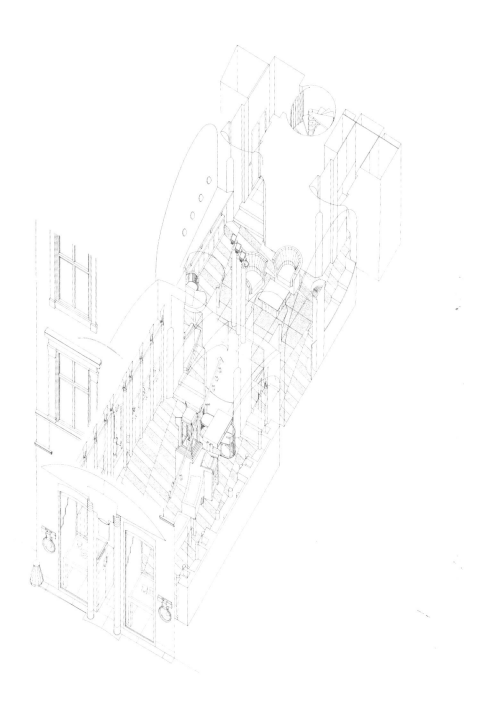

02

Hans Hollein, Schullin II jewelry store, Vienna, Austria, 1981–1982.
All: Archive Hans Hollein, Az W and MAK, Vienna.

01 View from front retail space towards the rear lounge
    with uplighters.

02 General view of ground floor, axonometry.
    Ink, pencil, and dot-screen foil on translucent paper.

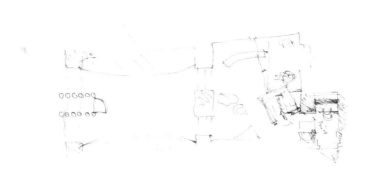

03

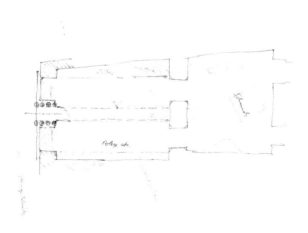

04

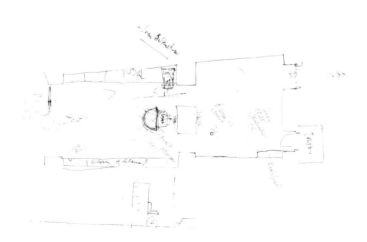

05

07

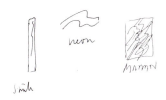

06

03   Study of entrance situation and floor plan.
     Felt-tip on translucent paper.

04   Study of floor plan. Felt-tip on translucent paper.

05   Study of surfaces: blue ceiling with stars and
     stainless-steel display cases, and fountain, sketch.
     Felt-tip on translucent paper.

06   Study of facade and overall material concept. Photocopy.

07   View along Kohlmarkt with Imperial Palace in the background.
     Photo: Franz Hubmann/Imagno/picturedesk.com

195

Frankfurt Museum of Modern Art
1982–1991

01

The city of Frankfurt organized an open competition in 1982 for the design of its new museum, to which Atelier Hollein was also invited. The task was very similar to that of the Abteiberg Museum in Mönchengladbach in terms of program, floor area, volume, and location in the center of the city, near a cathedral. Hollein's team, which had already gained some experience in building museums with the realized projects in Tehran and Mönchengladbach, won the competition with a design that was closely related to the urban context. Here, as with the Abteiberg Museum, the planning and construction phase extended over a period of almost a decade. The compact triangular building was conceived to make maximum use of the site. It is defined by a complex internal spatial structure: a series of spaces run diagonally around a three-sided central hall, merging into each other. The external appearance is determined by the tension between the clear, block-like form and the varied formulation of the facades, corners, and roof lines. While the building is conceptually aligned with earlier themes such as the Aircraft Carrier City in Landscape (1964), it establishes a connection between the interior world of the museum and the surrounding urban landscape in a variety of ways. Its closed facade, articulated only by narrow horizontal cornices, is punctuated by indentations, protrusions, and projections—rows of columns, arcades, glazed fronts, balconies, and oriels—that open up to the urban space, setting up individual sightlines onto the historic Old Town and the dominant presence of Frankfurt Cathedral.

Location Domstraße 10, Frankfurt am Main, Germany
Type Museum/cultural building
Client City of Frankfurt am Main, Peter Iden
(Founding Director)

ARCHITEKT HANS HOLLEIN   MUSEUM FÜR MODERNE KUNST FRANKFURT

02

Hans Hollein, Frankfurt Museum of Modern Art, Frankfurt
am Main, Germany, 1982–1991. 01–02, 04: Archive Hans Hollein,
Az W and MAK, Vienna.

01   View of building tip and facade along Berliner Straße.
      Photo: Richard Bryant/Arcaid Images

02   Main entrance with pedestrian zone (not realized),
      perspective. Color pencil on photocopy.

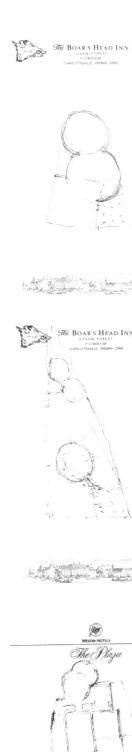

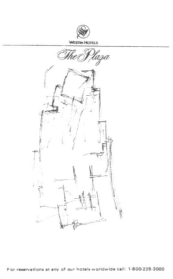

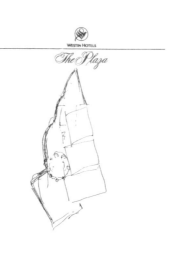

03

04

03 Concept development sketches on hotel notepads.
 All: Private Archive Hollein.

04 Hans Hollein and colleagues photographing the competition
 model. Photo: Sina Baniahmad

Haas Haus
1985–1990

01

The construction of the Haas Haus on one of the most prominent corner sites in the center of Vienna, near Stephansplatz, was not Atelier Hollein's first engagement with a historically charged urban space. Already in the late 1970s, a project by Hollein had addressed the redesign of Stock-im-Eisen-Platz, opposite the Haas Haus, in the context of the opening of a new metro station. In terms of urban design, and specifically in its attempt to strengthen the situation of the square, the Haas Haus ties in with that earlier project. Through its powerful presence, the much-discussed new building (which was initially planned as simply a conversion of the existing Haas Haus) became a feature that dominated the space and in the process redefined the adjacent square. The importance Hollein attached to the relationship between the building and the square is expressed not only in his meticulous analysis of the history of the site but also in the way he incorporated the public space in front of the building into the design. Special paving, furniture, and lighting underscored the idea of a distinct urban space that could be read as complementary to the multi-faceted interior. The five-story central atrium, with its continuous luminous ceiling and dramatic staircase, evoked a metropolitan outdoor space realized in neon, highly polished stone, and stainless steel. Twenty years after the opening of the building, the central atrium was destroyed by a consolidation of the retail space. In turn, with the creation of the pedestrian zone in the 2000s, the independent architecture of the square was dismantled in favor of a consistent design concept for the city center. Given the erosion of the basic concept of Hollein's design, it is no longer possible to recognize in this place his architectural vision of the city as a juxtaposition of distinctive places and defined squares.

Location Stock-im-Eisen-Platz 12, 1010 Vienna, Austria
Type Office and commercial building
Client Zentralsparkasse, Wiener Städtische, Wiener Verein

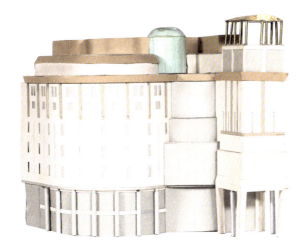

02

03

Hans Hollein, Haas Haus, Vienna, Austria, 1985–1990.
All: Archive Hans Hollein, Az W and MAK, Vienna.

01   Bay window element facing St. Stephen's Cathedral
     and side elevation facing Goldschmiedgasse.
     Photo: Franz Hubmann/Imagno/picturedesk.com

02   Building study, 1986 version, model. Foamboard, card,
     cardboard, plastic, Styrofoam, and metal. Photo: Elmar Bertsch

03   Site model with proposed square design (not realized).
     Plastic, foam block, acrylic glass, wood, metal, and acrylic glass.
     Photo: Elmar Bertsch

04

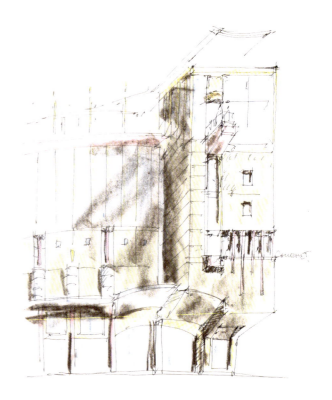

05

04   Facade study of the bay window element facing St. Stephen's
     Cathedral, undated version with stepped underside.
     Ink and pastel crayon on translucent paper.

05   Facade study of the bay window element facing St. Stephen's
     Cathedral, undated version with curved underside.
     Ink and pastel crayon on translucent paper.

06

06 Volumetric studies, a selection of eighteen models
from a larger number of variants. Styrofoam, foamboard,
cardboard, paper, and wood. Photos: Elmar Bertsch

Vulcania — European Park of Volcanism
1994–2002

01

Hollein was invited by former French President Valéry Giscard d'Estaing to participate in the competition for a European center for volcanism in Auvergne. After designing the Guggenheim Museum in Mönchsberg, Salzburg (1989), Atelier Hollein was considered an expert in subterranean museum buildings. Although the proposal came second in the competition, it was deemed the most suitable project for realization, subject to certain revisions. Hollein's team was the only one to arrange much of the program underground, which was viewed very positively. Conversely, there was criticism of the form of a key element of the design, the soaring central cone, which was thought to be too reminiscent of the cooling tower of a nuclear power plant and so had to be changed. Visitors enter the building complex via a ramp made of volcanic rock. Initially, all they see is the split cone, clad in basalt, and the glazed panoramic restaurant of the museum. Descending further into the artificially formed underground landscape of basalt and concrete, they reach a space dominated by the shimmering golden interior of the 36m-high cone. This marks the center of the museum complex, both below and above ground. Grouped in a circle around the cone are the five main sections of the museum. The organization of the complex aligns with Hollein's fundamental approach to museum buildings and can be understood as an interpretation of his concept for an "Imaginary Museum" from 1987, which was also based on a circular, three-dimensional matrix. Both projects allow for the possibility of open circulation. Visitors can decide for themselves the order in which they engage with the exhibits and the time they spend in the different parts of the museum.

Location 2 route de Mazayes, 63230 Saint-Ours-Les-Roches, France
Type Museum / cultural building
Client Region d'Auvergne, Valéry Giscard d'Estaing

02

03

04

Hans Hollein, Vulcania, European Park of Volcanism, Saint-Ours-Les-Roches, France, 1994–2002. With Atelier 4, Clermont-Ferrand, France. All: Archive Hans Hollein, Az W and MAK, Vienna.

01 Aerial view of complex with conservatory in the foreground.

02 Ramp descending the artificial crater leading to the main entrance of the underground exhibition. Opening ceremony on February 2, 2002, where more than 1,200 schoolchildren took part.

03 Conceptual collage of crater and cone. Color pencil on photocopy.

04 Perspective view from artificial crater back towards the golden cone and the restaurant building. Color print.

05

05 Site model showing overall complex, detail. Basalt cast.
Photo: Elmar Bertsch

06 Nine model studies of the central cone. Various materials,
Styrofoam, paper, and pins. Photos: Elmar Bertsch

06

Hans Hollein 1934–2014

1934
Born March 30 in Vienna, Austria.

1953
Graduates from vocational school, Vienna, Austria.

1956
Diploma, masterclass Prof. Clemens Holzmeister, Academy of Fine Arts, Vienna, Austria.

1958
Works in the office of AOS Arkitekter (Magnus Ahlgren, Torbjörn Olsson, and Sven Silow) Stockholm, Sweden.

1958
Harkness Fellowship from the Commonwealth Fund.

1958–1959
Studies at the Illinois Institute of Technology, Chicago, United States.

1960
Master of architecture from the College of Environmental Design, University of California, Berkeley, United States.

1962
Lecture "Zurück zur Architektur" (Return to Architecture) at Galerie nächst St. Stephan, Vienna, Austria.

1963–1964, 1966
Guest professorships at Washington University, School of Architecture, St. Louis, United States.

1964
Obtains professional license.

1965–1970
Member of the editorial board of *BAU*, Vienna, Austria.

1966
R.S. Reynolds Memorial Award for Retti candle shop.

1967
Manifesto "Alles ist Architektur" (Everything is Architecture) (*BAU*, no. 1–2 (1968): 1048).

1967–1976
Professor at the Academy of Fine Arts, Düsseldorf, Germany.

1976–1979
Head of masterclass for industrial design and of the Institute of Design at the University of Applied Arts, Vienna, Austria.

1978–1990
Austrian commissioner for the Venice Biennale, Italy.

1979–2002
Head of masterclass for architecture at the University of Applied Arts, Vienna, Austria.

1984
R.S. Reynolds Memorial Award for Abteiberg Municipal Museum.

1985
Pritzker Prize, United States.

1990
Chicago Architecture Award, Chicago, United States.

1991
Austrian commissioner for the Venice Architecture Biennale, Venice, Italy.

1993
Honorary Fellow of Royal Institute of British Architects.

1995–1999
Head of the Institute of Architecture, University of Applied Arts, Vienna, Austria.

1996
Austrian commissioner for the Venice Architecture Biennale, Venice, Italy.

1996
Director of the sixth Venice Architecture Biennale, *Sensing the Future–The Architect as Seismograph*, Venice, Italy.

1999–2012
President of the Kunstsenates (Senate for the Arts).

2010
Founding of Hans Hollein & Partner ZT-GmbH with Christoph Monschein.

2014
Dies on April 24.

Selected Works and Exhibitions

1963
Exhibition *Architektur* (*Architecture*) with Walter Pichler, Galerie nächst St. Stephan, Vienna, Austria.

1964–1965
Retti candle shop, Vienna, Austria.

1966–1967
Boutique Christa Metek, Vienna, Austria.

1967
Group show with Buckminster Fuller, Frei Otto, Claes Oldenburg, and Christo, Richard Feigen Gallery, New York, United States.

1967–1969
Richard Feigen Gallery, New York, United States.

1967–1968
Exhibition *Architectural Fantasies: Drawings from the Museum Collection* with Walter Pichler and Raimund Abraham, MoMA, New York, United States.

1968
Austriennale, Austrian contribution to the XIV Triennale di Milano, Milan, Italy.

1969–1972
Carl Friedrich von Siemens Foundation, Munich, Germany.

1970
Exhibition *Tod (Death)*, Abteiberg Municipal Museum, Möchengladbach, Germany.

1971–1972
Media Lines, Olympic Village, Munich, Germany.

1972
Exhibition *Werk und Verhalten–Leben und Tod. Alltägliche Situationen* (*Work and Behavior–Life and Death. Everyday Situations*), 36th Venice Art Biennale, Italy.

1972–1974
Schullin I jewelry store, Vienna, Austria.

1972–1982
Abteiberg Municipal Museum, Mönchengladbach, Germany.

1974–1976
MAN transFORMS, inaugural exhibition of the Cooper Hewitt, Smithsonian Design Museum, New York, United States.

1976–1979
Austrian Travel Agency, Vienna and Vösendorf, Austria.

1977–1978
Glassware and Ceramic Museum, Tehran, Iran.

1979–1990
Köhlergasse elementary school, Vienna, Austria.

1980
Set design for *Komödie der Verführung* (*Comedy of Seduction)* by Arthur Schnitzler, Burgtheater, Vienna, Austria.

1981–1982
Schullin II jewelry store, Vienna, Austria.

1982–1983
Exhibition *Die Türken vor Wien: Europa und die Entscheidung an der Donau 1683-1983* (*The Turks before Vienna: Europe and the Decision at the Danube 1683-1984*), Künstlerhaus, Vienna, Austria.

1982–1991
Frankfurt Museum of Modern Art, Frankfurt am Main, Germany.

1984–1985
Exhibition *Traum und Wirklichkeit: Wien 1870-1930* (*Dream and Reality: Vienna 1870-1930*), Künstlerhaus/Historisches Museum der Stadt Wien, Austria.

1985–1990
Haas Haus, Vienna, Austria.

1986–1988
Touring exhibition *Metaphern und Metamorphosen* (*Metaphors and Metamorphoses)*, Centre Georges Pompidou, Paris, France, Museum of the 20th Century (20er Haus), Vienna, Austria, and Nationalgalerie, Berlin, Germany.

1987–1993
Erste Allgemeine Generali, Bregenz, Austria.

1988
Exhibition *Hans Hollein*, Academia delle Arti del Disegno, Florence, Italy.

1988–1993
Banco Santander, Madrid, Spain.

1898
Exhibition *Hans Hollein,* Yurakucho Art Forum, Tokyo, Japan.

1989–2002
Museum im Fels (Museum in the Rock), unrealized, Mönchsberg, Salzburg, Austria.

1990
Exhibition, Tsukashin Hall, Hyogo, Osaka, Japan.

1991–1992
Archaeological grounds at Michaelerplatz, Vienna, Austria.

1992–2002
Cultural quarter and Lower Austria Museum, St. Pölten, Austria.

1994–2000
Media Tower (Generali Tower), Vienna, Austria.

1994–2002
Vulcania, European Park of Volcanism, Saint-Ours-Les-Roches, France.

1995
Exhibition *Hans Hollein,* Historisches Museum der Stadt Wien (now Wien Museum), Austria.

1995–2001
Torre Interbank, Lima, Peru.

1996–2001
Austrian Embassy, Berlin, Germany.

1997–2002
Centrum Bank, Vaduz, Liechtenstein.

2001–2003
Albertina, entrance area (Soravia Wing) and café, Vienna, Austria.

2002
Adaptation and vertical extension of Hilton Hotel, Vienna, Austria.

2012
Exhibition *Hans Hollein*, Neue Galerie Graz at the Universalmuseum Joanneum, Graz, Austria.

2014
Exhibition *Hollein*, MAK, Vienna, Austria.

2014
Exhibition *Hans Hollein: Alles ist Architektur*, Abteiberg Municipal Museum, Mönchengladbach, Germany.

Mark Lee

Hans Hollein and America

When I was a student of architecture in 1989, I traveled to Vienna and had the opportunity to meet with Hans Hollein at the University of Applied Arts. He was at the peak of his career: he had been awarded the Pritzker Prize in 1985, the same year his *A+U* monograph was published; the Abteiberg Museum in Mönchengladbach had opened a few years before, and Haas Haus and Frankfurt Museum for Modern Art were in their respective planning and construction stages. Already long established in Europe, Hollein was now at the center of the field internationally.

Although I was merely a young student of architecture, he generously agreed to the meeting and conveyed a courteous sense of gentle-manliness. Hearing that I came from Los Angeles, he mentioned that California had a special place in his heart as it "bookended" his career to date—it was where he had gone to study, at UC Berkeley, as well as to receive the Pritzker Prize, at the Huntington Library in Pasadena. And I already knew that Hollein had been instrumental in reviving interest in the work of Rudolph Schindler in Los Angeles at a time when many of the buildings were in neglect or falling apart. Alongside his publications on Schindler, he also facilitated the first publication and exhibition on John Lautner, bringing attention to a body of work that was then unknown in Europe.

Beyond California, Hollein was already very present on the American scene. He designed the Feigen Gallery in New York in 1969 and co-curated the seminal *MAN transFORMS* exhibition at the Cooper Hewitt in 1974. Jaquelin Robertson invited him to a two-day conference at the University of Virginia in 1982, the transcript of which was later published as the influential book, *The Charlottesville Tapes*. Hollein, alongside O.M. Ungers, Rafael Moneo, the Krier brothers, and Rem Koolhaas, presented a European perspective that heavily influenced American architectural culture at the time.

To the American audience, Hollein was an intriguing figure. Beyond being simply an architect, designer, artist, or writer, he was someone who curated culture. He designed everything from buildings and interiors to exhibitions, furniture, and glasses—the embodiment of *gesamtkunstwerk*. His slogan of "everything is architecture" echoed Joseph Beuys's empowering dictum that "every man is an artist." Most importantly, it allowed one to recognize that other solutions, besides an architectural one, might better address the issue at hand.

During our meeting Hollein asked me about my work, my thoughts on architecture, and my impressions of Los Angeles with an almost child-like curiosity. I remember leaving the meeting feeling both exhilarated and reassured about my pursuit of an architectural vocation. My first and only encounter with him left me with a sense of intrigue and positiveness that has endured and evolved over the years of my practice and my thinking. My knowledge and appreciation of Hollein has continued to grow. In particular, I appreciate his provision of a critical model for practice, one that matched an extraordinary breadth in the approach to a project with an insistence on depth and rigor in whatever medium he chose to deploy. This characteristic of his work, its constant oscillation between the poles of intensive disciplinary practice and a sense of freedom, is something for our own generation and beyond to aspire to.

Currently a younger generation of American architects are looking at Hollein's work in fresh and profound ways. Practices with diverse output, from LADG, Sean Canty, Bureau Spectacular, and Andrew Kovács to First Office, Besler & Sons, Para Projects, and Michelle Chang, are all directly or indirectly affected by and indebted to Hollein in more ways than one. Watching their practices grow and develop reminds me of that afternoon in Vienna in 1989, and of how Hans Hollein's generosity and curiosity continues to expand across generations over the decades.

Appendix

Image Credits

© All objects Hans Hollein by Archive Hans Hollein,
Az W and MAK, Vienna/Architekturzentrum Wien, Collection,
unless otherwise stated in the caption.

We thank all the photographers as well as Dorothea Apovnik/
Private Archive Hollein, Sina Baniahmad, Axel Hubmann,
Christoph Molin Pradel, Georg Riha, Jerzy Surwillo, and Sabine
Haase-Zugmann for their valued support.

Every reasonable attempt has been made by the authors
and publishers to identify owners of copyrights. Photographers
not mentioned in the credits are kindly asked to contact
the Architekturzentrum Wien (office@azw.at) and recompense
will be made according to the standard practice.

Index of Persons

Index of Persons

Bibliography

Friedrich Achleitner, *Die rückwärtsgewandte Utopie: Motor des Fortschritts in der Wiener Architektur?* (Vienna: Picus, 1993).

Friedrich Achleitner, *Österreichische Architektur im 20. Jahrhundert,* vols. 1–3: *Wien 1.–23. Bezirk,* ed. Architekturzentrum Wien (Vienna: Residenz, 2010).

Friedrich Achleitner, "Viennese Positions with Particular Reference to the Problem of the Transformation of Historic Environments," *Lotus International Review of Architecture,* no. 29 (1981).

Architekturzentrum Wien, *The Austrian Phenomenon: Architektur Avantgarde Österreich 1956–1973* (Vienna/Basel: Az W/Birkhäuser, 2009).

B.J. Archer and Anthony Vidler, eds., *Follies: Architecture for the Late-Twentieth-Century Landscape* (New York: Rizzoli, 1983).

aut. Architektur und tirol, Arno Ritter, Claudia Wedekind, Alexa Baumgartner, Birgit Brauner, Günther Dankl, Albrecht Dornauer, et al., *Widerstand und Wandel: Über die 1970er-Jahre in Tirol* (Innsbruck: aut. Architektur und tirol, 2020).

La Biennale di Venezia and Giovanni Keller, *Sensing the Future: The Architect as Seismograph—The 6th International Architecture Exhibition, La Biennale di Venezia* (Milan: Electa, 1997).

Eva Branscome, *Hans Hollein and Postmodernism: Art and Architecture in Austria 1958–1985* (London: Routledge, 2017).

Craig Buckley, "Everything is Architecture: Hans Hollein's Media Assemblages," *Montage, Media, and Experimental Architecture in the 1960s* (Minneapolis: University of Minnesota Press, 2019).

Francois Burkhardt and Paulus Manker, *Hans Hollein: Schriften & Manifeste* (Vienna: Universität für angewandte Kunst Wien, 2002).

Aslı Çiçek, Jantje Engels, and Maarten Liefooghe, eds., *Staging the Museum, OASE,* no. 111 (May 2022).

Aslı Çiçek, "Calculated Aesthetics," *Practices of Drawing, OASE,* no. 105 (April 2020).

Kristin Feireiss and Hans-Jürgen Commerell, *Hollein: Aufbauen und Aushöhlen* (Berlin: Aedes, 2003).

Angelika Fitz, Monika Platzer, *Hot Questions–Cold Storage: Architecture from Austria. The Permanent Exhibition at the Az W,* ed. Architekturzentrum Wien (Zurich: Park Books, 2023).

Robert Fleck, *Avantgarde in Wien 1945–1981: Die Galerie nächst St. Stephan 1954–1981: Chronik* (Vienna: Löcker, 1982).

Kenneth Frampton, "Meditations on an Aircraft Carrier: Hans Hollein's Mönchengladbach," *A+U Tokyo* (1985): 142–144.

Galerie Ulysses, *Städtisches Museum Abteiberg Mönchengladbach: Entwurf des Neubaus von Architekt Prof. Hans Hollein—Aspekte der musealen Aktivität unter Leitung von Dr. Johannes Cladders* (Vienna: Galerie Ulysses 1979).

Kersten Geers, "Model Architecture," *Innocence, San Rocco,* no. 0 (Summer 2010): 66–70.

Hans Hollein, Dietmar Steiner, Historisches Museum der Stadt Wien, *Hans Hollein: Eine Ausstellung, 197. Sonderausstellung des Historischen Museum der Stadt Wien* (Vienna: Eigenverlag der Museen der Stadt Wien, 1995).

Hochschule für angewandte Kunst, *Hans Hollein: Design MAN transFORMS—Konzepte einer Ausstellung/Concepts of an Exhibition* (Vienna: Löcker, 1989).

Wilhelm Holzbauer and Hans Hollein, *Ort und Platz: Stadträumliche Architekturanalysen* (Vienna: Universität für angewandte Kunst Wien, 1989).

Franz Hubmann, Carl Aigner, André Heller, Hans Hollein, and Wilfried Seipel, *Franz Hubmann: Das photographische Werk: Mit einem Interview von Wilfried Seipel und Textbeiträgen von Carl Aigner, Otto Breicha, Andre Heller u. a.* (Vienna: Christian Brandstätter, 1999).

Otto Kapfinger and Adolf Krischanitz, "Versuch über die Semantik in der Architektur von Hans Hollein," *UMBAU,* no. 8 (1984).

Samuel Korn, Wilfried Kuehn, and Susanne Titz, *Alles ist Architektur? Ausstellen und Forschen: Hans Hollein und das Museum Abteiberg* (Mönchengladbach: Museum Abteiberg, 2015).

Steffen Krämer, *Die Postmoderne Architekturlandschaft: Museumsprojekte von James Stirling und Hans Hollein. Studien zur Kunstgeschichte*, vol. 120 (Hildesheim/Zurich/New York: Georg Olms, 1998).

Wilfried Kuehn, Christoph Thun-Hohenstein, Susanne Titz, and Marlies Wirth*, Hans Hollein: Photographed by Aglaia Konrad and Armin Linke (*Milan/London: Mousse Publishing/Koenig Books, 2014).

Wilfried Kuehn, et al., "Exhibition Extension," *Displayer*, no. 3, ed. Wilfried Kuehn and Stephan Trüby/Staatliche Hochschule für Gestaltung Karlsruhe (Karlsruhe: Hfg Karlsruhe, Ausstellungsdesign und Kuratorische Praxis, 2009): 131–136.

Alessandro Mendini, "Colloquio con Hans Hollein," *Domus*, no. 645 (1983): 1.

Ákos Moravánszky and Torsten Lange, *Re-Framing Identities: Architecture's Turn to History, 1970–1990*, 1st ed. (Basel: Birkhäuser, 2016).

Museum Abteiberg Mönchengladbach and Hannelore Kersing, *Städtisches Museum Abteiberg, Mönchengladbach: Ein kommentierter Bildband* (Mönchengladbach: Städtisches Museum Abteiberg, 2001).

Österreichischer Fachzeitschriften Verlag, *BAU: Schrift für Architektur und Städtebau (1965–1970)*.

Wolfgang Pehnt, *Hans Hollein: Museum in Mönchengladbach–Architektur als Collage,* 5th ed. (Frankfurt am Main: Fischer Taschenbuch, 1993).

Gianni Pettena, *Hans Hollein Opere/Works 1960–1988* (Milan: Idea Books, 1988).

Monika Platzer, *Cold War and Architecture: The Competing Forces that Reshaped Austria after 1945,* ed. Architekturzentrum Wien (Zurich: Park Books, 2020).

Jaquelin Robertson and Stanley Tigerman, *Der postmoderne Salon: Architekten über Architekten* (Basel: Birkhäuser, 1991).

Wilfried Skreiner, *Hollein: Austria XXXVI Biennale di Venezia 1972* (Bundesministerium für Unterricht und Kunst, 1972).

Gerfried Sperl, *Österreichische Architekten im Gespräch mit Gerfried Sperl* (Salzburg/Munich: Anton Pustet, 2000).

James Stirling, "Showcases of an Exhibition," *Domus*, no. 607 (June 1980).

Stephan Trüby, "'Everything is Architecture' Versus 'Absolute Architecture,'" *Displayer*, no. 3, ed. Wilfried Kuehn and Stephan Trüby/Staatliche Hochschule für Gestaltung Karlsruhe (Karlsruhe: Hfg Karlsruhe, Ausstellungsdesign und Kuratorische Praxis, 2009): 136–140.

Peter Weibel and Hans Hollein, *Hans Hollein* (Ostfildern: Hatje Cantz, 2012).

About the Authors

Architekturzentrum Wien

The Architekturzentrum Wien is the Austrian museum of architecture. Located in the MuseumsQuartier in the heart of Vienna, the Architekturzentrum Wien exhibits, discusses, and researches the ways in which architecture and urban development shape the daily life of each one of us. The broad program of the Architekturzentrum Wien is seen as a bridge between the specialist world and everyday experts. What can architecture do? This is a question of great relevance to all of us. The program comprises more than five hundred events a year, ranging from international exhibitions, symposia, workshops, and lectures to guided tours, city expeditions, film series, and hands-on formats. The museum's facilities include a unique collection on Austrian architecture of the twentieth and twenty-first centuries and a public architecture library.

Lorenzo De Chiffre

is an architect, Senior Scientist at the TU Wien, and author of numerous texts on architecture in international publications. He studied at the Royal Danish Academy of Fine Arts and the University of East London. In 2016 he completed his doctoral thesis on the Viennese *Terrassenhaus* (terrace house), and in 2017 curated the exhibition, *The Terrassenhaus: A Viennese Fetish?*, at the Architekturzentrum Wien.

Benni Eder

studied architecture at the Academy of Fine Arts in Vienna and the PUC Santiago de Chile and works as an independent architect at studio eder krenn in Vienna. He has received several prizes and awards, including the City of Vienna's Förderungspreis für Architektur. In addition to his practice, he teaches at the TU Wien.

Angelika Fitz

is the Director of the Architekturzentrum Wien. Since the late 1990s she has worked as a curator and author in the fields of architecture, art, and urbanism. She focuses on the societal contextualization of architecture, planetary and feminist perspectives. In 2022 she was awarded the Julius Posener Prize for architectural theory. Recent exhibitions and publications include *Critical Care: Architecture for a Broken Planet* (2019), co-edited with Elke Krasny, and *Yasmeen Lari: Architecture for the Future* (2023), co-edited with E. Krasny and M. Mazhar, both published by MIT Press.

Theresa Krenn

studied architecture at the TU Wien and Academy of Fine Arts in Vienna and works as an independent architect at studio eder krenn in Vienna. She has received several prizes and awards, including the City of Vienna's Förderungspreis für Architektur. In addition to her practice, she teaches at the TU Wien.

Mark Lee

is a principal and founding partner of the Los Angeles-based architecture firm Johnston Marklee. He has taught at numerous schools in North America and Europe, including Harvard GSD, where he is Professor of Architecture and held the Chair of the Department of Architecture until 2022, Princeton University, University of California, Technical University of Berlin, and ETH Zurich. Together with partner Sharon Johnston, Mark Lee was the Artistic Director for the 2017 Chicago Architecture Biennial.

Monika Platzer

is head of collections and curator at the Architekturzentrum Wien. Studied art history and holds a doctorate from the University of Vienna. Her research focuses on the history of twentieth-century Austrian architecture and cultural history. International curatorial and research activity at leading institutions such as the Canadian Centre for Architecture and the Getty Research Institute.

Colophon

© 2023 Architekturzentrum Wien and Park Books AG, Zurich
All texts © the authors.

ISBN 978-3-03860-340-5

Editors: Lorenzo De Chiffre, Benni Eder, Theresa Krenn, and Architekturzentrum Wien
Project management: Katrin Stingl, Claudia Lingenhöl (Archive Hans Hollein, Az W and MAK, Vienna/Architekturzentrum Wien, Collection)
Book design: Polimekanos, Lisa Stephanides, Stefan Kraus
Texts: Lorenzo De Chiffre, Benni Eder, Angelika Fitz, Theresa Krenn, Mark Lee, Monika Platzer
Interviews: Reem Almannai and Florian Fischer, Aslı Çiçek, Pier Paolo Tamburelli, Dirk Somers, Claudia Cavallar, Maria Conen and Raoul Sigl, David Kohn, Stefanie Everaert and Caroline Lateur, Andreas Rumpfhuber, Wilfried Kuehn, Oliver Lütjens and Thomas Padmanabhan, Beate Hølmebakk, Martin Feiersinger, Job Floris, Kersten Geers
Translation (German–English) and copyediting (English): Pamela Johnston
Copyediting (German): Sonja Pisarik
Interview transcription: Lorenzo De Chiffre, Benni Eder, Theresa Krenn
Image editing: Elmar Bertsch, Iris Ranzinger

Printed by Gerin Druck Gmbh
Bound by Papyrus
Paper: Arctic Volume White
Typefaces: Suisse Neue, Suisse International, Union

Architekturzentrum Wien, Museumsplatz 1, 1070 Vienna,
www.azw.at
Park Books, Niederdorfstrasse 54, 8001 Zurich, Switzerland,
www.park-books.com
Park Books is being supported by the Federal Office of Culture with a general subsidy for the years 2021–2024.

This book was published on the occasion of the exhibition *Hollein Calling: Architectural Dialogues* (September 21, 2023– February 12, 2024), Architekturzentrum Wien.

Director Architekturzentrum Wien: Angelika Fitz
Executive Director Architekturzentrum Wien: Karin Lux

Curators: Lorenzo De Chiffre, Benni Eder, Theresa Krenn
Exhibition design: studio eder krenn and Lorenzo De Chiffre
Graphic design: Polimekanos, Lisa Stephanides, Stefan Kraus
Project management: Katrin Stingl, Claudia Lingenhöl (Archive Hans Hollein, Az W and MAK, Vienna/Architekturzentrum Wien, Collection)
Production management: Andreas Kurz

Acknowledgments:
Dorothea Apovnik, Sina Baniahmad, Liselotte Bilak, Michael M. Boschner, Hermann Czech, Mechthild Ebert, Thomas Hasler, Sophie Hiesberger, Noemie Hitz, Katharina Hövelmann, Philip Kaloumenos, Barbara Kapsammer, Christoph Monschein, Peter Noever, Eva Mair, Karoline Mayer, Katharina Ritter, Viola Rösch, Alberto Sánchez, Max Samida, Alexandra Scheibl, Astrid Staufer, Christian Teckert, and students in the "Re-drawing Hans Hollein" course at TU Wien.

The research project Dialogues on Hans Hollein was funded by: *Hans-Hollein-Projektstipendium* (Bundeskanzleramt, Sektion II–Kunst und Kultur, Abteilung II/6–Bildende Kunst, Architektur, Design, Mode, Foto und Medienkunst) and Stadt Wien Kultur

Public funding Architekturzentrum Wien (Az W)

Stadt Wien

Bundesministerium
Kunst, Kultur,
öffentlicher Dienst und Sport

Colophon

Az W is supported by

ARCHITECTURE LOUNGE

Architekturzentrum Wien

A good part of the Architekturzentrum Wien's comprehensive program is supported by the contributions from its membership program, particularly the contributions from its Architecture Lounge partners. This platform for highly committed companies and associations attributes top priority to knowledge exchanges and networking. Learning, networking, and hospitality are the terms that best describe this field of communication at the nexus of architecture, business, and politics.

Architecture Lounge Members:
ARWAG Holding AG
BDN Fleissner & Partner
Bundesimmobiliengesellschaft m.b.H.
Buwog Group
EGW Erste gemeinn. Wohnungsgesellschaft
Gesiba, Gemeinn. Siedlungs- & BAU AG
Gewog–Neue Heimat
Grohe Ges.m.b.H.
iC Projektentwicklung
Immobilien Privatstiftung
Kallco Development GmbH
Kallinger Projekte GmbH
Mischek Bauträger Service GmbH
Neues Leben Gemeinn. Bau-, Wohn- und Siedlungsgen.
Österreichisches Siedlungswerk AG
Österreichisches Volkswohnungswerk
Sozialbau AG
Strabag Real Estate GmbH
Swisspearl Österreich GmbH
Vasko+Partner Ingenieure
WBV–GPA Wohnbauv. f. Privatangestellte
WKÖ–Fachverband Steine-Keramik
Wien 3420 Aspern Development AG
Wienerberger Österreich GmbH
wohnfonds_wien
WSE Wiener Standortentwicklung GmbH